Deaf Ministry: Ministry Models for Expanding the Kingdom of God by Leo Yates, Jr. describes the many facets of ministry with people who have hearing loss and their families, friends and faith communities. It is a tool box of practical information and resources for developing local ministries. It also includes a discussion about ministry with people with disabilities with an emphasis on advocacy and hospitality. By including the different ministry models of Deaf ministry in one book, this provides a plethora of suggestions to both pastors and laity so they can either begin or expand their own Deaf ministry. Rev. Yates does a wonderful job of capturing what the various ministries are and gives readers an inside look at what Deaf ministry is all about. The giftedness of the Deaf, hard-of-hearing, late-deafened and Deaf-blind community has yet to be fully engaged in the ministry and the life of the church. When I teach about Deaf ministry, this book will be one of my go to resources for the students to read, as it provides a broad overview of Deaf ministry. This book explains how the Body of Christ can achieve that goal of empowerment while further expanding the Kingdom of God.

Bishop Peggy A. Johnson

Table of Contents

Chapter 1 – An Introduction to Deaf Ministry

Welcome to Deaf ministry. Deaf ministry is an umbrella term for doing ministry with d/Deaf, hard-of-hearing, late-deafened, and Deaf-blind individuals and their families. In Deaf culture, Deaf people share a language, deaf school experiences, social customs (e.g. flashing lights & being direct in their conversations), shared recreational activities, & other aspects. In addition to these, when one sees a capital 'D' in the word deaf, it indicates cultural deafness within what is discussed or stated. Besides indicating hearing loss, the small 'd' in deaf indicates someone who is not culturally Deaf.

In general, Deaf ministry is often used as a generalized term that means a church has a ministry with Deaf, hard-of-hearing, late-deafened, and Deaf-blind people, often by welcoming, providing care, in ministry with, and including in the life of the church. In addition, it is also seen as a church program that is inclusive of Deaf people.

One definition for the word *ministry* by the Random House Dictionary is the service, functions, or profession of a minister. By the virtue of our baptism, we are all ministers, in which the apostle Peter shared with the Early Church, calling us a priesthood of all believers (1 Peter 2:5).

Historically, the Church has had a negative view of Deaf people, in which often they were oppressed and deemed as incapable of doing for themselves. Many first world countries have changed in how they view d/Deaf people, recognizing the gifts and graces they have and that communication no longer has to be a barrier in serving together for the wider church.

The gospel writer, Mark, includes Jesus healing a deaf man and He provides more than a healing, but also inclusion. Mark 7: 31-37.

> *31 Then Jesus left the vicinity of Tyre and went through Sidon, down to the Sea of Galilee and into the region of the Decapolis. 32 There some people brought to him a man who was deaf and could hardly talk, and they begged Jesus to place his hand on him. 33 After he took him aside, away from the crowd, Jesus put his fingers into the man's ears. Then he spit and touched the man's tongue. 34 He looked up to heaven and with a deep sigh said to him, "Ephphatha!" (which means "Be opened!"). 35 At this, the man's ears were opened, his tongue was loosened and he began to speak plainly.*
> *36 Jesus commanded them not to tell anyone. But the more he did so, the more they kept talking about it. 37 People were overwhelmed with amazement. "He has done everything well," they said. "He even makes the deaf hear and the mute speak."* (NIV)

Upon the first glance, many readers see this passage as Jesus "fixing" the deaf man; however, one point of the story was the man who once lived in isolation has now become a part of the community-at-large. Inclusion is the emphasis of this story, not just the healing.

Along with inclusion, is the need to recognize the grace that Christ offered the deaf man, in which he is shown as being a part of the family of God. This grace does not stop with just Deaf people, but is given to all people, regardless of race, creed, color, ethnicity, national origin, religion, gender expression, sexual orientation, gender expression, age, height, weight, physical or mental ability, veteran status, military obligations, marital status, and so on. There are no barriers to God's love and grace; moreover, Christ showed grace time and time again and exemplified it further through his death on the cross. The apostle Paul tells us this in Romans 5:8 (NIV), *"But God demonstrates his own love for us in this: While we were still sinners, Christ died for us."*

Deaf ministry is another way of sharing God's grace with all people. When we do the Lord's work, aren't we too fulfilled? It goes both ways. In fact, the apostle Peter shared with his community, "Each of you should use whatever gift you have received to serve others, as faithful stewards of God's grace in its various forms" (1 Peter 4:10).

Deaf Culture

Deaf people do not perceive themselves as having lost something (i.e., hearing) and do not think of themselves as handicapped, impaired, or disabled. They celebrate and cherish their culture because it gives them the unique privilege of sharing a common history and language.

As with any culture, there are shared values, beliefs, and experiences that people have in common. This holds true for many in the Deaf community – they have their own Deaf culture and their own language – American

Sign Language (ASL). In fact, there are sub-cultures that include: Deaf poetry, Deaf African American history and traditions, Deaf Latino history and traditions, Deaf religious traditions, and so on.

Deaf culture has four components to it. They are language, behavioral norms, values and traditions.[i] In Deaf culture, vision plays a significant role in each of the four components. People who are Deaf rely strongly on their vision to communicate and gather information.

ASL is:	**ASL is not:**
☐ The preferred language of the Deaf community	☐ Signs in English word order
☐ A visual gestural language	☐ An auditory or written language
☐ A language with its own syntax and grammatical structure	☐ A universal language[ii]

Historically, ASL has been passed from one generation to the next in schools and communities. Even when ASL was not allowed in the classroom, Deaf staff and peers discreetly used their cherished language to communicate. ASL has also been preserved through church and other social gatherings.

Behavioral Norms – Making eye contact is necessary in communicating. Reasons include:[iii]

☐ Essential for effective communication.
☐ Important because people who are Deaf read the nuances of facial expressions and body language for additional information.

Attention getting – This is a common feature of Deaf culture, which includes:[iv]

- ☐ Hand waving is most common.
- ☐ Tapping the shoulder or arm is acceptable.
- ☐ Flickering lights on and off is also common.
- ☐ Tapping on a table or stomping foot on a floor is done occasionally.
- ☐ Using a third person to relay attention is sometimes used in a crowded room.

Meeting others within the Deaf Community – This can include:[v]

- ☐ Greetings often include hugs instead of handshakes.
- ☐ Conversations tend to include elaboration about lives and daily occurrences.
- ☐ Conversations tend to be open and direct.
- ☐ There is an interest in other people's connection with the Deaf community.

Values – like in other cultures, values play an important distinction in culture. The following are highly valued and vital aspects of everyday living by the Deaf community. Notice the value comparisons between people who are Deaf and hearing.[vi]

Deaf Values	Hearing Values
ASL	Spoken language
Eyes (rely on vision)	Ears (rely on sound)
Hands/signs	Mouth/speech
Videophone (VP); Relay Service; pagers	Telephone/Cell phones
Visual/vibrating alerting systems	Sound alerting system
Video mail	Voice mail
Interpreters	Audio speakers
Captioning	Concerts
Deaf clubs, Deaf civic and social organizations	Civic and social organizations

Traditions – of the Deaf community are a reflection of their cultural values. It is understandable that many of their traditions are based on the face-to-face gathering of people who are Deaf, because communication—the lifeblood of any culture—only happens visually in this community.[vii]

The traditions materialize in the strong family-like ties and lifelong camaraderie that develops between individuals. Some examples include their strong devotion to community Deaf club/events, Deaf alumni events, senior citizen gatherings, religious activities, conferences, and sporting events at the local, regional and national level. These provide a social gathering opportunity, a mechanism for participation in the political and economic decision-making trends affecting Deaf citizens and a means for grooming new leaders to carry on Deaf community traditions. Events are frequently filled with entertainment such as Deaf folklore, arts, history, ASL poetry, songs and joke-telling.

Models of Deafness

Over the past several decades, a few models of deafness have been identified, which indicate how deaf individuals may be viewed and/or treated. Three models of deafness are listed here, which includes medical, social, and cultural aspects of deafness.[viii]

Medical Model – In this model, being deaf is mostly viewed as undesirable and should be avoided. Those favoring this model often experience hearing loss later in life. Restoring their hearing is preferable.

Social Model – This model emphasizes deafness as a disability, which is different from the medical model of deafness. Social factors influence this model, as well as the environment often disables the individual. If the environment was improved, then the individual would be less disabled or not be disabled at all. Integrating deaf individuals with society is desired.

Cultural Model – This is the standing model within the Deaf community, having acceptance, as well as enrichment from the cultural aspects of deafness. Deafness is celebrated (e.g. Deaf pride) and the Deaf community does not see itself as a disability group. The use of sign language is the preferred mode of communication within this model. Restoring any hearing is less likely with this model as well.

Deaf Identity

Author, N.S. Glickman (1996), has identified four different types of deaf identity. Deaf identity can evolve in any direction depending on the circumstances of the individual, as well as the acculturation process between

Deaf and hearing culture. [ix] The four types are listed here to better understand the deaf-hearing dynamics that influence people.[x]

1. **Culturally hearing** – Hearing norms are the reference point for normality and the role of deafness in one's identity is not emphasized.
2. **Culturally marginal** – Those who do not fit into either hearing or Deaf societies as demonstrated through their behaviors. Their identities emerge as confused, without clear notions of connections with deaf or hearing societies. Often, saying they feel they do not belong in either society.
3. **Immersed in Deaf culture** – A positive and uncritical identification with Deaf people. Hearing values are denigrated and the Deaf world is idealized.
4. **Bicultural** – The ability to comfortably negotiate hearing and Deaf settings. These people embrace Deaf culture and also value hearing contacts.

Audism

Most people in the hearing world see deafness as a disability, a cross to bear, a *missing* part. They think about all of the things that Deaf people miss: music, easy banter, telephone conversation and inclusiveness (or lack thereof). They see deafness as an inferior and suboptimal way of life over hearing. There's even a term in the Deaf culture for this called *audism*. Simply put, it is a negative and/or oppressive attitude towards Deaf people by either deaf or hearing people and organizations, and a failure to accommodate them. People who have audist attitudes are considered to be audists. For example, the refusal or failure to use sign language in the presence of a person who uses sign language is considered audism.

Discriminatory practices often occur at the individual level and institutional level.[xi]

American Sign Language

American Sign Language (ASL) is a visual – gestural – spatial language composed of hand shapes and hand movements. This language also includes facial expressions and body language as integral parts of the communication process. ASL has grammatical features (e.g., subject and verb agreements) that distinguish it as a formal language. In addition, ASL has linguistic components such as phonology, morphology, semantics, syntax, and cultural history which provide a foundation for the language.

Generally, signs have a tendency to be context specific, and in order to produce the appropriate sign, a user of ASL will need to understand the concept and not just the word to be conveyed. Many religious signs symbolize the concept they represent, while others do not. *Iconic* signs (signs that resemble the word) are typically formed more often than *arbitrary* signs (signs not resembling the word). Some religious signs have historical relevance and may not necessarily correlate with a more modern representation (e.g., the sign for "Protestant."). Morphological rules (a subfield of linguistics) state that when two signs are combined to make a compound sign, a new meaning will emerge. For example, combining the signs "farm" and "house" can make the sign for "stable." Generally, two or more users must agree on a new or temporary sign. There are religious signs that may not be recognized in some areas of the country due to regional variations. Furthermore, ASL is predominantly used in the United States and parts of Canada.

Deaf Ministry Models

There are multiples ways of doing this specialized ministry and this book provides an overview of several common types of Deaf ministries. Fortunately, there is not a one-size fits all and there is not a need to try to fit circles into square pegs. Deaf ministry can include the following models: (1) The Deaf church, (2) an interpreted ministry, (3) a hard-of-hearing and late-deafened ministry, (4) Deaf-blind ministry, (5) a multicultural church, (6) Deaf advocacy, (7) Deaf missions, and (8) a disability ministry.

Deaf Church

In the Deaf church model, Deaf people are mostly the leaders and/or are at the forefront of doing pastoral and servant ministry. Most often, the congregation is made up of mostly d/Deaf, hard-of-hearing, late-deafened and Deaf-blind individuals and their families with a few or some hearing members. A Deaf congregation may share facilities with a hearing church, while some have their own building that is owned or leased. Deaf congregations without their own church building or who is a part of a hearing church's ministry is included in this ministry model because they have their own Deaf worship service, their own Deaf leadership committee/board, and are mostly autonomous. Also, Deaf culture is often prominent in this ministry model.

Interpreted Ministry

Deaf ministries include within its umbrella the interpreted ministry model. A chapter in this text goes into more detail of what an interpreted ministry is and what it often looks like. An interpreted ministry is where the church provides a sign language interpreter (or a team of interpreters) to provide communication access for both d/Deaf and hearing congregants in worship and other church events.

Hard-of-Hearing Ministry

Frequently, the hard-of-hearing ministry model, which often includes those who are late-deafened, ranges from inclusion (e.g. hospitality or invitations to events), to communication access (e.g. assisted listening devices, providing printed materials, or having an interpreter), and/or advocacy when it's asked for. It's best to inquire what the individual's communication needs are.

Deaf-blind Ministry

The Deaf-blind ministry model includes individuals with both a hearing loss and a vision loss. Since one does not have to be fully deaf and/or fully blind, this category of Deaf ministry can fit in each of the other ministries already mentioned, yet, depending on the communication needs and services can certainly be its own ministry altogether. Additional to the communication aspect of the ministry, there may be needs of needing a support service provider (SSP) to assist the Deaf-blind individual, transportation to and from the church, and other support needs outside of worship, such as assisting with basic life needs (e.g. advocacy, providing friendship, connecting to support systems, and assisted technology).

Multicultural Church

In a multicultural church model, the congregation and leadership will be made up of both d/Deaf and hearing individuals, including those leading worship. This multicultural setting attempts to be inclusive of d/Deaf, hard-of-hearing, late-deafened, Deaf-blind, and hearing people. Barriers to communication are typically removed in this venue and all people are seen as equal.

Deaf Advocacy

The Deaf advocacy model supports Deaf churches and/or organizations through a variety of means, such as providing case management, financial or material assistance, direct advocacy, and by empowerment. Deaf advocates, sometimes seen as Deaf allies, are typically individuals, Deaf or hearing churches, organizations, hearing family members of church members who are supportive of Deaf values and inclusion in mainstream society and/or within the church. Other examples of this type of ministry are prayer, financial partnerships with Deaf churches and/or organizations that support their mission and ministry, and by offering assistance through resources so it may be autonomous. Often, Deaf advocates also provide human service work to the Deaf community.

Deaf Missions

The Deaf missions model will range from doing outreach to marginalized individuals in the community (e.g. bringing dinner to group homes or visits to a nursing home), to planning or joining mission trips abroad (e.g. Kenya or Jamaica) or domestically. Also, it can be considered a one time or an irregularly scheduled type of outreach ministry or support.

Disability Ministry

The disability ministry model is a church's pledge to serving those with disabilities, which can be to a specific disability group, like hearing loss, or various disabilities. Often, a church provides accommodations so individual(s) and their families can participate in the life of the church and/or its community.

Negative Church Experiences

As children, many Deaf people went to church with their families. For the majority of them in the pre-ADA generation (prior to the passing of the American with Disabilities Act), there were no interpreters provided, which made their worship experience boring, and for some, feeling begrudged. Also, some d/Deaf individuals were brought to church and healings were attempted in order to restore their hearing loss.[xii] When the healing did not occur, they often were ignored due to not having enough faith. Having these negative church experiences, it has left some Deaf people disinterested in church. Loving them and showing grace can welcome them back to the church. Seeing they are accepted as they are (not needing to be healed, but are valued), some are returning.

Challenges of Deaf Ministry

Like with hearing ministry, Deaf ministry has its challenges. Church blogger, Marshall Lawrence, raises good points in the challenges of doing Deaf ministry.[xiii]

❑ *Deaf people are invisible to most hearing people.* Deaf people are just not on the radar of most hearing people. They know Deaf people exist, but they have given little or no thought to how very different their lives must be. Consequently, they make false assumptions about how much access Deaf really have to the world. They ASSUME most parents of Deaf children will learn how to communicate in sign language. (The truth: 80% of Deaf kids grow up in families where sign language is not used in the home.) They ASSUME religious instruction is carried on by the parents or the churches, but we've already shared that this is really rare for Deaf kids.

❑ *Hearing people believe that Deaf children can now be "cured" by cochlear implants and improvements in hearing aid technologies.* This is NOT true. There is no "cure" for deafness. Indeed, the surgery required to implant the cochlear devices actually destroys any residual hearing the person may have. I am NOT totally against these devices. They certainly have their place and they have been a blessing to many! But it is vital that you understand that the "hearing" offered by these devices is VERY different from what we would consider natural human hearing. The depth, the breadth, the power, the dynamic range, the rejection of unwanted sound elements — all of which the human ear working in tandem with the human brain can deliver — these elements are just not

14

present for those who use the implants. There is NO "cure" for deafness and, despite what the surgeons will tell you, when a deaf child is forced to rely ONLY on the implants and is not permitted to learn and use sign language, that child is almost certainly destined to struggle more with language comprehension and is far more likely to live a lonely and socially isolated life than is a child who learns to sign at a young age.

❑ *There is a real shortage of well-trained ASL users in North American churches.* Most church interpreters are poorly trained volunteers who may have a heart of gold, but do not have the skills needed to clearly communicate important spiritual truths in sign language. Others (and I know this is going to sound very harsh but it is far more prevalent than you would imagine) are motivated by the emotional kick they receive by being in such a conspicuous position of benevolent leadership to these "poor pitiful disabled people" and fail to exhibit the winsome spirit of true Christ-like servanthood. Such people often turn off the Deaf who may attend for a short time. Even if they have excellent skills and a true servant's heart, they may be thwarted by pastors, worship leaders, or others who see the addition of sign language as a complication and a detriment to the worship experience of the hearing majority.

❑ *There is a lack of Deaf Christian leadership and a great need for more Deaf led churches.* Just as English speaking hearing people can get so much more out of the experience worshiping in a congregation where nearly everyone can communicate freely in English; many Deaf people prefer to worship in a place where

American Sign Language is the native language of the congregants. But Deaf churches (or separate Deaf worship services and small group opportunities) are still rare, and those that do exist are almost always found in larger communities — often towns with a residential Deaf school nearby.

❑ *In-fighting within the ministry.* This can easily happen between interpreters, between leadership, and by having conflict over ministry or program ideas. The whole vision can be dampened due to tensions and initial passion can be depleted rather quickly.

❑ *The cost of ministry.* Many hearing churches wish to draw the circle wide and have Deaf, hard-of-hearing, late-deafened, and Deaf-blind people attend their church, but often time's interpreters need to be budgeted for. If it is a small church, then it can be difficult to afford an interpreter. Prioritizing Deaf ministry when it comes time to making the budget is essential.

❑ *Slow growth.* Sometimes ministries are slow to grow and the same can hold true for starting a Deaf ministry. It is about building relationships – this is the heart of Deaf ministry (relationships). Don't give up five minutes before the miracle.

Deaf Ministry Listing

There are a couple of somewhat reliable websites that offer (an almost) up-to-date list of Deaf ministries and Deaf churches. If your church has a Deaf ministry, contact the two websites to add to their list.

Deaf Ministries Connections
Harrisonburg, VA
https://deafministriesconnection.wordpress.com/

Interpreted Ministries List
https://deafministriesconnection.wordpress.com/interpr
eted-services/

The OHSOEZ.com website
Listed by denomination.
www.ohsoez.com/churches/churchtitle.htm

Questions for Reflection

1. What model of Deaf ministry interests you and why?
2. Do you believe God may be calling your church to a different form of Deaf ministry, one that may expand your current ministry? Why do you feel this way?
3. Where do you see God's grace in your ministry? Provide examples.
4. What experiences do you have with a variety of Deaf people? What have you learned from these experiences?
5. In what ways can your church incorporate facets of Deaf culture, including the linguistic aspect?
6. Romans 8:31 reads, *What then shall we say to these things? If God is for us, who can be against us?* (NIV) How do you see God supporting your faith community in doing Deaf ministry?

Conclusion

In conclusion, an older article by the National Council of Churches states that approximately ten percent of d/Deaf and hard-of-hearing people attend church, indicating a large population is unserved.[xiv] Deaf culture was also discussed providing some insight to the Deaf community and the culture's richness. In addition, the following Deaf ministry models were introduced: The Deaf church model, the interpreted ministry model, the hard-of-hearing ministry model, the Deaf-blind ministry model, the Deaf missions model, the multicultural church model, the Deaf advocacy ministry model, and the disability ministry model. In addition, typical negative church experiences by d/Deaf, hard-of-hearing, late-deafened, and Deaf-blind individuals, as well as some common challenges of having a Deaf ministry were discussed.

Chapter 2 – Overview of the Deaf Church Model

Like other language minority groups, many Deaf people congregate in a church setting for spiritual and fellowship reasons. Generations ago, Deaf people who attended Deaf residential schools usually had some type of church exposure, usually on Sunday mornings or Sunday afternoons, when a minister or priest came to the school campus. Others attended hearing churches, without having an interpreter, with family members. Some Deaf people had good church experiences; others did not. In matters of faith, each experience was different.

Worship services to the Deaf community were perceived as a ministry for the church. Centuries have gone by since the Episcopal Church organized the first Deaf congregation in the United States; next was the Catholic Church, soon followed by the Lutheran Church. Not far behind these three denominations came the Methodist Church and the Baptist Church, both of which had established Deaf worship services by the turn of the twentieth century.[xv]

Deaf worship services, where the dominant language is ASL, sometimes adapt liturgy (a prescribed format for worship) to better suit congregations. For instance, contemporary praise services popularize the worship service with music, whereas some Deaf congregations may give less emphasis to music and more to drama, an extension of ASL storytelling. Because ASL is a visual and spatial language, it is not uncommon for Deaf worship services to include dramas more frequently than hearing worship services do, perhaps during Scripture readings or as sermon illustrations. A number of Deaf congregations incorporate a drum during a song that is being signed so that vibrations ripple through the worship space, a cultural practice that may be somewhat annoying or distracting for hearing people but enhances the experience for Deaf worshipers.

Most Deaf congregations will welcome hearing visitors. A hearing person learning to sign can expect common questions from Deaf church members, such as the following:

- ❏ Your first and last name?
- ❏ Are you Deaf, hard-of-hearing, or hearing?
- ❏ Are there Deaf people in your family?
- ❏ Why are you learning sign language?
- ❏ Who is teaching you the language and culture?

It is normal for a hearing person to feel intimidated because of not knowing the language; most first-time visitors to any church, Deaf or hearing, usually feel awkward. An interpreter can assist the minority language user to feel more at ease because communication can take place between the parties. As an interpreter facilitates communication, hearing people can clear up common misconceptions about Deaf people.[1]

Cultural aspects that differ from hearing culture can be observed within Deaf congregations. Whether a Deaf church member shares with others an anecdote about a Video Relay Service (VRS) call with a child or announces to others the upcoming homecoming event at the Deaf school, Deaf culture is a major influence in the dynamics of a Deaf congregation. Deaf culture, with similar experiences, common language, and shared traditions, often differentiates a Deaf congregation from a hearing congregation.

Deaf Fellowship

Since d/Deaf individuals come from various backgrounds, it is likely d/Deaf individuals come from various faith traditions as well. In fact, quite often, denominational affiliation is secondary, while having a Deaf fellowship can be of primary importance to those serving and being a part of the church. Fellowship is a cultural tradition where Deaf people would gather in various locations, in which they catch up on news events, receive encouragement, and in a sense feel supported by other Deaf people.[xvi] Hearing churches often have potlucks, which is similar to the idea of being in fellowship with one another. Having a sense of belonging is important to most people and it is no different for Deaf people.

Along with the socialization aspect, there is a sense of community within this fellowship. Whenever there is

---

[1] Common misconceptions: (a) Can Deaf people drive? (b) How do Deaf parents know when their child is crying? (c) Will their children be Deaf?

no pastor or priest to oversee the Deaf congregation or church, leadership is often shared among the membership, which includes preaching.

Deaf Leadership

Within a Deaf church, the leadership is made up of primarily d/Deaf individuals. In fact, there may be a d/Deaf pastor (or a hearing pastor who is fluent in sign language) overseeing the Deaf congregation's needs in terms of: spiritual life, pastoral care, family ministries, fellowship, and discipleship activities. Lay leaders (or deacons like in the Baptist tradition) are usually d/Deaf and provide support depending on their gifts, talents, interests, and/or need. Clergy and laity work together in the life of the faith community, whether it is made up of Deaf and/or hearing people.

Lay-Led Deaf Ministry

The Lutheran Deaf Mission Society of the Lutheran Church – Missouri Synod – describes a common Deaf ministry model that is led by mostly Deaf lay people.[xvii] It describes it as a trained d/Deaf lay minister, who in most respects functions as the pastor of a Deaf congregation. The lay minister is certified for ministry by the district. The title of the office which the lay minister holds varies among the Districts.

The Lay-minister often serves under remote supervision of a pastor. The lay-led ministry model has many advantages and disadvantages in common with the bi-vocational model, with the following aspects unique to Lay-led Deaf ministry.

Advantages – A few advantages for this type of Deaf ministry include:

1. The lay minister is a d/Deaf person who is familiar with the local deaf community. He or she will typically have a better rapport with the community than would a hearing pastor serving in the same location.
2. This model typically raises up leaders for ministry from within the congregation, effectively utilizing God's gifts for ministry within the Body of Christ.

Disadvantages – A few disadvantages of this model include:

1. The quality and quantity of pastor supervision of a lay minister varies greatly. Ideally, the supervising pastor knows Sign and understands Deaf culture, but this may not always be the case.
2. The depth and breadth of theological training which the lay minister receives varies greatly. A lay minister may serve without an adequate understanding of Law/Gospel hermeneutics.
3. Limitations determined by the District and by State Law may restrict some aspects of the lay minister's functions, e.g. performing weddings.

Deaf Ministry Leadership Training

There are a number of venues that offer training in doing Deaf ministry. Besides the apprenticeship or mentorship type training, **Deaf Missions** offers on-going training courses in a variety of topics through their Deaf Missions Training Center. By doing to their website (www.deafmissions.org), information about the training is on the training webpage.

Deaf Pah classes, the **Deaf Institute of Theology Pre-Seminary Program**, is offered by the Deaf Lutheran Mission Society (DLMS), Concordia Seminary, affiliated with the St. Louis, and The Lutheran Church—Missouri Synod Deaf Missions. Their website is www.csl.edu/admissions/academics/altrt/deaf-institute-of-theology/. The alternate website is www.deafjesus.org/courses/courses.html.

The **Sunset International Bible Institute** offers a Deaf program that trains ministry leaders in doing Deaf ministry. It also provides sign language classes and interpreting training. Their website is www.sibi.cc.

Cultural Worship

In a Deaf worship setting, the order of service and/or liturgy is often culturally adapted to a Deaf congregation. For example, a former Deaf Church that I served at bangs a gong at the beginning of the service. (Gong) In the name of the Father. (Gong) In the name of the Son. (Gong) In the name of the Holy Spirit, three-in-one. Amen.

Another cultural adaptation can be seen in the **litany**. Where there is a leader who signs/reads, a lay person representing the people would sign/read the words of the people, in which the congregation copy signs the lay person. It makes sense because hearing people often read the litany from a bulletin; yet, Deaf people need their hands free to sign the words of the litany. While some congregations will have two individuals for this, others will stick with one person who simply roles shifts the two aspects of the litany (leader and people).

Still, another cultural adaptation is in the **Scripture reading**. While hearing churches have a hearing person read aloud the Scripture passage, it is common for some Deaf faith communities to perform a <u>Biblical drama</u>. It can be as simple as two people to a handful of people acting out a scene from the Biblical passage. Often props are used in some way that brings the reading to life (e.g. long blue fabric representing water). When doing a Biblical drama, it is a wonderful way to include others from the Deaf congregation, giving them a sense of ownership and involvement in their worship service.

Music in the Deaf church is sometimes culturally adapted by using a drum while a choir signs the music. By using a drum, it often provides a vibration to those seated in the audience and to the choir members themselves. While most Deaf people enjoy feeling the vibration, it can be loud to some hearing people who are not used to it. Since Deaf people need their hands free (not holding a hymnal), a d/Deaf person will lead music by signing a song for the congregation to copy sign (following along to what the lead signer is signing). Including music videos since they are often captioned is also used by some Deaf churches.

Including **visuals** or **props** are often expressions in Deaf culture and this holds true in Deaf worship. Including props, banners, and the like are frequently used as illustrations in the **sermon** that is preached. For example, a white t-shirt was used once in a sermon where I sprayed red ink (disappearing ink) to illustrate that sin causes blemishes in our spiritual life; however, a relationship with Christ helps to clean these blemishes. The congregation was amazed to see the ink stains gone. Still, storytelling and/or wearing costumes when preaching sermons are often used as well.

Outreach Ministry

Often, members from the Deaf church or Deaf ministry will have an outreach ministry to the Deaf community. The following are some suggestions.[xviii]

- ❑ Visit group homes (consider bringing dinner, refreshments, and/or playing Bible bingo)
- ❑ Visit shut-ins (bring a church newsletter to a person's home, at a hospital, assisted living facility, or at a nursing home, as many people like to stay informed)
- ❑ Visit d/Deaf, hard-of-hearing, late-deafened, and/or Deaf-blind patients on a psychiatric unit (Bringing refreshments and playing Bible bingo works well)
- ❑ Provide basic religious education at a Deaf school in the area, usually an after school event
- ❑ Lead or participate in an after school sign language club at an area school or at your church
- ❑ Prison ministry, in which a Bible study and/or pastoral care are provided to the d/Deaf prisoners. Prison programs are usually arranged through a volunteer coordinator at the prison or through a chaplain
- ❑ Summer camps that specifically host d/Deaf campers (most kids are d/Deaf).[2] If it is not an all Deaf camp, then it may be a blended group of kids (made up of hearing and d/Deaf kids) that will utilize interpreters
- ❑ Host or participate in a Deaf adult camp is gaining more popularity where adults who are d/Deaf and have disabilities attend
- ❑ There are a number of Deaf-blind adult camps that are also hosted around the country that some churches are affiliated with as well.

---

[2] A list of Deaf-related camps can be found at Gallaudet University's website. www.gallaudet.edu/clerc-center/info-to-go/national-resources-and-directories/summer-camps.html.

Deaf Prison Ministry

Prison ministry is often seen as a form of outreach ministry. There are a number of Deaf ministries around the country that are involved in prison ministry. The involvement often depends on the cooperation from the prison. Some prisons are more flexible than others. One caveat is some prisons do not allow persons from the outside to conduct prisoner visits and conduct Bible studies or other activities, as the latter is frequently considered a part of the prison volunteer initiative. When in doubt, it is best to ask what the prison policy is.

The Christian Lutheran Church of the Deaf in Silver Spring, MD has an active prison ministry. They partner with other area Christian ministries in providing:[xix]

1. Weekly Bible study with male d/Deaf inmates.
2. Educational tutoring at the prison, helping some to improve their competence in English literacy, and others who are hard-of-hearing and late-deafened to learn Sign.
3. Correspondence ("pen pal") with d/Deaf inmates in State and Federal facilities.
4. After-Care mentoring for newly released inmates.
5. Community awareness and advocacy in the criminal justice system, addressing the unique and often neglected needs of incarcerated Deaf people.

The Deaf Lutheran church is also affiliated with the

❑ Deaf Prison Ministry Network (http://deafprison.org/)
❑ Embracing Lambs Ministries (www.freewebs.com/embracinglambs/)
❑ Deaf Prison Coalition (Facebook group)

The **Healing Hands Ranch**, north of Houston, Texas, is a men's residential program for ex-offenders needing after-care services. They accept both hearing and d/Deaf men. Services they provide are discipleship training, GED preparation classes, mentoring, addiction counseling, and on-site job training. For more information can be found at their website at www.healinghandsranch.org.

Bi-vocational Ministry

Some Deaf congregations are made up of individuals and families who do not earn large salaries, which influence their offerings and tithes to the church. This is similar to hearing churches as well. It is common that some d/Deaf pastors and ministers work a second job to help support him/herself and his/her family. The apostle Paul did the same thing; moreover, when he was an apostle, he had a tent-making business.

CODA/KODA Ministry

Children of Deaf Adults (CODA) are adults and Kids of Deaf Adults are children and youth. If your church includes the d/Deaf, hard-of-hearing, late-deafened, and Deaf-blind parents, then there is a likelihood of needing a children's ministry, which might be a CODA or KODA ministry. Some Deaf churches have a ministries specifically set up for CODAs and KODAs, which often includes acceptance of them being bilingual and bicultural (Deaf and hearing culture). Whether it is a children's program or a youth program, consider the language and cultural needs of these children.

In their work, <u>A Guide for Professionals Serving Hearing Children with Deaf Parents</u> (2001), Jenny

Singleton and Matthew Tittle point out a few key understandings about children with Deaf parents.[xx] Some distinctions of CODAs are as follows:

1. Bilingual/bicultural, CODAs are born to Deaf parents and potentially share the language and culture of their Deaf parents, but are also members of the hearing community and acquire English.
2. Protective and frequently advocate for their Deaf parents and the Deaf community, often concerned for their parents' image and protect them from insults or ignorance from hearing people. At times, CODAs provided cross-cultural mediation between Deaf and hearing people.
3. Some CODAs struggle with two different cultures as they develop their cultural identity. Some have found support in connecting with either a youth community (through KODAheart.com) or an adult community (through CODA International), as they share similar circumstances (it normalizes their experiences).
4. CODAs from the pre-ADA (American Disabilities Act) generation often interpreted for their Deaf parents (it was the norm), while post-ADA generation of CODAs did so less frequently. It is best to provide a sign language interpreter for the d/Deaf parents than to have the child interpret.

CODA International hosts an annual conference in different parts of the country. CODAs who attend feel such a belonging and it helps to build their sense of identity. Their website is www.coda-international.org. KODA-Heart is an organization and they list KODA camps and KODA organizations, in which many are listed by state. Their website is http://kodaheart.com/resources/koda-organizations/.

Funerals and Memorial Services

When a member of the Deaf community passes, it is often a time of remembrance and many Deaf people usually turn out for the service. There is a fellowship aspect to the death, in which Deaf people gather and socialize. In fact, it is not uncommon for the Deaf people to be the last ones to leave a funeral home, even standing outside under the street light to finish conversations.[xxi] It is not unusual for there to be an additional memorial service for the d/Deaf person who passed, in part, because the initial service was mostly a culturally hearing type of service. To pay tribute to the d/Deaf person, a culturally Deaf memorial service is sometimes hosted by a Deaf church after the funeral.

Questions for the Future

In Roger Hitching's book, The Church and Deaf People, Hitching includes an interview with Chaplain Shrine, a Deaf chaplain in the Church of England. Shrine indicates three potential concerns for the Deaf church.[xxii]

1. Its members are aging, which suggests that many Deaf churches will die out in the next twenty years or so. Younger people are not joining.
2. The church has a poor image in the Deaf community, where it is often regarded as irrelevant, old-fashioned, and stuck on English and hearing ways of doing things.
3. The Deaf church is generally ignored and marginalized by the wider church.[xxiii]

Shrine's concerns are valid. Historically, Deaf churches were geographically located near Deaf clubs and Deaf schools. Most Deaf clubs, which were more prominent in the early and mid-twentieth century, have folded, and with more Deaf children being mainstreamed, in part because of having cochlear implants, in public schools, there is a potential need for more interpreters in churches in the near future.

Case Study – Bishop Peggy Johnson

Before Bishop Peggy Johnson served as a United Methodist bishop, she served as a local pastor at a Deaf church in Baltimore, MD. The church is Christ United Methodist Church of the Deaf. Bishop Johnson served from 1988 to 2008. In the twenty years she served, Bishop Johnson turned a small congregation into a large, multicultural, and vibrant Deaf church that served not only her congregation and her community. Bishop Johnson felt that part of the ministry's success is doing ministry with Deaf people.

Aside from making the building accessible, she helped to ensure that worship offered captioning, that it had a voice interpreter for the "sign language impaired," large print bulletins, having an assisted listening device system, and interpreters for the Deaf-blind individuals who attended the service. Modeling inclusion and accessibility was an important aspect of Christ Church's ministry.

Bishop Johnson would ask herself, "Who are missing from the pews?" Growing the congregation was important and ensuring that all were welcomed was key to the church's growth. Providing a space for fellowship before and after worship was an important aspect to the church's growth. Along with fellowship, providing education regarding current events and basic life needs (e.g. how to have a last will and testament, HIV prevention, and substance abuse prevention).

Relationships are important and this is seen in Bishop Johnson's outreach efforts where she was involved in Christian education at the area Deaf schools, involved in prison ministry, visiting the deaf unit at the state psychiatric hospital, visiting shut-ins, visited Deaf group homes, Deaf missions, hosting a religious interpreter's workshop, and establishing Deaf camp (one for youth and one for adults with disabilities) and a Deaf-blind camp for adults. Bishop Johnson also helped to establish the Deaf Shalom Zone, a non-profit organization associated with the Deaf church that provided case management needs to the Deaf community.

Along with personal relationships is considering ecumenical Deaf ministry that denominations work and serve together in ministry together. Bishop Johnson frequently served with other denominational ministers in doing ministry, such as prison ministry, Christian Education at the Deaf school, and at camps. Also, volunteers are crucial and recruiting people to be involved in the ministry is crucial. For example, when Bishop Johnson visited a shut-in, she often brought a d/Deaf person to accompany her.

Educating hearing people and hearing churches about Deaf ministry was also important to the church's outreach efforts. Bishop Johnson and her Deaf choir would visit hearing churches and share the importance of Deaf ministry and deaf awareness. Educating the churches on how to have their own deaf ministry, preaching about valuing Deaf people (e.g. often preaching

Bishop Peggy Johnson

from Paul's scripture in 1 Corinthians 12:12-31 on the body of Christ), and basic inclusion strategies.

Part of Bishop Johnson's strategy was not having her own agenda, but asking the people what was important to them. Good advice that helped to grow the church to an average attendance of 150 each Sunday and have a global outreach.

Case Study – Immigrant Deaf Church

Marlene Windham says, "God gave me a vision. So, I just dropped everything and came to Los Angeles." She moved to Los Angeles to restart the ministry for Deaf people. Windham was joined by Fred Crews, pastor at Calvary Community Church of the Deaf in nearby Norwalk, and Ron Renusch, a Deaf evangelist who moved to California from Colorado, in restarting Pilgrim's ministry, which is now called Los Angeles Deaf Church. Windham shares that the new Deaf ministry exploded with Deaf immigrants who live nearby. "I've seen Deaf people reached by the gospel for the first time," she says. According to Christian organization Heart for the Deaf, fewer than 5 percent of d/Deaf people are Christians. "To watch some of these people develop into vibrant servants of the Lord - to see them pick up on what God can do, and what you can do for God-I'm seeing it happen." These people are getting outside of themselves to reach other Deaf people, and that's what it's all about. That just brings tears to my eyes."[xxiv]

Los Angeles Deaf Church and Calvary Community Church of the Deaf, which Windham are co-churches, they have established an Internet ministry to the d/Deaf (www.deafchurch.net) that is flourishing and reaches thousands. Worship services that include sign language are broadcast live online. "We're being watched all over-- China, Japan, France, Scandinavian countries, everywhere," says Windham. "Just last February, a team of 10 people was asked to come to India – Deaf people – and they went there and did a missionary trip. Deaf ministry is just busting out all over. It has been the most amazing journey--just amazing," Windham says. "I don't know what else to say, except that all my life I've waited on the Lord and let Him design my path, and there's no way I could have come up with all this!"

Questions for Reflection

1. Do you have any Deaf churches in your area? How might you collaborate with them?
2. What experiences do you have with culturally Deaf people?
3. Where do you see Christ in the Deaf community?
4. What deaf-related outreach ministry can your church implement and when?
5. Matthew 25:36 reads, (Jesus said,) *I needed clothes and you clothed me, I was sick and you looked after me, I was in prison and you came to visit me.* (NIV) How can you provide care like this to d/Deaf, hard-of-hearing, late-deafened, and Deaf-blind people in your community?

Conclusion

This chapter discussed the different aspects of the Deaf church model, which often includes the importance of Deaf fellowship, Deaf leadership and training, and how ASL and Deaf culture are at the heart of this ministry model. Outreach ministry and prison ministry was also discussed that encouraged the involvement of pastoral and laity leadership in these ministries. It is important to note that some features of the other ministry models may include some aspects of the Deaf church model in order to broaden the accessibility of those attending worship, to encourage participation in the life of the church, and to extend inclusion and hospitality to individuals and families who are d/Deaf, hard-of-hearing, late-deafened, and/or Deaf-blind. For example, in a multicultural ministry setting, the congregation is made up of both d/Deaf people and hearing people. There is a strong likelihood facets of the Deaf church model are incorporated in the multicultural church or congregation (i.e. involvement in a Deaf prison ministry, fostering fellowship, and/or utilizing a Deaf liturgist during worship).

Chapter 3 – Overview of an Interpreted Ministry

A widespread form of Deaf ministry is the interpreted ministry model. The reasons for this can include there may be no local Deaf church; d/Deaf, hard-of-hearing, late-deafened, or Deaf-blind individuals attend a hearing church with hearing family members, or simply for preference sake. Quite often, the interpreter or team of interpreters helps lead efforts to include d/Deaf, hard-of-hearing, late-deafened, and/or Deaf-blind individuals in the life of the church. Examples are such as planning fellowship opportunities, teaching a sign language class, and coordinating outreach ministry (see p. 25). The following briefly explains the interpreted ministry, the interpreter role, interpreting competencies, and it offers ways for how to work as an interpreter. This chapter will help churches understand the idiosyncrasies of the interpreter.

Interpreted Ministry

The Lutheran Deaf Mission Society describes what the interpreted ministry model often looks like. Consider the following.[xxv]

Description - This ministry model is characterized by a hearing congregation providing an interpreter (paid or volunteer) for worship services and other activities.

Advantages – A few advantages of this model include:

1. Those Deaf young people who are (were) mainstreamed in school may feel more comfortable when mainstreamed in church.
2. This model provides for integration of Deaf people into the life of the hearing congregation.
3. This model provides greater opportunity for a congregation to serve the needs of hearing members of the family, particularly deaf children of hearing parents.
4. This model often provides opportunities for deaf Christians to worship and fellowship in a location nearer to their residence than the nearest Deaf church.
5. This model utilizes unique gifts for ministry which God has given to members of Christian congregations.
6. This model is well suited for serving small groups of people at little cost.

Disadvantages – A few disadvantages of this model include:

1. This model generally limits the participation of Deaf people in the life of the congregation to

those activities which are interpreted, typically the Sunday morning worship services.

2. Deaf people are dependent upon the availability and the ability of the interpreters for meaningful participation.

3. The language barrier that a pastor experiences when he is not conversant in Sign gives him and the Deaf members a sense of isolation from each other.

4. Pastoral counseling for Deaf members is prolonged or complicated (and often avoided by Deaf people) because of the "intrusion" of a third party (the interpreter).

5. The interpreter may acquire the role of "assistant pastor" even though he/she is not qualified for that role.

6. Denominations using this model have discovered that little outreach and growth results from this model, with groups remaining generally at ten people or less.

7. Interpreters are often difficult to locate in communities where this model would be most feasible (those with small Deaf populations).

8. Interpreters often do not receive adequate training and support.

9. A large majority of Deaf people do not favor interpreted worship. Just like hearing people, they prefer to receive the Word of God and to worship Him in their own heart-language, rather than constantly receiving only a translated message that was prepared and presented for another language and another culture.

Comments – Additional comments regarding this model include:

1. The low cost of implementing this model should not be the primary factor in choosing it for a situation.
2. The congregation must be encouraged to see the needs within the congregation, e.g., a family with a Deaf member.
3. The pastor must be strongly supportive and approachable.
4. The interpreters must continually upgrade their interpreting skills.
5. Opportunity should be provided for occasional separate times of fellowship for Deaf members, including Bible studies and worship events.

The Professional Interpreter

The remaining chapter gives focus to the interpreting role and competencies, much of which is from the book, Interpreting at Church, 4th Edition (2016). Industry professionals generally call persons who provide interpreting services *interpreters* or *practitioners*. From time to time, the term "signer" may be referenced; however, interpreters are encouraged to educate consumers with the proper title. When one provides interpreting services, it is much more than signing. It involves consultation, preparation, delivery of services, and follow-up in the setting where the interpreter works.

Religious interpreting has a place in society, as it assists in the spiritual transformation of a congregation and provides inclusion in a populated religious setting. Whether a Deaf congregation is providing American Sign Language (ASL)-to-English interpretation for hearing participants or a hearing congregation is providing

English-to-ASL interpretation for Deaf participants, religious interpreters are needed to make communication possible between two languages. An inclusive setting within the church is essential where the congregation can be open to diverse cultural and linguistic alternatives.

The decision to have an interpreter present for Christian worship services is one of many steps in the transcendent process that enables congregations to invite others who might have a different modality of language and cultural experiences. "Everyone is important, and all people are welcome here" is the view people should perceive. When the church provides professional interpreters for church services and programs, the doors widen with linguistic ambiance and hospitality for those whose language capabilities might otherwise place them in the minority. The professional interpreter, who provides religious interpreting or transliterating services, helps to fill a fundamental human need and enables seekers to develop their faith further in their faith communities.

"It is a calling," is what some say motivated them to learn sign language. Others may be influenced by a fascination that stems from seeing interpreters at work, or from having an encounter with a Deaf person at church that sparked an interest in learning the language. Another typical story is that of befriending a Deaf individual during childhood. Whatever the motivation, interpreters in faith-based settings are a crucial link in the chain of communication.

Interpreters provide communications access at a worship service, one reason they are valued in Christian settings. Faith, believing in a higher power, and experiencing spiritual renewal are still important for most faith communities. Religion may be less emphasized today than it was a century ago, but religious themes, ideas, and influences still saturate society. When a crisis occurs, whether personal or public, people feel compelled to seek guidance, hope, and support from the Church. Millions of visitors, for example, attended church following the catastrophic events of 9/11. Some visitors became church members, while others received what they needed and left again. Interpreters help to bridge hearing and Deaf communities, which includes both parts of the Church.

Interpreting in an unfamiliar church setting might make the practitioner a little leery. Whether the congregations are made up of mostly older church members or are young, thriving, multicultural congregations including a variety of people of different ethnicities, ages, backgrounds, and cultures, churches have dynamics just like family dynamics. Parts of the underlying culture can include environment (the church location), values (is the church more member-driven or doctrine-driven), and rituals. Each congregation is different, and the interpreter will need to work in accord with these cultural distinctions. As stated, each congregation has unique dynamics. There might be similarities with other congregations, but every church will have observable distinctions. Each congregation has a history, its own culture and sub-cultures, and its own expectations and preferences, which set it apart from other churches. Social, intellectual, or moral influences affect the dynamics as well. Qualities that help make the interpreter successful in settings with changing dynamics are flexibility, diplomacy, and good manners. The knack to communicate one's needs to make the church setting more conducive to interpretation activities is also essential. The ability and willingness to adapt in various contexts enables the interpreter to be comfortable and more accessible for interpreting assignments in his or her faith tradition.

History of RID

Before the establishment of the Registry of Interpreters for the Deaf (RID), most interpreters either had Deaf family members or were associated with the Deaf community. Perhaps they worked at the residential Deaf school or an area church. These early interpreters performed informal interpreting services, typically as a favor. Other venues for interpreting included meetings, special doctors' appointments, legal proceedings, and churches.

Pre-RID interpreters knew English and sign language, and this was thought to be the only prerequisite necessary to interpret for friends, family members, or colleagues. It is important to note that before the RID was formed, no interpreting training programs (ITPs) existed. There was no official registry of interpreters, and ASL was not considered an official language.

In June of 1964, at Ball State University (formerly Ball State Teachers College), a group of people with a common interest in formalizing the profession met during a teachers' conference where they were interpreting.[xxvi] Those present agreed that it would be necessary to have the following:

- ❑ A registry of "qualified" interpreters
- ❑ A set of standards (ethics)
- ❑ Interpreter training
- ❑ Testing and licensure
- ❑ Promotion of awareness for interpreting services

By the end of the conference, these Deaf and hearing participants established the Professional Registry of Interpreters for the Deaf. In 1972, the organization was incorporated, its goals and mission were further refined, and the name was slightly changed to become the RID of today.[xxvii]

Professional Accountability

Sign language interpreting is considered a profession. Qualified and licensed interpreters provide professional services to Deaf, Deaf-blind, hard-of-hearing, late-deafened, and hearing people. Like other professions such as medicine or teaching, the interpreting profession has four attributes that establish it as a legitimate profession. These are as follows:

- ❑ Specialized knowledge and skills
- ❑ Fulfillment of a fundamental human need
- ❑ Accountability structure
- ❑ Placement of another's interests before one's own[xxviii]

These attributes underscore professionalism in the interpreting setting. The interpreter must market him- or herself as a legitimate professional in the Deaf and hearing communities and assume responsibility for the work in order to interpret in the faith community.

Through RID, interpreters remain accountable when they participate in the Certification Maintenance Program (CMP) for certified members and the Associate Continuing Education Tracking (ACET) for non-certified members.[xxix] These essential programs were established to help ensure that interpreters remain proficient and updated with regard to changes in the profession. It is mandatory for certified interpreters to participate, while participation for associate members is optional. For the sake of accountability, associate members should also take part in the program because it helps to be exposed to best practices, to be associated with the profession, and help keep track of their professional development.[xxx]

Interpreting Certification

Unless the practitioner is a *generalist interpreter* (having a minimum amount of competence in various settings), he or she usually works in a specific field such as mental health, religion, education, law, or medical. The *specialist interpreter* has advanced education, additional knowledge and/or experience in a specialized setting. Because there is no other specialist certificate offered at this time, it is not uncommon for interpreters to have a post-secondary education, degree, or training in their specified field. The certifications offered to practitioners are the National Interpreter Certificate (NIC) and the Certified Deaf Interpreter (CDI), which is offered through the Center for the Assessment of Sign Language Interpretation (CASLI), an RID supported LLC. The prerequisite for national certification is a bachelor's degree, unless one is eligible for the Alternative Pathway track (see RID's website for additional information).[xxxi]

As in other professions, licensure requirements have evolved since the inception of RID. Some certifications that are no longer offered, yet are still accepted in the profession, are:

- ❑ Comprehensive Skills Certificate (CSC)
- ❑ Interpretation Certificate (IC) [partial certificate of the CSC]
- ❑ Transliteration Certificate (TC) [partial certificate of the CSC]
- ❑ Master Comprehensive Skills Certificate (MCSC)
- ❑ Specialist Certificate: Performing Arts (SC: PA)
- ❑ Specialist Certificate: Legal (SC: L)
- ❑ Certificate of Interpreting (CI)

- ❑ Certificate of Transliteration (CT)
- ❑ National Interpreter Certificate Advanced (NIC Advanced)
- ❑ National Interpreter Certificate Master (NIC Master)[xxxii]
- ❑ Oral Transliteration Certificate (OTC)

Deaf and hard-of-hearing interpreters, working as relay interpreters and/or interpreting for Deaf-blind individuals, were awarded the Reverse Skills Certificate (RSC), but that certification is replaced by the Certified Deaf Interpreter (CDI). The Conditional Legal Interpreting Permit – Relay (CLIP-R) certificate used to be awarded to Deaf and hard-of-hearing individuals working as relay interpreters in legal settings.[xxxiii] The National Association of the Deaf (NAD) used to offer national certifications, which were the NAD III (Generalist), NAD IV (Advanced), and the NAD V (Master). Those interpreters who continue to hold these certifications have registered them through RID.

Many interpreters are what the profession considers generalists. A generalist works as a practitioner in the community, either as a contract employee (freelance interpreter) or as a staff interpreter. As a staff interpreter, the practitioner may be employed by an interpreting agency or an organization. Freelance interpreters commonly contract their services with an interpreting agency or directly with the business or organization. When working in multiple settings (e.g., VRS, church, government, medical, etc..), many generalists are adaptive and possess a general knowledge in various disciplines.

National Interpreter Certificate

New and seasoned interpreters seeking certification are offered the National Interpreter Certification (NIC) through the CASLI. The computerized test is taken first; upon passing, the candidate for certification takes the interview and performance testing concomitantly. Successful candidates achieve the NIC. At one time this certification had three levels – the NIC, NIC Advanced, and NIC Master, but transitioned to the single-level NIC, in part for clarity and to streamline the scoring process.[xxxiv] This licensure was developed in a collaboration between the National Association of the Deaf (NAD) and RID.[3] The two organizations forged a partnership called the NAD-RID National Council on Interpreting (NCI).[xxxv] Prior to this collaboration, each organization tested and awarded its own certifications. NAD and RID agreed to establish a joint task force to study and implement a new certification system. They recommended redesigning the testing process to include a psychometric test that examines the interpreter's knowledge (computerized or written test), ethical standards (interview portion), and performance.

Ethical Standards

The ability to make ethical choices is necessary, not only for full-time interpreters, but for part-time interpreters as well. The Code of Professional Conduct (formerly known as the Code of Ethics) delineates seven tenets for the professional.[xxxvi]

---

[3] Before this collaboration, NAD had its own process for awarding certification. Holders of NAD certification were awarded a NAD III (Generalist), NAD IV (Advanced), or NAD V (Master). NAD certified members maintained their certification status and CMP when they transferred to the RID CMP system. NAD no longer awards certification.

TENETS

1. Interpreters adhere to standards of confidential communication.
2. Interpreters possess the professional skills and knowledge required for the specific interpreting situation.
3. Interpreters conduct themselves in a manner appropriate to the specific interpreting situation.
4. Interpreters demonstrate respect for consumers.
5. Interpreters demonstrate respect for colleagues, interns, and students of the profession.
6. Interpreters maintain ethical business practices.
7. Interpreters engage in professional development.

A full version with explications of the Code of Professional Conduct (CPC) tenets is accessible from RID's website.

During the interview portion of the National Interpreting Certification test, the interpreter must demonstrate the ability to adhere to ethical standards by giving possible solutions to circumstances that compromise one or more of these tenets. To ensure that the quality of interpreting services is at least adequate, if not better, RID has put in place the Ethical Practice System (EPS) for consumers or other interested parties to file complaints.

Interpreting & Transliterating

One section of the performance test rates the interpreter on language assessment. During this assessment, the interpreter must produce the right language for the Deaf or hard-of-hearing individual and determine whether to interpret or transliterate the message from the *source language* into the *target languages* (e.g., interpreting from English into ASL).

Between 1989 and 2005, candidates for certification (those who passed the written test) had a choice between two sign language certifications (the CI and CT) offered through RID.[xxxvii] Many practitioners chose to take both tests. When successfully completed, the certification test validates the person's ability to meet the minimum professional standards required of interpreters. A candidate who is able to interpret from ASL to spoken English as well as from spoken English to ASL would be awarded the CI. Candidates taking the CT had to exhibit the ability to transliterate between an English-based sign language and spoken English as well as transliterate between spoken English and an English-based sign language.[xxxviii] These two certifications replaced the CSC, and in turn are now replaced by the National Interpreter Certification (NIC).

There are a number of reasons for implementation of the NIC. One reason is that the candidate should be able to not only meet but exceed the minimum standards. Included in the NIC test is a scoring process, which differentiates itself from the last test that was pass/fail. New interpreters must take one test that incorporates both interpreting and transliterating in order to be awarded certification. Interpreters must be able to demonstrate their ability to interpret and transliterate to meet the diverse language needs of consumers. The Deaf community is populated with both ASL and Signed English users, which mean qualified interpreters, are also needed in the church setting.

Different Contexts

MULTIPLE VENUES

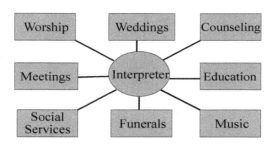

Church settings can offer a variety of genres; however, spiritual venues are predominately take place in the context of worship. For hearing churches with a thriving Deaf ministry, Deaf consumers may participate in other programs and services offered by the church, such as:

- ❑ Performing arts such as music and drama
- ❑ Pastoral care and counseling
- ❑ Weddings (possibly including pre-marriage counseling and the reception)
- ❑ Funerals and memorial services
- ❑ Retreats (e.g., a day long, overnight, and weekly retreats are common)
- ❑ Committee meetings (e.g., finance or leadership)
- ❑ Special worship services (e.g., Ash Wednesday or Good Friday)
- ❑ Sunday School (e.g., children or adult) or Bible study
- ❑ Church-related programs (e.g., fundraiser or youth trips)

❑ Social services (e.g., food pantry, referral services, self-help groups, and case management assistance)

Newer interpreters will need to be mentored and have additional experience in order to interpret in pastoral counseling settings, weddings, funerals, and committee meetings. Some contexts (e.g., weddings) will require additional preparation than others.

It is recommended that professional interpreters who work in settings that have liability risks purchase professional liability insurance.[xxxix] If the practitioner interprets regularly in pastoral counseling settings, the interpreter should consider the need for insurance coverage. In fact, most priests and ministers carry professional liability insurance for protection purposes. RID has an arrangement with an insurance agency to sell insurance to RID interpreters (another good reason to be a member).[4] Practitioners can obtain a referral to the insurance agency by contacting RID. Professional liability coverage is in the best interest of the interpreter.

Educating the Congregation

When an interpreter enters the church for the first time, he or she is often unfamiliar with the dynamics of the congregation. Most churches that encounter a d/Deaf individual or family for the first time are unacquainted with resources available to them. It is necessary at times to switch hats in order to educate consumers (e.g., church leaders) about interpreters.

---

[4] DHH Insurance provides liability insurance policies to RID members. Their website is www.DHHInsurance.com .

From interpreter to educator, the practitioner will work to make the environment accessible to the parties involved. RID provides general information about the profession of sign language interpreting. A copy of their publication given to those working with the interpreter for the first time might be helpful and prevent undermining or undervaluing the interpreting services. Hearing people who have never interacted with Deaf people may also need to be advised what to expect.[5]

From time to time, interpreters may be the only link to finding community resources. Church leaders who inquire will need to be made aware of what resources are available in the community. Resources that might be helpful to know and share include:

- ❑ Department of Rehabilitation Services (V.R.) locations[6]
- ❑ Area interpreting agencies
- ❑ Area churches that have Deaf ministries (for consultation)
- ❑ Textbooks on Deaf culture and sign language
- ❑ Information on the American Disabilities Act (ADA) for advocacy purposes[7]
- ❑ The state relay service (711)[8] and video relay service

---

[5] For instance, interpreters can explain cultural distinctions and language differences.

[6] To locate V.R. offices by state, go to http://www2.ed.gov/about/contacts/state/index.html. V.R. can provide employment search, job training assistance, and give referrals.

[7] For more information on the ADA can be read at www.ada.gov/cguide.htm .

[8] For d/Deaf members who are active in the church, a TTY or a video phone in the church office may be necessary so out-going

Education comes with the territory. Churches are sometimes at a loss in knowing that a newcomer who is d/Deaf needs accommodations such as sufficient lighting, removing visual distractions or barriers, and reserved seating. One form of Deaf empowerment is to ask the Deaf consumer (if present) to do the educating so as to allow the practitioner to remain in the interpreting role.

Logistics for Interpreter Placement

Generally, the interpreter will want to consult with the consumers, both Deaf and hearing, regarding physical logistics. Often the interpreter stands near the front of the sanctuary, close to either the pulpit or the lectern.[xl] However, the interpreter may need to make adjustments and relocate when there is interference such as a procession or liturgical dance. Furthermore, the interpreter will want to be placed away from lighting that illuminates from directly behind, such as a window.

Another consideration for placement is where the consumer is seated. Ask an usher or someone in charge to reserve seats for the consumers. If you are filling in for another interpreter, inquire where the consumers usually sit (seats may already be reserved). This will ensure the consumers can adequately see the interpreter. While it is important that the consumer to be able to see the interpreter, it is equally important for the interpreter to be able to hear the speakers. The interpreter should be prepared to discuss other logistical arrangements (e.g., length of the service and use of sound systems) when

---

calls can be made. Also, IP Relay on the Internet is an alternative for d/Deaf members who can access the Internet through a computer.

needed.[9]

Standard Practice Papers

RID's Standard Practice Paper: Interpreting in Religious Settings is not only informative, it delineates the skills, factors, and logistical concerns interpreters will want to think about in this work. It, and other practice papers, can be located at RID's website. Experienced interpreters from various religious backgrounds met as a committee to collaborate and draft a document that provides approaches and issues the profession and those with interpreting needs will want to consider when they work in a religious setting. New interpreters with a Christian faith who want to work in church settings will find the Standard Practice Paper to be useful because of the guidance, considerations, and resources that it includes. Other Standard Practice Papers are referenced throughout the document; these are worth reading for better insight and clarity about the role of an interpreter. Such papers are:

- ❑ Standard Practice Paper: Professional Sign Language Interpreting
- ❑ Standard Practice Paper: Business Practices: Billing Considerations
- ❑ Standard Practice Paper: Multiple Roles
- ❑ Standard Practice Paper: Team Interpreting

---

[9] If the service were traditional, it is suggested to stand close to the pulpit so Deaf parishioners can see both the preacher and the interpreter. When interpreting in a contemporary praise service that incorporates multimedia, and if the multimedia is used quite frequently, stand near the screen. If there is a praise band which is located near the deaf congregants, then the interpreter can relocate to where the band is and not be stationary.

STANDARD PRACTICE PAPER

> The Registry of Interpreters for the Deaf, Inc., (RID) Standard Practice Paper (SPP) provides a framework of basic, respectable standards for RID members' professional work and conduct with consumers. This paper also provides specific information about the practice setting. This document is intended to raise awareness, educate, guide and encourage sound basic methods of professional practice. The SPP should be considered by members in arriving at an appropriate course of action with respect to their practice and professional conduct.
>
> It is hoped that the standards will promote commitment to the pursuit of excellence in the practice of interpreting and be used for public distribution and advocacy.

About Interpreting in Religious Settings

Religious interpreting occurs in settings which are spiritual in nature. These settings can include worship services, religious education, workshops, conferences, retreats, confession, scripture study, youth activities, counseling, tours and pilgrimages, weddings, funerals and other special ceremonies. Religious interpreting poses unique challenges and requires specific skills and knowledge to address those needs. Special consideration should also be given to the interpreting environment and to interpreter compensation.

Specialized Skills

Professionals interpreting in a religious context should have fluency in a signed language (e.g. American Sign Language or Signed English) and a spoken language (e.g. English or Spanish). In addition, knowledge of a source language of an original text found in scripture such as Arabic, Hebrew, Latin or others would enhance the overall interpretation. It is ideal for the interpreter to have familiarity with the sacred text; however, the interpreter may need to work with an English translation.

Some interpreters enter the field by working in a religious venue. For some persons, interpreting in a religious setting is a spiritual calling. Interpreters are strongly encouraged to enhance their skills by working with a religious mentor who is a seasoned and/or certified interpreter before working independently. For additional information about mentoring, read RID's SPP titled, *Mentoring*.

333 Commerce Street ■ Alexandria, VA 22314
PH: 703.838.0030 ■ FAX: 703.838.0454 ■ TTY: 703.838.0459
www.rid.org

Specialized Knowledge

Interpreters will want to be aware of the consumer's cultural expectations and preferences that are specific to the environment. Interpreters in religious settings should also have access to and familiarize themselves with:

- Specialized vocabulary both signed and spoken that relate to the specific setting
- Texts specific to the setting (e.g. Koran, Torah, Bible)
- Materials used (e.g. sermon notes, homilies, multimedia presentations)
- Belief system(s), doctrine(s), creed(s) and ceremonial prayer(s)

Interpreters should be aware of how their own beliefs may potentially conflict with the beliefs of a different faith. Interpreters will want to accept assignments in a religious setting where they can faithfully and impartially interpret the message. Whether an interpreter needs to be a practicing member of a certain faith or follower of its precepts is a decision made by those requesting interpreting services. These issues should always be discussed with the interpreter and consumers prior to delivery of interpreting services.

In addition, interpreters who are members of RID must adhere to the NAD-RID Code of Professional Conduct regarding confidentiality. The interpreter should keep all interpreted information confidential, such as confessions, counseling and private meetings.

Working Environment

The religious interpreting environment requires advance preparation and cooperation on several fronts. Prior communication with a specific on-site contact along with access to the person(s) in charge of the presentations and presenters themselves is critical. The members affiliated with the particular setting should also be made aware of the interpreting services to be rendered, and all parties should understand the role of the interpreter.

The contact person should ensure the interpreter is provided with the necessary materials needed for the interpreter to appropriately prepare and assist in the logistics, placement and smooth integration of the interpreter's services into the religious activity. These arrangements should be made in advance of the date of the service or event.

Preparation

Each interpreter's access to all the materials, along with the order of each event/ceremony, with sufficient time to prepare appropriately, is central to the interpreting function.

Specific musical arrangements, lyrics and the meaning behind poetic language require analysis and rehearsal. This level of preparation by the interpreter is necessary in order to render a piece of music or poetic expression that is accurate, artistic, culturally modified and as visually inspiring and insightful as the audio portion. In this specialized setting, preparation by the interpreter requires commitment to ensure quality interpreting, such as matching the music flow, using the correct sign modality, providing an accurate rendition of the frozen text, displaying the appropriate emotions and actions, etc.

Long or complex events may require a team of two or more interpreters. Additionally, a musical or dramatic program may require weeks of preparation that may necessitate involvement of the interpreter (s) in the rehearsals. Preparation would also include information and detailed attention as to what is or is not acceptable, permissible to (or not to) interpret and appropriate attire.

Materials

Materials include but are not limited to music, sacred text or readings, along with the translations.

These materials can be provided in a printed and/or recorded format. Subsequently, the contact person will want to ensure the interpreter(s) are provided with lists of names that may be read, the agenda, announcements, copies of sermons, speeches, poetry, scripts of any artistic performances, songs and the like in advance.

Placement of Interpreter:

While the interpreter's placement may vary, it is important for the interpreter to consider acoustics, sight line, lighting, background, location and availability of equipment, but special consideration should be given to a religion's accepted protocol in a religious service. For the benefit of the participants, the interpreter should be sensitive to the following:

STANDARD PRACTICE PAPER

3   Interpreting in Religious Settings

- Space for a music stand to place materials
- Hierarchy
- Gender roles
- Areas deemed sacred
- Multimedia
- Videotaping
- Physical movement inherent to the service

Compensation

If a professional interpreter views religious interpreting as service/ministry to the organization or a charitable contribution, she/he may not expect payment. In situations when interpreters do not charge for their services, interpreters may want to consider educating their religious communities about potential expenses of services to develop awareness. Some interpreters accept payment but may donate it back to the religious establishment. For additional information about billing practices, read RID's SPP titled, *Business Practices: Hiring an Interpreter/Billing Considerations.*

ADDITIONAL RESOURCES

El Paso CC National Multicultural (Formerly National Interpreting Project)
Mary L. Mooney, Project Director
El Paso Community College
P.O. Box 20500
El Paso, TX 79998
(915) 831-2432 V/TTY
(915) 831-2095 FAX
E-mail: marym@epcc.edu
www.epcc.edu/Community/NMIP/Welcome.html

National Catholic Office for the Deaf
7202 Buchanan Street
Landover Hills, MD 20784-2236
(301) 577-1684 V/Fax
(301) 577-4184 TTY/Video Phone
E-mail: info@ncod.org
Email: homeoffice@icda-us.org
www.ncod.org

Jewish Deaf Congress (Congress of Jewish Deaf)
(718) 740-0470 TTY
(718) 740-4994 FAX
E-mail: DCCNEWS@aol.com
www.jirs.org/jirs/jirs0005ys.html

Episcopal Conference for the Deaf
E-mail: JLCroft@juno.com
www.ecdeaf.com

International Catholic Deaf Association
United States Section
7202 Buchanan Street
Landover Hills, MD 20784
(301) 429-0697 TTY
(301) 429-0698 FAX
www.icda-us.org

TEXT RESOURCES

Blake, Joan *SIGNING THE SCRIPTURES: A Starting Point for Interpreting the Sunday Readings for the Deaf (Year A).* Liturgy Training Publications, 2004.

Blake, Joan *SIGNING THE SCRIPTURES: A Starting Point for Interpreting the Sunday Readings for the Deaf (Year B).* Liturgy Training Publications, 2005.

Blake, Joan *SIGNING THE SCRIPTURES: A Starting Point for Interpreting the Sunday Readings for the Deaf (Year C).* Liturgy Training Publications, 2003.

Yates, Jr., Leo *INTERPRETING AT CHURCH: A Paradigm for Sign Language Interpreters.* BookSurge, LLC, 2007.

Interpreter Interview

Some churches establish a Deaf ministry committee or taskforce, which may include a subcommittee whose task it is to hire an interpreter.[10] An informal interview with the interpreter may be done over the phone, through e-mail, or in person. Interpreters may expect the following interview questions:[xli]

1. Do you hold professional certification? If not, what experience do you have? (Although it is not always necessary to have, licensure is an indication of the interpreter's professional abilities.)
2. Can you explain the role of an interpreter so that we can understand it? (Include information about your responsibilities.)
3. Do you have a degree or certificate from an Interpreter Training Program? (Attending an Interpreter Training Program is not absolutely necessary for hiring interpreters, but does provide a better understanding of the interpreter's background.)
4. How does the level of your education compare to the education level in the church? (This is important, because the interpreter must be able to comprehend and match the language appropriately when interpreting.)
5. Do you speak in a professional manner? Do you exhibit a paternalistic attitude or condescending

---

[10] An interpreter may be on the committee or have a role in the interpreter search and interview. Also, Deaf people should be on the Deaf ministry committee.

behaviors toward Deaf persons? (This is a red flag.)

6. Can you work at most worship services?
7. Are you a member of any professional organizations?
8. Do you have experience working in this type of setting?
9. Have you been active in a state organization or an RID affiliate chapter? (This shows a commitment to the interpreting field and a desire for professional development.)
10. Do you know the Code of Professional Conduct (code of ethics)?

There are additional questions that a hiring committee could ask; moreover, they are likely to ask questions specific to the church's needs. For example, if there is a need, will you interpret at mid-week activities?

Considerations before Accepting

Most assignments in the church setting are for provision of interpreting during worship services. Before accepting the assignment, the interpreter should consider a few ethical questions such as the following:[xlii]

1. Do I have the ability to accurately and efficiently interpret the service?
2. Is this denomination different, or is it similar to what I am used to interpreting?
3. If this church's doctrine and theology is different than my own, will my biases interfere with the integrity of the message?
4. Are there any potential conflicts or boundary issues with the consumers (d/Deaf and hearing individuals are considered consumers)?

5. Will I have adequate preparation time before the day of the service?

Only assignments with which the interpreter feels comfortable and competent should be accepted.

Accepting the Assignment

To get information that will enable the interpreter to better prepare for the upcoming service, he or she will need to ask some initial questions when services are requested by the church or parish.[xliii]

1. What is the time and date of the event?
2. How long will the service run? (Consider using a co-interpreter if it is beyond 1½ to 2 hours long.)
3. How do people typically dress for the service, formal or casual?
4. Where is the church located? Can directions be given?
5. Who is the contact person upon arrival at the church? What is the contact person's cell phone number?
6. Will any rehearsals or earlier services be held that the interpreter may attend and view? Will materials be given (e.g., sermon, music, etc.)?
7. When can the interpreter obtain the bulletin, any special music, scripts, and the sermon?
8. Does the consumer have any special needs (e.g., low vision)?
9. What is the consumer's name?
10. What is the fee to be paid to the interpreter? Will it include travel reimbursement?

It is crucial to receive bulletins, music, and sermons in advance. The interpreter may need to be persistent in order to get these materials, but they will help with overall job performance. Also, keeping track of hours worked and request types (e.g., meeting or worship), like through an excel spreadsheet, may help the treasurer or committee with budget planning.

Many interpreters organize their preparation materials (bulletin, music sheets, etc.) in a three-ring notebook.[xliv] This helps to ensure that sheets of paper do not fly off the music stand while interpreting. The interpreter can see the material more easily if it is enlarged to a 16-point or 20-point font and will be less likely to lose the place on the page.[xlv] Different colored one-inch sticky notes placed on the materials can differentiate between music, prayers, creeds (e.g., Apostle's Creed), Scripture, and the sermon and make the materials more visible as the interpreter flips to the needed page. In addition, with these materials anchored in a notebook, the interpreter can be a little more at ease, knowing the materials are safeguarded from breezes.

Music Stand

The interpreter should request a music stand, one that is sturdy, in which to place the bulletin, any notes (e.g. the 3-ring notebook), hymnal, or music sheets. The height of the stand may need to be adjusted so the interpreter can easily read these materials, yet not so high that it interferes with the interpreter's signing space. Some interpreters actually store a portable music stand in the trunk, just in case the church cannot provide one. Having a flashlight on hand may be helpful for when special moments call for the lights to be dimmed.

Worship Space

Architecture for sanctuaries varies greatly from one building to another. Where there is a commonality to some sanctuary layouts, some worship services are now being held in such locations as schools, store fronts, and movie theaters. Upon arrival, the interpreter must determine the best location to stand or sit in order for consumers to best utilize the interpreting services. If the church has experience with interpreters, then there will be a pre-determined location for the interpreter. Visual barriers that could prevent the consumer from seeing the interpreter (e.g. flags or banners) should be moved before the service begins. Some sanctuaries have one pulpit for both the laity and the clergy to share, while other sanctuaries have a lectern (for laity) and a pulpit (for clergy). The following is one common layout, where the Communion table is in front of the pulpit; however, it can either be in front of the pulpit or behind it.

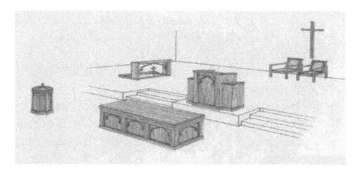

CHURCH FLOOR PLAN EXAMPLE^{xlvi}

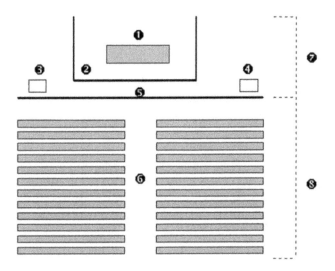

Index
1. Communion table, most often called the altar.
2. Communion railing, also called the chancel railing, with provisions for kneeling.
3. Pulpit, used by clergy for gospel readings and sermons.
4. Lectern with Bible used by lay readers for scripture readings.
5. Boundary between nave and sanctuary; usually the floor of the chancel is three steps higher than the floor of the nave. In Orthodox churches, the boundary may be in a slightly different location and may consist of a screen covered with icons.
6. Congregation. Western churches have pews, but in most Orthodox churches the congregation still stands.
7. The sanctuary or chancel.
8. The nave, where the congregation sits.

An interpreter might be placed in front of the pulpit (3) or the lectern (4), after first consulting with consumers.

More and more churches have websites. This is a great resource, with pictures of the worship space that will enable the practitioner to assess the space ahead of time. Upon arrival on the premises, there may be certain spaces in the sanctuary that are considered sacred, and clergy may be the only individuals to enter them. Interpreters must respect these sacred spaces. There may be occasions when negotiation with church officials becomes necessary so that clear message delivery can occur.

Is the interpreter supposed to stand or sit? Interpreters that were surveyed have given both answers. It is easier for the interpreter to more fully make use of the interpreting space, dance in place while interpreting a song, or take small steps to accentuate the message while standing. Deaf congregants sitting in the third row or further back will be able to better see the interpreter who is standing. Consumers should be consulted regarding their preferences; however, either is acceptable.

Choice of Language

Before the assignment begins, it is advantageous for the interpreter to meet the consumer and assess the consumer's choice of language. Like hearing people, Deaf people's use of language varies due to influences of education and background. Language preference is predicated by several factors including age, ethnicity, region, education, gender, and context. Observation of the consumer's communication style enables the interpreter to better gauge where choice of language is on the language continuum.

During this language assessment, there are indicators the interpreter can observe in order to determine whether interpreting or transliterating is warranted. If the interpreter arrives to the assignment and finds consumers with various language styles (e.g. Signed English, Contact Sign, and ASL), the rule of thumb is to sign ASL.[xlvii] It is best to have one linguistic choice (e.g. ASL) and not try to code-switch (move back and forth between Signed English and ASL); this prevents the consumers from becoming confused.[xlviii] Some language and cultural indicators to look for are the following:

- ❏ The consumer's choice of syntax (English grammar or ASL grammar)
- ❏ Use of initialized signs continuously throughout the conversation (indicating Signed English)
- ❏ Has a sign name (indicates an ASL user)
- ❏ Use of a cochlear implant (may indicate Signed English)
- ❏ Mention of attendance at a Deaf residential school or having been mainstreamed in a public school

After the conclusion of the language assessment, consultation with the consumer can validate the interpreter's observation. An assertive consumer may even sign his or her language preference to the interpreter without being asked.

Meeting the Speaker

Interpreters will want to meet the speaker(s) who participate in the worship service. Interpreters usually interpret for liturgists, choir directors/music coordinators, and clergy. Participants not accustomed to having an interpreter might feel awkward at first or feel the need to speak more slowly for the interpreter. If this is the case, the interpreter may want to reassure the speaker that he or she is experienced with interpreting at a normal pace.

Furthermore, the interpreter can ask if there are any changes in the liturgy, as well as where the speaker will stand when speaking[11]. Meeting the participants will enable the interpreter to be aware of the dynamics in the worship service.

In essence, the interpreter is part of the worship team. The interpreter's role is as important as that of others who preside over the worship service. Consultation with the other speakers displays the interpreter's professionalism and models a commitment to the interpreting role in the service. Each member of the worship team has a critical role.

Conclusion of the Service

It is not uncommon for those who do not know sign language to come up and thank the interpreter. After all, sign language is a visual language that captivates many first-time onlookers. In contrast, if the assignment did not go well for some reason, saying farewell is still a dignified professional behavior that the interpreter should exhibit.

Interpreters should not be surprised if feedback is given by the consumer; in fact, a new interpreter might want to ask for feedback. Feedback may include additional signs to add to the lexicon, encouragement to continue as an interpreter, and/or helpful resources (e.g., newsletter or church directory) to educate the interpreter with the congregation's psychodynamics. It is best for the interpreter to accept the feedback gracefully in the hope it will be of some benefit.

---

[11] Some speakers remain at the lectern or pulpit, while some walk around. If the speaker does walk around while speaking, a gentle reminder not to walk in front of the sightline may be needed.

Reflection is a helpful process that enables the interpreter to monitor professional growth. The interpreter may want to keep a journal, which can help pinpoint ambiguous concepts, difficulties during the service (e.g., not being able to hear), and unfamiliar words or signs. Study and reflection can help the interpreter to reduce future errors and mistakes. Writing in a journal assists the interpreter to better understand the work and helps to monitor professional development. In addition, consultation with colleagues is another reflection technique that some interpreters engage in within their community. Internet message boards are helpful, too (e.g. Yahoo groups). All interpreters will benefit from reflection.

Intricacies of Interpreting

Having background information about interpreting is helpful for practitioners to know. Here we will begin to lay the foundation for the knowledge portion of religious interpreting in addition to offering pointers for skill development. Included are mastering language skills, fluency in American Sign Language, having a general knowledge of interpreting, familiarity of interpreting models, understanding the interpreting process, along with other helpful information.

Mastering Language Skills

In order for the message to be understood, analyzed, and delivered to consumers, working interpreters must have language fluency in ASL and English. Language in itself is only part of the framework for interpreters. Furthermore, interpreting involves an intrinsic process that incorporates cognitive abilities and dexterity. The ability to combine skills and knowledge, along with being bilingual and bicultural, is a must for a successful interpreter.

Effective interpreters must have an extensive English vocabulary and repertoire of signs. Just imagine driving a car on two wheels; eventually the car will flip over and crash because vehicles must drive on four wheels. Likewise, interpreters must be fluent in both languages, or they risk "crashing."

Professionals in all industries rely on informational resources, and this is particularly true for sign language interpreters. A few helpful resources for interpreters working in religious settings are as follows:

1. <u>American Sign Language Dictionary: Unabridged Edition</u> by Martin Sternberg. (1998)
2. <u>601 Words You Need to Know to Pass Your Exam</u> by Murray Bromberg and Julius Liebb. (2005)
3. <u>Holman Illustrated Bible Dictionary</u> by editors: Butler, Brand, Draper, and England. (2003)
4. <u>Interpretation SKILLS: English to American Sign Language</u> by Marty M. Taylor, Ph.D. (1993)
5. <u>SO YOU WANT TO BE AN INTERPRETER?</u> 4th ed. by Janice H. Humphrey and Bob Alcorn (2007)
6. <u>Interpreting at Church: A Paradigm for Sign Language Interpreters, 4th Edition</u> by Leo Yates, Jr. (2016)

These resources, though not exhaustive, will benefit new and seasoned interpreters alike. Online resources such as ASLPro.com might be helpful as well. Having extra-linguistic knowledge is imperative for interpreters who work in specialized fields like religion.

American Sign Language

ASL is a visual-gestural language composed of handshapes and hand movements. Each sign has five general *parameters* (characteristics):

1. Handshape
2. Orientation (palm)
3. Location
4. Movement
5. Facial expressions

A common sentence structure in ASL is *topicalization*. This is used when the object of the sentence is at the beginning.

> ASL: ALL SIN, GOD FORGIVES.
> English: God forgives all sins.

Another frequently used sentence structure is *rhetorical questions*; these are similar to questions, yet are statements.

> ASL: JEREMIAH FRUSTRATED, WHY?
> HE FEELS OVERWHELMED.
> English: Jeremiah is frustrated because he is overwhelmed.

When a subject precedes a verb and ends with where, what, why, or who, it is a *Wh-question*.

> ASL: ISRAELITES TRAVELED, WHERE?
> English: Where did the Israelites travel?

If a reference to time is part of the sentence, then the *time marker* is signed at the beginning. This is a TIME + SUBJECT + VERB sentence structure.

ASL: 33AD, JESUS CRUCIFIED, DIED,
BURIED.
English: Jesus was crucified, died, and buried
in 33AD.

These are only a few of many sentence structure examples
in ASL.

When users of ASL communicate, they typically
leave out articles (the, a, an) and the verb "to be" (is, are).
Grammatical rules for ASL leave out these two linguistic
features. When one does sign an article or a "to be" it is
for purposes of specificity.

Non-manual signs (certain facial expressions) and
classifiers (specific handshapes) are part of ASL.
Classifiers and non-manual signs are used as adjectives
and adverbs (descriptors), which provide clarity to the
concept or idea being signed.[xlix]

EXAMPLES OF ASL CLASSIFIERS

Language users can borrow words from another
language; this typically occurs because there is no
equivalent sign or word in the user's native language. An
example of no equivalent sign is the word BANK. There
is no common sign in ASL for BANK, so most users will
fingerspell the word. According to the rules of
fingerspelling, it is acceptable to borrow from written
English for communication purposes. ASL users not only
borrow from written forms of language, but also borrow
signs from other sign languages. Examples of loan signs
from other sign languages are the newer signs for
JAPAN, ITALY, and RUSSIA.[l]

Enthusiasts have the option to learn ASL online at a website such as ASL University at www.lifeprint.com. An easy-to-read book for students who want to learn ASL is by authors, Barbara Bernstein Fant, Betty Miller, and Lou Fant titled, <u>The American Sign Language Phrase Book</u> (2008)[li] However, the best way to learn ASL is still conversing with Deaf and ASL users or in a formal educational setting and immersing oneself in the culture.

Signed English is a model of the English language, not intended to represent the mechanics of the language, but to produce sign words and markers of what is spoken.[lii] Generally, Signed English follows the rules of English grammar. Users of Signed English may have attended an oral school, were mainstreamed (attended a public school), or perhaps learned it after a progression of hearing loss. ASL and Signed English share many of the same lexicons of signs, but are distinguished mostly by syntax and culture. In addition, Signed English includes the heavy use of initialized signs, whereas ASL relies on these much less frequently. English is the native language for many Signed English users.

Contact signing, traditionally known as Pidgin Signed English (PSE), is another language-based system that uses features from both ASL and English.[liii] A variety of people, Deaf and hearing, use contact signing as a mode of communication. Contact signing features signing in an English word order, English words uttered on the mouth, fingerspelling, the use of non-manual signs, and body shifting. The system borrows lexical items from ASL and Signed English.[liv]

General Knowledge

Beyond reading books or journals, many professionals enroll in college classes in order to further their education. Students explore various subjects when they enroll in general studies classes (e.g. English, psychology, political science, humanities, etc.) at a community college or university. This higher education enables interpreters to work more effectively in numerous settings. Those who have not been in school for many years can start out as special students and take only one class just to get their feet wet.

Enrollment in classes such as public speaking, English, or a class in one's discipline (i.e. your religion) will improve the interpreter's language – this is imperative for working interpreters. Professionals across the board now enroll in online college classes to take classes from home or at work to make education a little more convenient. It cannot be overstated; higher education is imperative for professionals in this industry.[12]

Interpreters also attend interpreting related workshops/seminars and conferences in order to improve upon their knowledge and skills (and meet CEU requirements). These interpreting workshops, seminars, and conferences provide opportunities to network and consult with other colleagues in the field. RID approved workshops, seminars, and conferences are listed on RID's website.[13] All interpreters need improvement in some

---

[12] Earning a higher education has helped me immensely as an interpreter. The general knowledge that I learned from my college classes and graduate level classes enables me to think critically, and, thus, to better analyze the discourse to be interpreted. When I first went back to college, I went with trepidation. I felt I did not have an adequate high school education and knowledge to enter college level classes. After all, it had been a number of years since I graduated from high school. To my surprise, the whole process was not as bad as I anticipated. There is a support system in place at most colleges, which includes advising, testing, tutoring, and counseling.

[13] RID approved workshops are located at www.rid.org.

area(s) of their work, and continued education is an essential approach to improvement.

It is also helpful for the interpreter to keep up with current events. Familiarity with the latest news and trends prepares the interpreter for moments when they are mentioned during a sermon, Sunday school class, or in casual conversations. People keep up with daily news by reading the newspaper in print or online, by watching the news, by reading magazines such as *Time* or *Newsweek*, and by listening to National Public Radio (NPR) while driving. Knowledge of what is going on in the world keeps the interpreter one step ahead.

Interpreting Models

The profession has adopted *interpreting models,* also known as *interpreting philosophies,* for interpretation. The interpreter's responsibility is to accommodate the psychodynamics of the congregation. The interpreter is supposed to use each model according to conditions surrounding the assignment. After choosing the model, the interpreter is able to draw upon the model and apply it to the work.

Interpreters, in whatever setting, are ethically obligated to be prudent as they determine which model[lv] is to be applied. Each model is briefly described here:

❑ The **Helper model** of interpreting involves concepts of pity, dependency, and paternalism. It can foster dependency, inhibit identity development, and alienate Deaf and hard-of-hearing participants from communicating directly with their hearing peers. [Use of this model has a tendency to disempower the Deaf person. One might possibly use this model with a Deaf person who has developmental disabilities.]

☐ In the **Conduit/Machine model** of interpreting, an interpreter conveys information from one language to another without any personal or cultural context. [With this model, the deaf consumer has already been enculturated into hearing culture and generally needs no cultural mediation.]

☐ In a **Bilingual-Bicultural model** (bi bi) of interpreting, cognitive processing between both English and ASL is required by the interpreter for semantic equivalency. [For example, if the Deaf person describes light flashing when the phone rang, the interpreter will either filter that by saying, "When the phone rang, I answered it." or add in, "When the strobe light signal flashed—that's a notification device—I answered the TTY."]

☐ In the **Ally model** of interpreting for adults, decisions about interpreting are made within the social and political culture surrounding Deaf and hard-of-hearing adults. The interpreter needs to make a conscious effort to be aware of power imbalances in the religious setting. [For instance, the interpreter will point it out to the hearing consumer if the Deaf person is not being treated equally.]

Typically, interpreters use the conduit and the bilingual/bicultural (bi bi) more frequently than other models. If the helper model is used, caution and additional consideration are needed.[14] New interpreters

---

[14] Interpreters that plan to take the computerized test (knowledge section) for the NIC ought to be familiar with four models: helper,

should become familiar not only with these four models, but with other available interpreting models as well. Exposures to what other professionals do will help diversify the interpreter's possible choices even more.

The mentioned four models are from the Education Interpreting Performance Assessment ® (EIPA).[15] EIPA established these guidelines for educational interpreters; however, religious interpreters may wish to consider adoption of these philosophies as well.

Before the establishment of RID, the helper model was the philosophy that most volunteers and amateurs used. Pioneers who established RID believed the helper model oppressed and subsequently influenced the exclusion of Deaf people from the dominant culture. The helper model is less commonly used; however, none of the models are to be discarded because each model serves a purpose. The interpreter determines which is the most suitable for any given situation.[16]

Interpreting Process

Outside the United States, a number of countries view interpreters as professionals. Great Britain considers

---

conduit (machine), communication facilitator, and bilingual and bicultural (bi bi).

[15] EIPA Diagnostic Center at Boys Town Research Hospital in Omaha, Nebraska, developed the EIPA for interpreters in educational settings in the early 1990s. Permission by Brenda Schick is granted for this citation.

[16] Some religious interpreters I have met (certainly not all) seem to follow the helper philosophy. The helper model includes a paternalistic attitude that wrongfully stigmatizes the deaf population. From my observation, the majority of the deaf community do not see themselves as having a disability; instead, they view communication to be the barrier, not their hearing loss.

British Sign Language (BSL) interpreting a legitimate profession that meets the communications need of Deaf and hearing parties. One British city government recognizes the intensive work by interpreters. An online article posted by the Bradford city government in the U.K. briefly summarizes the interpreting process.

The Interpreting Process

Sign language interpreters may look very active with their hands, but in actual fact most of the hard work is going on in their heads. They have to listen carefully, watch for the message, extract the meaning and then find an appropriate way to express this in the second language. As with any other interpreted language, every English word doesn't necessarily have a corresponding sign in BSL and each language has its own grammatical structure. The interpreting process involves expressing the same meaning using a different vocabulary and grammatical structure. This means

- ❏ *Only ONE message can be interpreted at a time. [This condition is a challenge for practitioners when interpreting music that has two different lyrics sung simultaneously.]*
- ❏ *Interpreting requires intense concentration and can be very tiring. At top speed, interpreters may be processing up to 20,000 words per hour. The recommended time for interpreting is 20 minutes. Interpreters can work longer than this, but over long periods the quality of the interpretation will suffer. [Some worship services and church programs extend beyond two hours. Interpreters should strongly consider working with a team in these situations.]*
- ❏ *For meetings and events longer than 2 hours at least two interpreters are necessary. [Ninety minutes is becoming the norm to have a team.]*

❏ *The mental processing takes time, and there will be a delay as the message passes from one language to another.*[lvi]

As stated in the online article, the interpreter's mental faculties begin to deteriorate from peak performance after twenty minutes. Interpreters must have mental agility in order for the interpreting process to be optimal. In addition, RID encourages interpreters to work as a team when the length of a worship service goes beyond one and a half to two hours.

Simultaneous and Consecutive Interpreting

Most interpreters perform simultaneous interpreting, also known as real-time interpreting, for consumers.[lvii] When simultaneous interpreting occurs, the interpreter begins to produce the message in the target language a few seconds, generally three to eight, after the speaker begins. This *lag time* is needed for the interpreter to comprehend, analyze, and then produce the communicated message. If the interpreter does not allow sufficient time to elapse after the speaker begins, the interpreter may need to make corrections to the delivered message because insufficient information was not first accumulated. In contrast, when music is to be sung or signed by the congregation, the lag time for simultaneous interpreting is usually shorter.

Consecutive interpreting involves a pause or a break between language conversions.[lviii] First the interpreter listens to the source language, usually a phrase or passage, and then the speaker pauses, so the practitioner can interpret the message into the target language. It is not surprising that some interpreters may feel pressure or anxiety when performing consecutive interpreting. This is because the speaker's long and possibly detailed message may result in accidental deletions by the interpreter. An accidental deletion may occur when the interpreter reaches process capacity in his or her short-term memory.[lix]

Even though some spoken language interpreters might do consecutive interpreting more often, there are occasions that sign language interpreters do it as well. An example might be when foreign missionaries share testimonies with congregations; or if the church has a ministry for immigrants, the interpreter may be asked to interpret a meeting with a Deaf immigrant, a translator, or a member of a ministry team.

Language Register

An interpreter needs to recognize the *language register* from the source language in order to produce the correct register for the target language. *Register* is the variation of a language, signed or spoken, that is normally used for a specific purpose or a social setting.[lx] For instance, when preaching a sermon, the preacher will normally use a formal register. This is recognized by grammatically correct choices, use of a higher vocabulary, and one-way participation (where the minister is the only person communicating).

There are five general classifications that language is assigned to, and each classification has a low degree and a high degree. Language registers[lxi] most commonly used can include:

- ❑ **Frozen:** Printed unchanging language such as bible quotations. [Examples: Scripture, creeds, and hymns]
- ❑ **Formal:** One-way participation, no interruption. Technical vocabulary; exact definitions are important. Includes introductions between

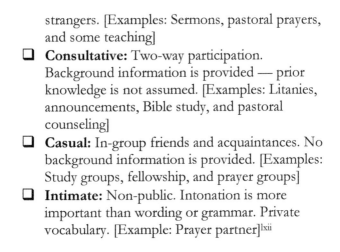

strangers. [Examples: Sermons, pastoral prayers, and some teaching]

❑ **Consultative:** Two-way participation. Background information is provided — prior knowledge is not assumed. [Examples: Litanies, announcements, Bible study, and pastoral counseling]

❑ **Casual:** In-group friends and acquaintances. No background information is provided. [Examples: Study groups, fellowship, and prayer groups]

❑ **Intimate:** Non-public. Intonation is more important than wording or grammar. Private vocabulary. [Example: Prayer partner][lxii]

Distinguishing the appropriate register enables the interpreter to produce an equivalent and coherent message. Language registers usually vary according to context. Using an example of a worship service, a minister will greet the congregation using a formal register.

Formal	**Casual**
Good morning	Wuz up

Again, within the context of worship, here is an example of a register that is consultative.

Consultative (this example is of a litany)
Leader: We are here to praise the Lord.
People: We praise the Lord.
Leader: It is right to give thanks.
People: We give thanks to the Lord.

The interpreter's competency is expanded when he or she is able to maneuver among registers.

Linguistic Expansion

Whatever *modality* of language is being interpreted (signed, spoken, or written), the interpreter will eventually face the circumstance of not having an equivalent word or sign (gloss) for the target language. This occurrence is common in all languages (i.e. translating from written Hebrew to written English). When there is no equivalent sign or word in the target language, the concept can be expressed by *using a phrase of words or signs*. Normally, this will not be a problem if the interpreter is not glossing or shadowing the source language (interpreting word for word).[lxiii]

It is acceptable to establish a temporary sign (create a new symbol) when a sign is not available, but it must be agreed upon between two or more language users. When a term or a name is repeated throughout a discourse, ASL users usually set up a sign for it. *Iconic* signs (a sign resembling the word) are typically formed more often than *arbitrary* signs (a sign *not* having any resemblance to the word). For example, there is no standardized sign for Jesus' earthly father, Joseph. The temporary sign MARY HUSBAND might be established to denote Joseph throughout a discourse.

Morphological rules (a subfield of linguistics) state when two signs are combined to make a *compound sign*, a new meaning will emerge.[lxiv] For instance, the sign PURPLE combined with the sign SPOT creates the sign BRUISE. When the interpreter processes the source language, and realizes there is no equivalent meaning in the target language, he or she might be able to express the idea through use of a compound sign. One theological term that this technique can be applied to is *repentance*. In its simplest form, *repentance* means to be sorry and to change one's ways. If the sign for SORRY and the sign for CHANGE are combined, the sign REPENT is created. In a sense, the interpreter is expanding his or her repertoire of signs.

Another linguistic rule that assists interpreters is *lexical borrowing.* This rule implies that a word can be borrowed from another language. Frequently, this is seen when the user fingerspells or signs a word from another language because there is not a gloss rendition in ASL.

ASL incorporates the use of *acronyms.* Acronyms are abbreviated letters of a full word. In both English and ASL, acronyms are used quite often. When a hearing person writes the name of a state onto an envelope, such as 'CA' (for California), an abbreviation is used. Some acronyms in ASL have been naturally inherited over decades. 'SS' (social security) and 'TH' for townhouse are common acronyms, and they are generally context specific. When the interpreter sets up an acronym for the first time, the full word is to be finger spelled (i.e. Book of Revelation = REV), followed by the acronym.

New interpreters are encouraged to consult with ASL users beforehand in order to include these features (sign choices). In some cases, there may already be signs established by the consumer.

Expansion Techniques

Professor Shelly Lawrence[17] presented seven expansion techniques during a Conference of Interpreters' Trainers (CIT) conference. [18] These techniques enable interpreters and users of ASL to elaborate (unpack) subjects and concepts, and

---

[17] The expansion system is borrowed by permission from Shelly Lawrence's 1996 and 2003 papers.
[18] Readers are recommended to read the full version in its entirety. It can be acquired by purchasing the CIT 1994 Proceedings journal through CIT"s website. The URL is www.cit-asl.org.

subsequently to give the message a deeper meaning. This is accomplished by using ASL features of location, space, height, and depth.[lxv]

1. **Contrasting**: This feature highlights an idea by juxtaposing two <u>opposite</u> ideas in order to emphasize one of them. For example, in English we might say, *"The Israelites worship the One True God."* Using the contrast feature in ASL can produce, *"Pagans worship various gods, and the Israelites worship the One True God."* With the addition of this contrasting idea, the original premise is emphasized. Sometimes this is done by stating the positive, then the negative (i.e., what something *is*, followed by what it *isn't*). Other times, the reverse occurs (i.e., a negative is followed by a positive).

2. **Faceting**: Faceting describes a feature whereby several different signs are given sequentially to express one idea more clearly. Although several signs are used, this feature actually narrows a concept to a more exact or specific image. The use of faceting often seems to cluster around the use of adjectives or adverbs. The multiple signs used in faceting, however, all serve to guide the viewer in a particular direction. The idea of *redemption*, for example, can be produced in ASL by signing: FORGIVE, LOVE, RECONCILE.

3. **Reiteration**: Reiteration refers to signs that are repeated in a text exactly the same way as they were initially stated. That is, a sign or signs are used again, reiterated, within a passage. It appears that reiteration implies emphasis: that something is important to the storyline, has cultural significance, or has high emotional impact to the signer. For the purpose of

emphasis, it seems that adjectives and adverbs are used and repeated. For instance, in English: *The Israelites traveled in the desert.* In ASL: WALK, JEWISH PEOPLE WALK DESERT.

4. **Utilizing 3-D Space:** Space is utilized to set up nouns that later get replaced with pronouns (referential space); space is also used to describe proximal relationships (topographical space). Moreover, because Deaf people view the world primarily through their eyes, visual description and detail is an important component of ASL discourse. Classifiers are one way visual information is conveyed. When looking at a whole utterance, space is used meaningfully to create cohesion in the text (spatial mapping). For instance, during a Scripture reading, cities are sometimes mentioned. Utilizing 3-D space can establish markers when cities are mentioned.

5. **Explaining by examples:** Another feature of ASL is to explain by the use of an example. If a term needs to be defined or a concept needs to be clarified, it is done by using many examples. In English, if a term needs to be explained, the initial approach would be to define the word; to say it in other words. In ASL however, a list of examples would follow the idea that requires explanation. In ASL, forming signs: PRAY, READ SCRIPTURE, SING will indicate the English word for *worship*.

6. **Couching or scaffolding**: "Couching" or "scaffolding" occurs by virtue of the differences between the two languages. One way ASL can expand vocabulary is to explain an item or give foundation or support to a concept. This can be done in a variety of ways that may include 3D space, explaining by example, contrasting, or by

simply explaining the concept. An example of this is *Jeremiah is a prophet. A prophet, called by God, speaks to the king and the people. Sometimes, a prophet predicts future events.*

7. **Describe, then Do**: The "Describe, then Do" feature can be observed when the signer shifts from a narrative style of discourse to direct style of discourse or from narrator to character. This occurs when an action or situation is described, then "acted out" with the use of a perspective shift. In English: *I left for church.* In ASL: I LOCK HOUSE - DOOR. I IN CAR AND DRIVE. I GO CHURCH.

Initially, new interpreters will have to visualize, experiment, and practice these features. Some techniques may be used more than others; however, each method will help the interpreter to produce a clearer and crisper message. Also, the opposite can be done by applying *compression techniques* by filtering a part of the message.

Errors and Omissions

Novice interpreters, as well as experienced interpreters, will have moments when an omission occurs. An omission is when part of the message (sentence, phrase, or concept) cannot be interpreted because it was not heard, understood, or retained.[lxvi] This frequently happens to new interpreters because of inexperience, distraction (emotional or environmental), and/or lack of concentration. The interpreter may feel a sense of panic but must keep his or her composure. Loss of composure may cause the consumer to lose confidence in the interpreter's ability.

Interpreters, first and foremost, are human. Interpreters cannot interpret one hundred percent of everything that is signed or spoken. There will be times when the interpreter misunderstands the speaker and interprets the wrong information. When the interpreter realizes there was a misinterpreted message, the most responsible (and ethical) thing to do is to repair the mistake. Consumers depend on the interpreter to produce the message accurately, and it is the interpreter's duty to recover the message.

One example is a situation that happened during a Christmas Eve service. The interpreter thought she heard the preacher say that Jesus ordered all the male babies two and under to be killed, and that is what she interpreted. Moments later, she realized she had corrupted the information. She corrected it with the right information (King Herod ordered the massacre, not Jesus).[lxvii] For her to leave uncorrected the first message that Jesus gave the order would have been detrimental to the entire sermon, as well as possibly damaging to the consumers' spiritual faith. No doubt, the interpreter made the right choice when she corrected the message.

Monitoring

Part of the process of interpreting includes self-monitoring by the interpreter. This important aspect of the process enables the interpreter to recognize potential problems and identify contributing factors that affect one's work. Once the interpreter is aware of hindrances, then adjustments can be made to lessen or eliminate them. Below is a short list of what to monitor when interpreting from English to ASL.[lxviii]

- ❑ Ensure the consumer's sightline is clear so the interpreter can be seen.
- ❑ The interpreter must be able to hear the speaker so there are no misunderstandings.

❑ Continue to match the speaker's register, and adjust the interpretation if needed.

❑ Look for acknowledgments, either a head nod or smile, to be sure that what the interpreter produces is being understood by the consumer. [During a natural break or pause, if no indication is seen, it is appropriate to consult with the consumer.]

❑ Articulate the message clearly.

❑ The interpreter must be aware of his or her own feelings so the delivered message is not accidentally contaminated.

❑ Form signs and movements so that they flow naturally and consistently.

❑ Watch for possible environmental intrusions, such as lights being turned down or a procession in the middle of the sightline.

This partial list is a good start. In addition, if the interpreter is working with a co-interpreter, both interpreters can work together to monitor the work.

When interpreting from ASL to English, part of the same list will be included as part of the self-monitoring process.

❑ Project your voice for the audience to hear.

❑ Speak clearly and naturally, so the Deaf person's affect is being matched by the interpreter.

❑ Omit filler words such as, "um." [i.e. "Um, today's Scripture, um, is from, um, Psalm 23. Um…"]

❑ Recover or repair the interpretation when needed.

For additional guidance, the interpreter can read over the certification rating scales on RID's website.[19] Even if the interpreter does not feel ready to take the certification exam, the rating scale is a helpful guide for understanding what is expected from interpreters in the profession.

Mentoring

Practical experience is one of the best tools for learning how to interpret. A mentor can provide invaluable insight and guidance for the new interpreter. Techniques, additional vocabulary, and feedback are just a few of the benefits that are gained from a mentor. Many professions require some type of apprenticeship for new professionals who enter the field, and the interpreting profession is no exception to this standard.[20]

For some novice interpreters, mentors may be hard to come by because of geographical and/or time constraints. Some professional interpreters are unwilling to step into the world of religious interpreting for fear they will be stereotyped[21], or they lack expertise (background knowledge), or they are inexperienced in this type of setting.

Some affiliated chapters of RID keep a list of interpreters who mentor new interpreters. Today's technology allows for professional mentoring to occur

---

[19] The rating scales are located at www.rid.org. This outline helps the interpreter know what to prepare for when taking the NIC test.

[20] The Standard Practice Paper: Mentoring is worth reading. It is at www.rid.org.

[21] Some interpreters (emphasizing only *some*) look down on religious interpreters for what they perceive to be lack of skill and competency, failure to follow the same professional standards (CPC), and accepting work before one is qualified.

from remote locations and even across different time zones. With web conferencing, for example, you can upload short video streams of your work and get feedback through email, phone and/or instantly through a video conversation like through Skype. One-on-one human contact and working as a team is the primary approach for mentors and mentees, because of the role modelling, immediate feedback from work, and the safety net that mentees have when working with a mentor. However, the Internet and free long distance plans through cell phone providers have made it easier for people to get in touch when geographical limitation becomes an issue. As stated in chapter two (Skill Development), Signs of Development offers virtual mentoring. The website is www.signs-of-development.org.

The National Consortiums of Interpreter Education Centers (NCEIC) offers **The Mentorship Toolkit** on its website. The Mentorship Toolkit includes activities, articles, videos, rubrics for evaluating performances, and other resources – a wealth of helpful information. There is no reason why a mentor and a mentee cannot establish a relationship over the phone and the Internet. The Mentorship Toolkit is located at www.interpretereducation.org/aspiring-interpreter/mentorship/mentoring-toolkit/.

Goals and Objectives

A mentor can help the mentee decide what goals to pursue and in what order. Every interpreter is different, and needs vary according to strengths and weaknesses. A few goals to consider are:

Signing:
- ❑ ASL/Sign vocabulary
- ❑ Structuring space

- ❑ Grammar
- ❑ Fluency and affect
- ❑ Clarity of signs

English:

- ❑ English vocabulary
- ❑ Eloquence of speech
- ❑ Fluency and affect
- ❑ Clarity

Message:

- ❑ Message content (is it equivalent)
- ❑ Message matches speaker's register
- ❑ Interpreting process
- ❑ Appropriate body composure

When working on goals, one or two (no more than three) will be worked on at one time. Self-assessment by the mentee, which can be guided by the mentor, is highly encouraged.

Work done with a mentor can help the new interpreter considerably. The mentor's experiences, specific[22] and effective[23] feedback, and a reasonable amount of encouragement are what the mentee should expect from a mentor. Obviously, the new interpreter needs a mentor with professional experience. The mentee will also want someone who can analyze work in an honest and objective manner. Humility on the part of

---

[22] *Specific feedback* is what new interpreters need to be proficient. An example is, "Your fingerspelling was not produced correctly. When you produce the letter 'e' it is to look like this."

[23] *Effective feedback* integrates specific information for improvement, along with acknowledgment of what is signed or interpreted correctly. Generally, there should be balance in the discussion between the interpreter's strengths and weaknesses. It is also beneficial if the mentor guides the mentee to assess his or her own work.

the mentee is necessary when hearing feedback. Some mentors prefer to charge a fee when they share their expertise, while others will not charge the new interpreter/ITP student because they see it as a professional obligation. Mentoring is crucial because it will help form a foundation for the budding interpreter.[24] Being mentored at the beginning of an interpreting career is the most responsible approach.

Team Interpreting

One or more interpreters can share the responsibility of a worship service, Sunday school/Bible study session, and other church-related activities. When the context and content of the interpreting assignment are complex, or when the assignment is over sixty or ninety minutes, working as a team[25] is highly recommended. Teamwork helps to lessen the risk of developing cumulative motion injury, which is common for interpreters who work alone for long periods of time.[26]

During a worship service, team interpreters can switch off every fifteen to thirty minutes, or they can divide parts of the service between themselves. While one interpreter is interpreting, the other will support, monitor, and provide (*feed*) missed information. The working

---

[24] My own mentoring experience has evolved over the last decade. There was a sense of intimidation I used to feel when meeting or working with my mentors; however, most of my mentors had a way of making me feel at ease. The expanded learning I received from mentoring is priceless.

[25] RID provides a Standard Practice Paper that is a helpful guide for team interpreters. It is at www.rid.org.

[26] Interpreters are encouraged to maintain healthy working standards. For more information, RID publishes a Standard Practice Paper on cumulative motion injury. It is located at www.rid.org.

relationship between the two interpreters should include communication, trust, mutual respect, flexibility, and support. Essentially, both interpreters will work in some fashion the entire time.

One instrument for communication for team interpreters is a writing journal. Used as a professional log, a journal is helpful for discussion purposes after the service; what worked well and suggestions for next time can be written down. Interpreters can feel support through written dialogue; moreover, it underscores teamwork between professionals.

EXAMPLE OF TEAM COMMUNICATION

11am – 11:15am I'm glad you started. I felt I am not able to keep up with the announcements.

11:15am – 11:30am Ron has repeated 'it is well with your soul' four times. Instead of fingerspelling 'soul' let's set up a sign for it. By the way, I loved your version of the Lord's Prayer.

11:30am – 11:45am Thanks for feeding me the name, Jeremiah. I couldn't make out what he was saying. Glad you signed the song. I learned something from ya.

11:45am – 12pm He is using the term 'prophet' as messenger. Instead of signing prophet as foretelling the future, let's set up the sign 'messenger.'

When a service or event goes longer than two hours, some consumers wish not to pay for two interpreters. If the event is four hours, some unscrupulous requestors will hire one interpreter for the first two hours and hire the second interpreter for the last two hours. Obviously, if this occurs, it is not considered teaming. The attempt to cut costs actually undermines everyone involved. After an hour or so the interpreting process is already breaking down, which means more mistakes will come about, and the consumer may not receive the correct message. In addition, the second interpreter, who comes into the assignment unable to consult and prepare as professionals do, will be at a loss.

Unfortunately, some people also have misperceptions about Christian interpreters. Some

Christians—sometimes the interpreters themselves—expect them to be martyrs and continue to interpret for hours on end with no relief.[27]

To promote a team approach, the interpreter must not only educate consumers and other participants that the integrity of the message will remain more intact (particularly when a service goes beyond an hour), but also must influence those in charge (usually a coordinator or the one who pays for the service) that Deaf ministry is a significant part of the overall mission of the church. Furthermore, a certain amount of flexibility and humility by the interpreters is needed, in part to build cohesion. Incorporation of an interpreting team can crack open a door of understanding for consumers. A team will help the congregation to understand that a cooperative approach is viable and necessary; it can help redefine standards of interpreting within religious settings. A professional service is being provided. Teamwork can help to establish an inclusive environment for all parties

---

[27] I was once contracted to provide services at a revival that was hosted by a televangelist, and the requestor only scheduled two hours for my services. After two and half hours, the televangelist began the sermon; I informed the deaf consumers that I was unable to continue because of mental and physical exhaustion. While one consumer understood, the other abruptly responded by saying, "That's why I asked for Christian interpreters." Apparently, a Christian interpreter must have interpreted much longer than what is recommended, thus establishing a precedent for unhealthy and inappropriate professional standards. Interpreters, and those who follow some faith tradition, are not expected to work in abusive situations, and they should not – ever.

involved.[28]

Balancing Faith and Profession

ETHICAL QUANDARIES

Qualified?   Multiple
                               Roles

Volunteer or   Faith Bias
Be Paid?

                               Mistakenly
Boundaries   Disempower

Some churches are more flexible in terms of level of
expertise when it comes to obtaining an interpreter, as the
cost for providing interpreting services can be prohibitive
for a small or under-funded congregation. This flexibility
enables new interpreters the opportunity to work within
the church. Is this wrong? No, not if the interpreter's
work is proficient and done in a professional manner. It is
helpful to keep in mind that public confidence in the
interpreter increases when the interpreter (1) has language
competency (e.g., possess a command of both the source
and target language), (2) the quality of interpreting is
adequate (e.g., only makes a few mistakes), (3) is ethical
(e.g., keeping information and situations confidential), and
(4) is professional (e.g., dependable and objective).

---

[28] For additional reading about team interpreting, RID published
an excellent resource titled, Team Interpreting as Collaboration
and Interdependence by Jack Hoza (2010).

Customarily, the pastor, minister, or priest is the staff person most thought of in churches; however, other roles or positions are commonly present in some churches. Of these roles, many of them have ethics from their specified disciplines. Other church staff disciplines with their code of ethics include, but are not limited to, pastoral counseling (The American Association of Pastoral Counselors), Christian education (Association of Christian Schools International), and parish nurses (International Parish Nurse Resource Center). With the religious interpreter (the practitioner who only works in church settings) in mind, having a code of ethics that RID recommends and upholds (the Code of Professional Conduct) can offer the religious interpreter industry-wide standards, collaboration with other practitioners in the field, and a network.

Interpreters frequently face ethical dilemmas as they provide services to consumers. Some CPC tenets are easier to follow than others; however, the interpreter must not only be aware of disturbing conditions as they arise, but must also deal with them in accordance with the tenets of the CPC. These tenets are to be followed at all times, even in settings where services are offered *pro bono*. Some people of deep and passionate faith may experience an inner struggle when faced with issues of confidentiality, for example, but the consumer's personal issues must be held in trust and boundaries be maintained.

As an example, at a religious workshop a participant shared a story with the group about a practitioner who interprets regularly in the community and at her church. This practitioner divulged confidential information to the congregation about a Deaf consumer she had interpreted for that past week. The interpreter told the congregation she had interpreted an appointment at an abortion clinic. She asked the congregation to forgive her for doing that.

She also requested prayers for the Deaf woman involved and disclosed the Deaf woman's name to the congregation. The roomful of workshop attendees gasped in shock when they heard that someone had done this; everyone agreed this matter should never have been made public. This story is a prime example of the need to keep certain information confidential. It is imperative that an interpreter be able to make good decisions about what to say and what not to say.

Interpreters need to consider their own tolerance threshold when they agree to an assignment outside of their own faith tradition. For example, some people of the Baptist tradition do not find it acceptable for women to be preachers. If an interpreter is not comfortable in a setting where women are permitted to preach, then the interpreter should decline the assignment. It is not appropriate for the interpreter to share personal opinions with the consumer about female preachers; the interpreter must remain impartial.

On RID's website, there are a number of documents that give guidance for specific settings.[29] One such document is the RID Standard Practice Paper for Interpreting in Religious Settings.[30] This document recommends that the interpreter research a church or denomination's theology and doctrines before deciding to accept an assignment. Some people do not find it easy to step outside of their own faith tradition, and it is the interpreter's personal responsibility to judge whether an assignment is acceptable.

---

[29] On the Internet, go to www.rid.org.
[30] The SSP: Interpreting in Religious Settings can be accessed at www.rid.org.

Boundaries

An obstacle for some interpreters is to maintain boundaries and remain in the interpreter role. It is highly possible that the Deaf person may mistakenly transfer the pastor's authority to the interpreter. This can happen because the interpreter shadows (sometimes stands next to) the minister and affects the minister's body language. Because the interpreter is able to communicate in the consumer's own language, this can contribute to the possibility of transference. Whatever the reason for transference, it is the interpreter's responsibility to stick to his or her role.

It is not unheard of for Deaf worshipers to share personal problems or issues with the interpreter. Being sensitive to the consumer is understandable, but a word of caution is needed here. Interpreters must be able to make appropriate judgments as to where the line is crossed. The switch from interpreter to pastoral counselor can occur quickly and without realization. It is advisable to request that both the interpreter and consumer go together to speak to the pastor about the worshiper's issue. This will enable the interpreter to remain in the professional role of interpreting for the worshiper and pastor. The pastor, not the interpreter, has the training and credentials for pastoral care and counseling, and it is important to allow the minister to perform these duties.

Though not all interpreters have difficulty setting limits and keeping boundaries, these are a problem for some. Sometimes personal circumstances prevent interpreters from maintaining boundaries; if this is the case, it is essential to be aware of triggers. One book that addresses this issue is titled <u>BOUNDARIES</u>.[31]   This book highlights behaviors to be aware of and suggests solutions one can use. It is possible to be liked and still keep healthy boundaries, but it takes awareness and practice.

Sermons can be seen as speeches of exhortation. Most preachers want their sermons to be inspirational so a lesson or application will be remembered. Sermons can be dry, humorous, tear-jerking, or even emotionally transforming. During emotional moments, interpreters need to be able to distance themselves somewhat so they are not pulled in along with the audience. This can be a real challenge, because the interpreter has to remain in the interpreting role while listening to illustrations and stories that are meant to affect the soul.

Like other professionals who work in the church, interpreters have a right to worship as well. The need to worship is understandable, and if the interpreter is not spiritually fed because of the work performed, he or she may want to follow in the footsteps of other professionals, such as clergy, some of whom worship outside their own church setting in order to be fed spiritually.

Multiple Roles

Faith-driven interpreters enjoy interpreting in religious settings. In fact, it is not uncommon for some

---

[31] The book <u>BOUNDARIES</u> (2002) is by authors Dr. Henry Cloud and Dr. John Townsend. <u>BOUNDARIES</u> is a relatively inexpensive book; it can be purchased at many bookstores. To view video presentations based on the authors' book, go to http://cloudtownsend.master.com/texis/master/search/?sufs=2 &s=.1&q=boundaries .

interpreters to have multiple roles within the church.[32] An interpreter might teach an ASL class to hearing parishioners, lead a Bible study, or shoulder responsibility for other church programs. Multiple roles can create uncertainty, however, about which role takes priority over the others. In the event of uncertainty, it is helpful to remember that communication is a fundamental human need, and the interpreter's prime duty is to meet that need between parties.

Before a conflict arises, interpreters and others involved should examine where the interpreter may have a conflict. If Deaf and hearing people are participants in a venue where the practitioner's other role takes precedence, such as teacher or facilitator, the interpreter should speak to the Deaf consumer prior to the event. Some people attempt to please both language users by using sim-com (signing and speaking at the same time); however, it is not usually recommended. This communication method typically has English as the dominate language, thus neglecting grammatical features of ASL. Some Deaf people do not mind when hearing people use sim-com, but others do. In cases where ASL users prefer sim-com not be used, an option is to host a second event for the hearing people. Working out communications needs is not an easy task at times, and it is best to work out the logistics *before* a conflict occurs.

Interpreter Compensation

Before the first assignment begins, the payment arrangements (paid or not) should be established between the practitioner and the church. The interpreter has a

---

[32] The Standard Practice Paper: Multiple Roles in Interpreting offers additional guidance as well. It can be read at www.rid.org/.

right to receive compensation; moreover, a fair and reasonable fee should be arranged in a professional manner. For some interpreters, a verbal consent is acceptable, while for others a signed agreement, such as a Memorandum of Understanding (MOU) is preferable. If a signed agreement seems too formal, submitting invoices (weekly or monthly) is another alternative.

Most Christian congregations are dependent upon weekly offerings in order to meet budget requirements. There are many congregations that have experienced a decline in membership, which affects budgetary matters. Because of this, some congregations may find it a challenge to pay competitive rates for interpreters. Interpreters may need to negotiate, in a professional manner, what is acceptable. Some interpreters charge a reduced rate, while others charge their regular rate. Chapter two includes additional considerations.

The process of interpretation in a church setting actually begins before arrival at the sanctuary. The interpreter has the responsibility to consider the ethical dimensions of an assignment prior to accepting it and must be able to think objectively, which can be ethically challenging. Often, interpreters wish to interpret in the church setting for personal reasons. Faith-driven motivation can be a good reason to interpret in such a setting; however, the new interpreter must be professionally competent and capable of stepping into the role of interpreter.

A common in-house debate among interpreters working in religious settings is whether services should or should not be performed gratis. RID's Standard Practice Paper for Interpreting in Religious Settings briefly addresses this subject. Whether to provide services *pro bono* is ultimately up to the practitioner.

Trying to manage the costs for interpreter compensation, especially when costs were not budgeted for, can be a challenge for church interpreter coordinators, even more so for small membership churches. It is not uncommon that the threshold of quality tends to fluctuate when utilizing volunteer interpreters. When this occurs, it's best to consult with the primary users of the interpreter. Ethically, compromising someone's spiritual life should not be an option and the primary user's input ought to be a part of the hiring or evaluation process to ensure minimum quality.

Some issues to consider, however, are the following:

❑ If an interpreter refuses payment, it may set a precedent (and an assumption) that all professional interpreting services will be free.
❑ If the interpreter accepts the payment, this allows the interpreter to make the choice to endorse the check and put it in the offering plate. The interpreter could use the donation as a tax deduction for contribution to a charitable organization.[33]
❑ Interpreting professionally is an interpreter's livelihood. It should be respected as such. Just as another ministerial staff member would be compensated, so should the interpreter.
❑ Even if the regular interpreter does not wish to be paid, church leaders responsible for the annual budget should add a line item for interpreters.[34] If

---

[33] Interpreters must report compensation to the IRS. Typically, interpreters are hired as independent contractors (freelance interpreters). Interpreters should receive a 1099 – MISC form from the church. For more information, go to www.irs.gov/pub/irs-pdf/p1779.pdf to access it online.
[34] PROFESSIONAL STANDARDS: The interpreter is customarily paid for a two-hour minimum, even if the service is

the regular interpreter needs to be off, there will be funding available to hire a substitute.

❑ A fundamental question to consider is whether the interpreter should be compensated when consumer(s) miss the service (and should the interpreter still interpret regardless)? Professional standards dictate that interpreters are still to be paid since the block of time was contracted for interpreting services.

Clearly, it may not be easy for small churches to pay an interpreter, especially if it wasn't budgeted for. These considerations can guide further discussions to address the issue. Also, the Business Practices: Billing Considerations by RID (under the Standard Practice Papers section on RID's website) can provide guidance as well. The bottom line is that it is entirely up to the interpreter whether or not to accept payment; there is no right or wrong answer.

Practitioners who bill churches for their interpreting services will want to keep a copy of the invoice (for their own records) that is sent. One method for generating invoices is in Microsoft Word or Excel. After printing the invoice, a notation (on the electronic copy) of the date the invoice was sent is recommended. Rates that are normally charged are dependent upon having certification, experience, education, interpreting setting, and region (economics - supply and demand). Typical rates range

---

only an hour (this includes time for preparation). A service that is complex or lasting over ninety minutes or two hours should have a team of interpreters. If consumers do not show up for the service, the interpreter is still to be paid. Also, an interpreter holding certification is paid more per hour compared to an interpreter without credentials. These are standards throughout the profession.

$15 to $75 per hour, which varies according to being employed (staff) or contracted, certified or non-certified, and setting (e.g conference). A sample invoice is provided.

	INVOICE

Jane Smith, CI & CT
433 Anywhere St.
Marion, NY 10007
Phone 405.555.0190   Fax 405.555.0191

DATE: 02/24/20xx
INVOICE # 100
FOR: *Interpreting Services*

Bill To:
First Church
Attn: Bookkeeper
101 Main St.
Marion, NY 10007

DESCRIPTION	AMOUNT
2/24/20xx Interpreting services provided during 11am worship service (2 hr minimum). $25 per hour (reduced rate)	$50.00
2/17/20xx Interpreting services provided during 11am worship service (2 hr minimum). $25 per hour (reduced rate)	$50.00
TOTAL	$ 100.00

Please make all checks payable to **Jane Smith**. Payment is due upon receipt.
If you have any questions concerning this invoice, contact Jane Smith, 405.555.0190.

Dress Attire for Interpreters

People come dressed for worship in a variety of ways these days. In a traditional setting, the interpreter dresses in business attire. At a minimum, female interpreters should wear a blouse with dress slacks or a skirt and avoid the use of nail polish; male interpreters should wear a dress shirt and tie with dress slacks. Interpreters need to dress in solid colors that contrast their skin color to allow for visual clarity. Avoid flashy pendants or jewelry, for they may be visually distracting. These recommendations emphasize a professional look for interpreters.

If interpreting a contemporary praise service, it is preferable to dress similarly to what most people are wearing; however, to lean towards dressing more conservatively is usually more professional. Again, use solid colors that contrast skin color. A good rule of thumb is to observe what the clergy wears and dress similarly. When there is still uncertainty, a quick email or a brief phone call to the church is certainly acceptable. Determining the dress code will assist the interpreter to fit in better. Keep in mind, the dress code (e.g., business, business casual, or casual) will depend on the request (e.g., worship, a meeting, or a church bazaar).

Participating in the Service

In most settings, the interpreter is not a participant and remains a neutral party; however, this is not always the case when interpreting a worship service. If the interpreter is a member of the congregation, he or she may participate in some fashion. For example, the interpreter could request prayers, give a financial donation, or accept a sacrament (e.g., Holy Communion). The CPC tenets do not speak directly to these examples, however, so the interpreter should speak beforehand with the consumer to see if participation would be viewed as a conflict.

In 2004, a religious interpreters' conference was held in Columbia, Maryland, during which an afternoon Deaf panel discussion addressed the topic of interpreter participation. There were, in addition to the Deaf panel, 250 interpreters present for this forum, all of whom were in consensus that it is permissible to consult with the consumer about participation, if participation would not interfere with the facilitation of communication. This, however, is not always the professional norm, so it is best to approach this issue on a case-by-case basis.

Interpreting Training

As stated before, many interpreters learn the trade through an apprenticeship like program in their church. For those seeking further interpreting training, there are a few colleges and schools that offer more in-depth training. Some are

- ❑ Church Interpreter Training Institute (CITI) through Concordia Theological Seminary. The CITI program offers a summer course that covers a range of topics related to religious interpreting. Their website is www.ctsfw.edu/page.aspx?pid=744.
- ❑ The Cincinnati Christian University offers a bachelor's degree in Biblical studies and interpreter training program. Their degree program can be viewed by going to this website http://ccuniversity.edu/?s=interpreter.

Considering Humility

Interpreters often find themselves humbled in their work, perhaps due to the presence of other more experienced interpreters in the congregation, working with interpreters who are better skilled, or receiving feedback or criticism from consumers. In this work, it is helpful to have some humility, in part because it helps to foster respect with consumers, the interpreting team, and other church staff. At times, the role of the interpreter can be misunderstood or undervalued; however, when the interpreter shows humility the potential for conflict can sometimes be avoided and negotiation and/or education (i.e., sharing of best practices) can take place.

Pride in our work does have a positive effect since it promotes self-confidence; the flip side to this notion is that when the interpreter has too much pride it can be a causal factor for interpersonal conflicts between the practitioner and his or her consumers, interpreting team, and/or church staff. Psychologically, a certain amount of ego is healthy, and balancing it with humility takes discipline. My advice: it is always better to take the road of humility.

Case Study – Good Shepherd Baptist Church

M. Laquita Smith-Robinson is the interpreter coordinator at Good Shepherd Baptist Church in Baltimore, Maryland. She has been serving at Good Shepherd for 24 years. Prior to this, she had served for thirteen years in her home country of Bermuda. When Ms. Smith-Robinson came to the U.S., she attended an interpreting preparation program where she obtained a certificate in interpreting and an associate's degree in the college's interpreter preparation program. At Good Shepherd, sign language classes are offered to the congregation and the community, which has proven to be a valuable outreach evangelistic tool to reaching the Deaf and hearing community. Good Shepherd Baptist Church Deaf ministry also makes home visits, visits the sick in hospitals and supports church families.

**Good Shepherd
Baptist Church**

Questions for Reflection

1. How might your church incorporate an interpreter? Would it be accepted? If your church

already utilizes interpreters, how can it be improved upon?

2. Healthy boundaries enable us to do ministry more effectively. What boundary issues might you or someone in your church have difficulty with?

3. What can you propose in your church for it to be more accommodating to d/Deaf, hard-of-hearing, late-deafened, and Deaf-blind people?

4. How might your church raise awareness to be more inclusive of d/Deaf, hard-of-hearing, late-deafened, and Deaf-blind people?

5. Isaiah 65 reads, **17** *"See, I will create new heavens and a new earth. The former things will not be remembered, nor will they come to mind. 8 But be glad and rejoice forever in what I will create, for I will create Jerusalem to be a delight and its people a joy.* (NIV) In what ways do you see God creating something new in your faith community? Are there any barriers that need to be removed in order to see this come to fruition?

Conclusion

This chapter provides a birds-eye view of the interpreted ministry, along with giving the interpreter a view of terms, history, processes, and approaches for this specialized work in the church setting. Those who contemplate becoming an interpreter ought to delve deeper into the art and science of interpreting. There are still other aspects of interpreting to be explored that are not covered in this chapter. Whether one studies independently by reading journals and textbooks or studies in a formalized venue, it is possible to learn the idiosyncrasies of language and interpreting.

Chapter 4 – Overview of a Hard-of-Hearing and Late-Deafened Ministry

This chapter introduces readers to the Hard-of-Hearing and Late-Deafened Ministry model. It describes these two types of hearing loss, what is helpful to know, some background to hearing loss, and suggestions for having a ministry with hard-of-hearing and late-deafened individuals and their families. While this is not exhaustive, it is a beginning that will provide some insight to be inclusive and sensitive with this population. Also included are some common accommodations that help some hard-of-hearing and late-deafened individuals to be better welcomed into the life of the church. It is always necessary to ask the person what accommodation is needed, as well as how he or she labels him or herself (e.g. hard-of-hearing, late-deafened, or for the few who still use the term, hearing impaired).

The following descriptions distinguishes the populations being discussed.

Hard-of -Hearing: Refers to people who can understand spoken speech with the help of amplified sound through an assisted listening device or hearing aid. Persons may be born hard-of-hearing or lose their hearing later in life. Some learn sign language, while some do not.

Late-Deafened: Refers to people who became deaf post-lingually (after learning to speak), and were raised in the hearing community. Most late-deafened people do not learn sign language.

Oral Deaf: Refers to people who are born deaf or become deaf prelingually and who received speech therapy and are taught to speak. Most do not use sign language as their primary mode of communication.

Real Time Captioning

The Lutheran Deaf Mission Society suggests the use of captioning as an accommodation for some who have hearing loss. Certainly, preference of the user is important. The following is a description, as well as the advantages and disadvantages of using captioning.

Description - Communication Access Real-Time Translation (CART) is the technical name for the service which provides hearing impaired consumers written text of spoken material.[lxix] The system requires a specially trained stenocaptioner, certified through the National Association of Court Reporters (NCRA), utilizing a stenotype machine, notebook computer, and real-time captioning software to display instant speech-to-text translation on a video monitor. [35] CART services are generally more expensive than interpreting services. A less expensive alternative to CART is **Computerized Assisted Notetaking (CAN)**, in which a person types plainly onto a computer (usually a laptop). The CAN technician can sit next to the consumer or project the text onto a screen. In addition to services, videos ought to have captions for viewers. Some churches customarily project a video image of the preacher and worship leaders include real-time captions at the bottom of the screen.

Advantage – Real-time captions benefit people who do not sign, in part since English may be their first language.

Disadvantages – Some disadvantages include:
1. Usually, only very large hearing churches can afford to provide real-time captioning because
   a. CART services can be very expensive.
   b. The display of captions requires specially installed equipment.
2. Given a choice, many Deaf people prefer sign language over real-time captioning, because of the following:
   a. English is a secondary language for many Deaf people. Common English idioms are easily lost.
   b. Written text lacks the speaker's inflection.

Causes of Hearing Loss

When it comes to hearing loss, there are some common causes. The following are some common ones. [lxx]

---

[35] To locate a service provider, go to the National Court Reporters Association (NCRA) website at www.ncrasourcebook.com.

Congenital Hearing Loss – Congenital hearing loss is any hearing loss that is present at birth. The cause can be genetic and hereditary, caused by issues during pregnancy or caused from an issue during the birthing process.

Genetic – More than 50 percent of the time it is believed that genetic factors cause pediatric hearing loss. Genetic or hereditary hearing loss occurs when a gene from one or both of the parents impacts the development of the intricate process of hearing. Genetic issues can affect any portion of the outer, middle or inner ear, and can cause varying degrees of loss. Options for genetic forms of hearing loss vary widely and can range from hearing aids, medication, surgery, cochlear implants or no treatment at all. Your health care providers will help you in your search to determine the cause of your child's hearing loss and what options are available for your child.

Prenatal Issues – There are non-genetic factors that can potentially cause hearing loss before the birth of your child. Factors such as in utero infection, illnesses, toxins consumed by the mother during pregnancy or cytomegalovirus (CMV) can be passed on to a child in utero and may cause hearing loss. During the birthing process, procedures performed to save a baby's life in an emergency, such as a ventilator or a strong antibiotic, can also affect hearing.

Acquired Hearing Loss – Hearing loss can occur after birth. There are several factors that can cause this to happen:

- ❏ Chronic ear infections, also called Otitis Media
- ❏ Medications (e.g. Ototoxic drugs)
- ❏ Diseases (e.g. Meningitis and mumps)
- ❏ Head injury

❑ Perforated

Unknown Causes – In many cases, you may never really know why your child is deaf or hard-of-hearing. It is important to act quickly to confirm a diagnosis, and ensure your child has access to language as early and frequently as possible.

Types of Hearing Loss

There are five common types of hearing loss.

1. **Conductive**: Sound waves are not able to pass through the outer and/or middle ear to the inner ear for processing.

2. **Sensorineural**: Caused by damage to the tiny hairs within the cochlea in the inner ear; sound is unable to be converted into electrical signals for the auditory nerve.

3. **Mixed**: A combination of conductive and sensorineural hearing loss.

4. **Neural**: A result of damage to the auditory nerve that connects the cochlea to the brain.

5. **Auditory Neuropathy**: Sound enters the ear normally, but the transmission from the ear to the brain is impaired.[lxxi]

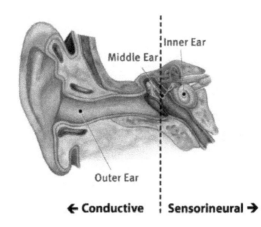

← Conductive ┊ Sensorineural →

Degrees of Hearing Loss

From time to time, a hard-of-hearing individual may share the degree of hearing loss he or she has. It can be helpful to know the degrees of hearing loss. The following numerical values are based on the average of the hearing loss at three frequencies: 500 Hz, 1,000 Hz, and 2,000 Hz, in the better ear without amplification. The following provides the degrees of hearing loss.[lxxii]

- ❑ Normal Hearing (-10 dB to 15 dB)
- ❑ Slight loss (16 dB to 25 dB)
- ❑ Mild loss (26 dB to 30 dB)
- ❑ Moderate (31 dB to 50 dB)
- ❑ Moderate/Severe (51 dB to 70 dB)
- ❑ Severe loss (71 dB to 90 dB)
- ❑ Profound loss (91 dB or more)

Mild loss: Person may miss 25% to 40% of speech sounds. The person has difficulty understanding someone with a soft voice and/or difficulty following conversations in a noisy environment.

Moderate loss: Person may miss 50% to 75% of speech sounds. The person has difficulty hearing normal conversations and hearing consonants in words.

Severe loss: Person may miss up to 100% of speech sounds. Conversations may be extremely difficult except one-on-one in a quiet setting.

Profound loss: Person may not hear at all. At this level, hearing aids may or may not help and cochlear implants are an option.[lxxiii]

Cochlear Implants

While hearing aids can be helpful for some people with hearing loss, there are many for whom hearing aids either do not help or help insufficiently. In such cases, cochlear implants can be helpful and are being used by more people with severe and profound hearing loss who no longer benefit from hearing aids.

A cochlear implant consists of an internal and external component. The internal component is surgically inserted under the skin behind the ear, and a narrow wire is threaded into the inner ear. The external component, which looks somewhat like a behind-the-ear hearing aid, is connected to the internal one through the skin via an external magnetic disk.[lxxiv]

Incoming sounds are converted to electrical currents and directed to a number of contact points on the internal wire. This operation creates an electrical field which directly stimulates the auditory nerve, thus bypassing the defective inner ear. Unlike hearing aids, cochlear implants convert sound waves to electrical impulses and transmit them to the inner ear, providing people with the ability to hear sounds and potentially better understand speech without reading lips.

The cochlear implant has become widely recognized and is used from small children to older adults.

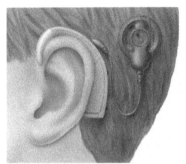
Cochlear Implant

Hearing Aids

Hearing aids help the many people with mild-to-severe hearing loss. The most common devices are hearing aids. These range from extremely tiny ones that fit completely in the ear canal, to ones that are placed behind a person's ear and that deliver sound into the ear canal via tubing and an ear mold.[lxxv] Some aids use just a tubing to deliver the sounds or locate a tiny loudspeaker right in the ear canal.

Hearing aids will not correct hearing like glasses correct vision.[lxxvi] They are not 20/20 hearing but they will help one hear in many situations. New hearing aids may require follow up visits for technical tweaks by your hearing professional.

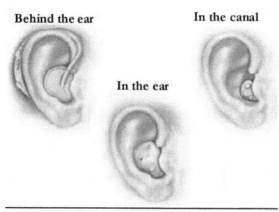

Behind the ear

In the canal

In the ear

Various Hearing Aid Styles

Financial Assistance for Hearing Aids

Foundations or organizations that have offered financial assistance:
Audient Alliance for Accessible Hearing Care
877-283-4368
www.audientalliance.org Affordable hearing aids; must meet low income guidelines

Hear Now Starkey Hearing Foundation
800-648-4327
Email: nonprofit@starkey.com
www.sotheworldmayhear.org/forms/hearnow.php
Affordable hearing aids; must meet low income guidelines.

Lions Affordable Hearing Aid Project (AHAP)
630-571-5466 ext 615
www.lionsear.org
The Lions developed a low cost, high quality hearing aid which at a little over $100 has proven to perform as well as aids that sell for $2,000; must meet guidelines

Hearing Guide Dogs

For some hard-of-hearing and late-deafened adults, having a hearing guide dog is helpful to them. This service dog, which is similar to a seeing-eye dog, is trained to alert his or her owner of a doorbell, alarm clock, someone calling a name, a smoke alarm, or other sounds. One national company that trains service dogs is Canine Companion. More information can be read by going to www.cci.org.

Helpful Hints for Communication

Hearing Loss Association of America (HLAA) provides some suggestions for communicating effectively. While these are general suggestions, it is always better to ask the hard-of-hearing or late-deafened individual.[lxxvii]

Approaching the Individual
- ❑ Face person directly
- ❑ Spotlight your face (no backlighting)
- ❑ Avoid noisy backgrounds
- ❑ Get attention first
- ❑ Ask how best to facilitate communication
- ❑ When audio and acoustics are poor, emphasize the visual

Communicating
- ❑ Don't shout
- ❑ Speak clearly, at moderate pace, not over-emphasizing words
- ❑ Don't hide your mouth, chew food, gum, or smoke while talking
- ❑ Re-phrase if you are not understood
- ❑ Use facial expressions, gestures

❑ Give clues when changing subjects or say "new
subject"

Establish Empathy with the Person
❑ Be patient if response seems slow
❑ Talk to a hard-of-hearing person, not about him
or her to another person
❑ Show respect to help build confidence and have a
constructive conversation
❑ Maintain a sense of humor, stay positive and
relaxed

Telecommunication Relay Service

Telecommunication Relay Services (TRS) use
operators or communication assistants, at no cost to the
callers, to facilitate calls between d/Deaf, hard-of-hearing,
late-deafened, and Deaf-blind individuals or those with a
speech disability and a hearing person on the telephone.
Teletypewriter (TTY), sometimes referred to as a TDD, is
device that a d/Deaf or hard-of-hearing, late-deafened,
and Deaf-blind caller uses to type messages to a relay
operator. The operator reads the message to the hearing
person on the other end of the call. The hearing person
responds and the operator types the message to the
d/Deaf caller using the TTY. What has become more
popular is the use of a computer, instead of a TTY, in
which the d/Deaf caller uses the IP relay (over the
internet). Many d/Deaf callers use the Video Relay
Services (VRS). This is when onscreen sign language
interpreter relays (interprets) the messages between a
d/Deaf, hard-of-hearing, late-deafened, or Deaf-blind
caller and a hearing caller. This method of placing calls
requires a high speed internet connection and a webcam
or a videophone.[lxxviii]

<u>Relay Service</u>

National Organizations

The **Association of Late-Deafened Adults** (ALDA) emphasizes a strong focus on the need for visual communication; using "whatever works" strategies such as captioning and computer assisted real time translation (CART), speech reading, sign language, and various kinds of assistive technologies.[lxxix] ALDA has annual meetings for individuals with hearing loss, as well as having chapters throughout the country. Their online community (email discussions) provides support and information for individuals with hearing loss. For people losing their hearing often feel isolated and connecting with others can be meaningful and supportive for many people. The ALDA chapter groups can be located by going to www.alda.org/resources/chapter-and-group.

The **Alexander Graham Bell Association for the Deaf and Hard-of-Hearing** (AG Bell) has been in existence for several decades. Like ALDA, AG Bell also has annual meetings and state chapters that individuals and families can connect with and receive support and information. It also has publications and newsletters. Through the Listening and Spoken Language Knowledge

Center, it emphasizes advocacy and restorative hearing through assisted listening devices and cochlear implants. To locate state chapters and support groups, go to their website (under the Connect tab) at www.listeningandspokenlanguage.org.

Assisted Listening Systems

Three common types of assistive listening devices that are typically used include:

- ❑ **FM System** - FM Systems work like a miniature radio station. The transmitter has a microphone and sends FM waves to a receiver. In the United States, special frequencies are set aside for users of FM systems so that there is no interference from outside FM transmissions.
- ❑ **Infrared System** - An **infrared system** uses invisible beams of light (like one's remote control). Infrared light waves are transmitted by an array of LED's (light emitting diodes) that are located on a panel. The receivers have a detector that senses the infrared light and converts the signal to sound.
- ❑ **Induction Loop** –Induction loop technology by magnetic induction is a basic principle of electronics. It works with an electrical current that is amplified and passed through a loop of wire. As a result, a magnetic field is generated around the area of the wire. The magnetic field that is created varies in direct proportion to the strength and frequency of the signal (or sound) being transmitted.[lxxx]

Normally, only one system is used. As technology continues to evolve, new revolutionary equipment will probably be invented. The practitioner can keep up to date on technology by remaining in touch with an organization such as *Hearing Loss Association of America* (formerly the *Self Help of the Hard-of-hearing*) or the *Alexander Graham Bell Association for the Deaf and Hard-of-Hearing.*

Church Accommodations

Not all hard-of-hearing and late-deafened individuals have the same needs. Having a disability coordinator can be helpful to find out what accommodations are needed. Some individuals may wish to have printed materials to accompany the bulletin, such as the PowerPoint slides, the sermon, and the anthem or special music that is not in the hymnal. Be sure to educate the church office about possible text relay service calls or video relay service calls by d/Deaf, hard-of-hearing, or Deaf-blind individuals so there will not be any confusion. Some individuals may want to sit in the first or second row so they can better speech read the speaker. Not having any light shining behind the speaker at the pulpit or lectern is recommended. Additional recommendations include:[lxxxi]

- ❏ Have printed materials available for meetings and Bible study.
- ❏ The room should be free of background noise. If a microphone is unavailable in a meeting, repeat the question before answering it.
- ❏ Have good quality sound systems.
- ❏ Have assistive listening devices available.
- ❏ Have sign-language interpreters and/or Communication Access Real Time Translation (CART) or Computer Assisted Notetaking (CAN) available.

- ❑ Dimming the lights may make it difficult for speech reading or to follow what is going on (like at a Christmas Eve service).
- ❑ Make sure the area is well lit.
- ❑ Captioning (either CART or CAN) can be displayed on a computer or a screen for the user.
- ❑ When advertising church events or special services, provide contact information for participants to request accommodations.
- ❑ Consider offering a sign language class.

Dictation App

With technology, there are a number of apps that can be helpful as a way of communicating through dictation (speech to text). Often this is done through one-on-one communication. One such app is the Dragon Dictation. It can be located by going to www.nuance.com/for-individuals/mobile-applications/dragon-dictation/index.htm.

Further information about the hard-of-hearing and late-deafened population can be found at the **Hearing Loss Association of America** website[36], **Association of Late-Deafened Adults**[37], or the **Alexander Graham Bell Association for the Deaf and Hard-of-hearing**[38] website. A plethora of information and resources is available from these advocacy organizations.

---

[36] Hearing Loss Association of America has a website. It can be accessed at www.hearingloss.org.

[37] Association of Late-Deafened Adults has a website at www.alda.org.

[38] The Alexander Graham Bell Association for the Deaf and Hard-of-Hearing promotes spoken language and hearing technologies. The organization's website can be accessed at www.agbell.com.

Church Accessibility Audit

Helpful is the survey by the United Methodist Congress of the Deaf titled, "Breaking the Sound Barrier: Ministry & Mission with People Who Are Hard-of-Hearing or Late-Deafened." The study by the subcommittee compiled and identified ways churches, facilities, and events can be more accessible for individuals with hearing loss.[lxxxii]

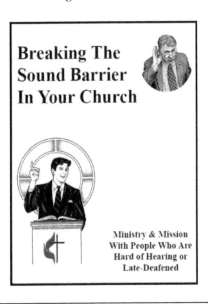

Breaking The Sound Barrier In Your Church

Ministry & Mission With People Who Are Hard of Hearing or Late-Deafened

---

How Accessible Is Your Church? Determining The Needs & Resources For Ministry & Mission With Hard-of-hearing & Late-Deafened People

PART ONE of this audit focuses on the needs of hard-of-hearing people who can use Assistive Listening Devices.

PART TWO focuses on the needs of late-deafened people who *must* have information communicated visually. The following audit checklist was developed by the United Methodist Congress of the Deaf and comes from the publication, *Breaking the Sound Barrier in Your Church.*

I. Which Of The Following Sound Adaptations Has Your Church Made To Encourage Participation By Hard-of-hearing People?

❑ ❑ Amplification for the whole congregation? NOTE: This does not substitute for an assistive listening system for hard-of-hearing people or those using cochlear implants.

❑ ❑ Microphone positioned away from speaker's lips, to accommodate people who are speech reading / lip reading)?

❑ ❑ Lavaliere (lapel) microphone worn by liturgists and/or preacher(s) not using a stationary microphone?

❑ ❑ Wireless microphone for use in the nave for sharing of joys and concerns or additional announcements?

❑ ❑ Strategically placed microphone(s) so that persons using assistive listening devices may hear organ/piano, soloists and choir?

❑ ❑ Assistive Listening System (FM, infrared, audio loop)?

❑ ❑ Receivers with jacks and neck loops for the assistive listening system (needed by people with cochlear implants or hearing aids with T-switches)?

❑ ❑ Person assigned to ensure that receiver batteries are charged (or replaced as the case may be) weekly?

❑ ❑ Assistive listening receivers set out on table in or close to sanctuary, making for easier access by hard-of-hearing people or those with cochlear implants?

❑ ❑ An attendant on hand to assist in selection of proper unit and explain its operation?

❑ ❑ Are posters placed at entry points telling of the availability of assistive listening devices, and where to find them?

❑ ❑ Lighting in front of liturgists, preachers, choir members, to facilitate easier speech reading?

Yes No In The Sanctuary:
❑ ❑ Using the church's Yellow Page, website, and newspaper advertisements to tell of its audio and visual enhancements for hard-of-hearing and late-deafened people?

❑ ❑ When remodeling or building new sanctuary, architect requested to research latest acoustical technology?

Yes No In Meeting Rooms:
❑ ❑ Meetings held in rooms with good acoustics (carpets, drapes)?

❑ ❑ Good lighting on speaker's face? (Should not have the light source behind the speaker.)

❑ ❑ Amplification used most of the time?

❑ ❑ Microphone positioned away from speaker's mouth?

❑ ❑ Microphone used by all speakers, including those in audience during feedback or discussion time?

❑ ❑ All presentations be done from the front (to facilitate hearing and speech reading)?

❑ ❑ Comments/questions from audience repeated by speaker (if microphone is not available to the audience)?

❑ ❑ Semicircular seating arrangement used for discussions to facilitate speech reading?

❑ ❑ FM or audio loop assistive listening system available?

❑ ❑ Receivers with jacks and neck loops available for assistive listening system?

❑ ❑ Videos selected for and presented in closed-captioned version?

❑ ❑ TV sets and VCR units equipped with closed-caption circuitry, remote control available, and instructions or attendant on hand to operate the system?

2. Does Your Church Supplement Sound with Sight for People Who Are Late-Deafened In The Following Ways? NOTE: These methods also benefit hard-of-hearing people *AND* the congregation at large!*

Yes No In Meetings

❑ ❑ Written agenda, even for "small" meetings.

❑ ❑ Graphic recording throughout meetings, even small ones

❑ ❑ Overhead projection, especially of action proposals

❑ ❑ Computer Assisted Note-taking or similar system, in "real time," and visible to all

Yes No During Worship:
Are the following visible to all worshipers? (Note that most hymnals and pew Bibles are in small print)

❑ ❑ Words of hymns?

❑ ❑ Words of anthem or solo?

❑ ❑ Litanies, prayers, scripture?

❑ ❑ Words of the liturgies?

❑ ❑ Children's moments?

❑ ❑ Sermon?

❑ ❑ Joys and concerns?

❑ ❑ Announcements?

Methods used to make the words of worship and other church events seen as well as heard:

❑ ❑ Handouts?

❑ ❑ Copies of the sermon available in advance?

❑ ❑ Overhead projection to large screen in sanctuary?

❑ ❑ Computer assisted note-taking (CAN or a similar system) projected onto large screen or a TV monitor?

3. Are Your Church Staff & Office *Hearing Accessible*?
Yes No

❑ ❑ Do you have at least one telephone with volume control/amplification?

❑ ❑ Do you have a TTY (telecommunication device for the deaf, also known as a TDD) or a video phone (VP)?

Advocating for Parents

It is of no surprise that some parents are at a disadvantage when it comes to navigating school systems. From time to time a pastor or minister can be helpful to the parents by informing them of their rights so they can advocate on behalf of their d/Deaf child.

The following describes what an individualized education program (IEP plan) is and what is considered when school experts with the parents discuss the plan for the child.

By law, a child with an IEP must be re-evaluated at least every three years or earlier when appropriate. The re-evaluation serves two key purposes: 1) to ensure that the child has a continued eligibility for the IEP, and 2) to assist in the development of the IEP.[lxxxiii] Parental consent to the evaluation/re-evaluation is required unless the parent has failed to respond to repeated requests for consent. According to Federal Regulation 34CFR 300.304, the criteria for IEP evaluation/re-evaluation are:[lxxxiv]

❑ Parents must receive notice that describes any evaluations the school district intends to conduct.

❑ The school district must:
- o Use a variety of assessment tools to assess functional, developmental and academic information, including information from the parents, to determine whether the child is eligible for special education and the contents of the IEP.
NOTE: The school district cannot use any single measure or assessment as the sole criterion.
- o Use technically sound instruments.

❑ The school district must ensure that:
- o Evaluation materials are selected so as not to be discriminatory on a racial or cultural basis.
- o The evaluation is administered in the child's native language or other mode of communication, and in the form to most likely yield accurate information regarding what the child knows and can do academically, developmentally, and functionally, unless it is not feasible to do so.
- o Evaluations that are used for the purpose for the assessments are valid and reliable.
- o Evaluations are administered by trained and knowledgeable personnel and administered in accordance with the assessment's protocol.
- o Assessments are tailored to assess specific areas of need and not merely those that provide a single general intelligence score.
- o Assessments are selected to best assure that if administered to a child with impaired sensory, manual or speaking skills, they accurately reflect the child's abilities rather than reflecting the child's impaired skills.
- o The child is evaluated in all areas related to the suspected disability.

o   The evaluation is sufficiently comprehensive to identify all of the child's special education and related service needs.[lxxxv]

Sunday School Classroom Tips

If a parent brings a hard-of-hearing child to a Sunday school class, it is helpful for the Sunday school teachers or superintendent to be aware of some helpful suggestions to ensure inclusion and accessibility. The following are sometimes helpful.

❑ Classroom directions may need to be repeated.
❑ Have people speak clearly and she's able to see their faces. Try not to cover your mouth with paper or books, or talk with your back towards the class.
❑ Do not necessarily draw attention to the hearing loss. If the teacher is concerned the child missed something, check with the child in a subtle way. For example, the child could signal you.
❑ When feasible, have the child sit close to the point of instruction whenever possible, whether it is the teacher, videos or other activities.
❑ The whole class understands that it's important to speak clearly and one at a time. Directions and assignments are available in writing.
❑ The child is able to share or compare notes with a classmate or you, as appropriate.
❑ Please remember to turn on captions for all videos.[lxxxvi]

Support Groups and Organizations

When a person begins to lose one of their senses, like hearing, it is quite common for the person to grieve over the loss. Frustration, anger, grief, and sadness are all common emotions due to hearing loss. Ideally, a support group at the church is recommended, yet, if the church does not have the capacity to do so, suggesting an outside support group may be helpful. The **Hearing Loss Association of America** has state chapters, in which some host support groups, along with information about hearing loss. This list can be found on its website at www.hearingloss.org.

Another online community that provides sharing, support and information can be found at **Hearing Like Me** (www.hearinglikeme.com). Videos and a plethora of information about hearing loss are provided for online viewers.

Case Study – Rev. Paul Crikelair

Rev. Paul Crikelair grew up hard-of-hearing. He used hearing aids and would often read lips in communicating with others. Having been ordained a United Methodist elder in the Eastern Pennsylvania Conference of the United Methodist Church, Rev. Crikelair shares he has had a successful ministry where he has served at churches that understand and accommodate his hearing loss.

What helps Rev. Crikelair, is using an assisted listening device system (both in the worship space and a personal device he carries with him), captioning, and asking others for clarity when something is missed. "Blessed are the flexible" is one way Rev. Crikelair puts it. He has never learned sign language, but believes one day he will.

Generally, speaking with individuals one-on-one is for the most part fine, but in small groups, such as a Bible study or in a committee meeting can be challenging at times. "I just ask the person to repeat him/herself. People understand and don't have a problem repeating themselves."

Rev. Crikelair is involved in The United Methodist Association of Ministers with Disabilities, a caucus of The United Methodist Church. He also wrote a chapter in the book, <u>Speaking Out: Gifts of Ministering Undeterred by Disabilities</u>. In his chapter, he goes into his experiences and challenges of being hard-of-hearing while serving in ministry.

Case Study – Marcus

An interview with a hard-of-hearing individual who wishes to remain anonymous provides some insight to some of the frustrations he experiences due to his hearing loss. Certainly his feelings are not shared by every person with a hearing loss, but there are others with similar experiences. Inclusion, showing patience, providing a community of belonging and extending grace are what can be learned from Marcus' story.

"I lost my hearing at 46 years of age, due to pressure medications. What I can say that I've never been this lonely in my life. Sometimes my phone does not ring for weeks at a time. I hear silence all day until I go out and put hearing aid on, and then I hear noise all day long. My family doesn't speak to me when I'm around. All my friends stopped speaking to me and it seems no one has patience for me. My hearing loss occurred on March 25, 2005. I have 16% in left ear and 0 in right ear. Not having any background noise helps me to hear more clearly. I no longer try to hear everything; I hear what I hear and what I don't hear I don't. My family said to me 'You don't want to hear what we talking about anyway.' Having others hear for me sucks, or make a call for that matter. I just started going to the movies since they are captioned with the glasses device. This is great as I can enjoy the movies again. All I can say is that it's very lonely and quiet being hard-of-hearing. I don't know ASL and I don't fit in the hearing world nor do I fit into the deaf community because I speak very well. I was 46 years old when lost my hearing."

Questions for Reflection

1. How can your church reach out to hard-of-hearing and late-deafened in your congregation and your community?
2. In what ways can your church promote awareness for this population?
3. What hope can you share with those who are losing their hearing?
4. Can you identify individuals (either in your church or in your community) who might be willing to provide typing (stenograph) so your church can offer captioning (CART or CAN) accommodation to those losing their hearing?
5. Isaiah 6:8 reads, *Then I heard the voice of the Lord saying, "Whom shall I send? And who will go for us?" And I said, "Here am I. Send me!"* (NIV) In what ways is God calling your church to be more open and accommodating to those who are hard-of-hearing and late-deafened?

Conclusion

In conclusion, this chapter gives an overview of the hard-of-hearing and late-deafened ministry model. It discussed the nuances of hearing loss and its possible causes, along with emphasizing the importance of accommodations and inclusion. Suggestions for providing accommodations are included, as well as an accommodation check-list to consider. Providing equal opportunities in the parish is important. Also, the case studies provide insight to some of the self-perceptions by hard-of-hearing and late-deafened individuals. The hard-of-hearing and late-deafened ministry is essential for helping to include individuals in the faith community, in part, because there are millions of people with this type of hearing loss (especially in older adults), as compared to those with profound hearing loss. For some hard-of-hearing and late-deafened individuals, they may feel in limbo between the Deaf community and hearing community (not fully belonging in either community), some may feel frustrated due to communication barriers and accommodations not being readily available. Leviticus 19:14 says, *"Thou shalt not curse the deaf, nor put a stumbling block before the blind, but shalt fear thy God: I am the LORD"* (KJV). The hard-of-hearing and late-deafened ministry helps the church to remove stumbling blocks so more people are welcomed and included in the life of the church. After all, a hard-of-hearing and late-deafened ministry can make a difference in some people's lives, even in some people's faith.

Chapter 5 – Overview of a Deaf-blind Ministry

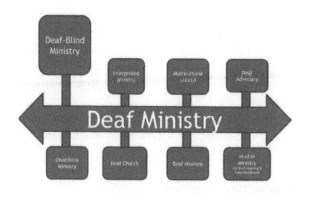

This chapter provides background information to vision loss that can accompany hearing loss, as well as some suggestions for accommodations, ways to be inclusive, and general ministry considerations for those who are Deaf-blind. Deaf-blind people are often overlooked when it comes to being in ministry.[lxxxvii] They are frequently missing from the pews, but they too are meant to be part of the church. People with hearing and vision loss need accommodations just like the rest of the Deaf and/or hearing community. The term 'Deaf-blind' can be somewhat misleading, because of the misconception that a person is fully blind and fully Deaf - this is not always the case. Deaf-blind individuals vary in hearing and visual loss, which means there is not one specific method for provision of accommodations. Meeting with the Deaf-blind individual beforehand in order to learn what accommodations are needed is recommended.

The term 'Deaf-blind' describes a condition that combines in varying degrees both hearing and visual loss. Two sensory losses multiply and intensify the impact each would have alone and create a severe disability, which is different and unique. There are four basic types of Deaf-blindness: (1) Being blind first and deaf later, (2) being deaf first and blind later, (3) being born deaf and blind, and (4) and being suddenly deaf and blind later in life (perhaps from an accident or an illness). These categories tell the world about how the Deaf-blind person will communicate. In general, Deaf-blind people experience problems with communications, access to information, and mobility. However, their specific needs vary enormously according to age, onset, and type of Deaf-blindness.

Communication Methods

The way a Deaf-blind individual communicates often depends on the type of vision or hearing loss he or she has, the communication method that was taught, comfortableness, and among other factors, such as education. The American Association of The Deaf-blind (AADB) is one of the leading organizations for promoting awareness in this area. AADB lists on its website common methods of communicating with a Deaf-blind person.

Sign Language

Some Deaf or hard-of-hearing people with low vision use American Sign Language or an English-based sign language. In some cases, people may need to sign or fingerspell more slowly than usual so the person with limited vision can see signs more clearly. Sometimes the person with low vision can see the signs better if the signer wears a shirt that contrasts with his or her skin color (e.g., a person with light skin needs to wear a dark-colored shirt).

Adapted Signs

Some Deaf-blind people with restricted peripheral vision may prefer the signer to sign in a very small space, usually at chest level. Some signs located at waist level may need to be adapted (e.g. signing "belt" at chest level rather than at waist level).[lxxxviii]

Tactile Sign Language

The Deaf-blind person puts his or her hands over the signer's hands to feel the shape, movement and location of the signs. Some signs and facial expressions may need to be modified (for example, signing "not understand" instead of signing "understand" and shaking one's head; spelling "dog" rather than signing "dog"). People can use one-handed or two-handed tactile sign language. People who grew up using ASL in the deaf community may prefer tactile ASL, while others who came from an oral background or learned signs later may prefer a more English-based tactile system.[lxxxix]

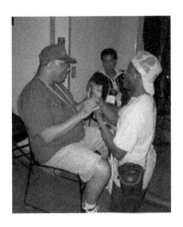

Pro-Tactile

Pro-Tactile involves a system of feedback cues called "back channeling" that provides the communicators with information about each other, their responses to what is being communicated, environment, etc. It is also an effective way to provide feedback to a Deaf-blind presenter about the audience's responses and reactions to their presentation in real time. For example, while the person is signing to the Deaf-blind individual, the Deaf-blind individual may tap with his/her index finger on the signer's hand indicating his/her understanding. Pro-tactile is new compared to the other modes of communication. Information can be found at www.visionlossresources.org/programs/dbsm/pro-tactile-training.

Tracking

Some Deaf-blind people with restricted but still usable vision (e.g., tunnel vision) may follow signs by holding the signer's forearm or wrist and using their eyes to follow the signs visually. This helps them follow signs more easily.[xc]

Tactile Fingerspelling

Usually blind or visually impaired people who lose their hearing later, or deaf or hard-of-hearing people who have depended on their speech reading and do not know how to sign, prefer tactile fingerspelling because sometimes sign language can be difficult to learn. The Deaf-blind person may prefer to put his or her hand over the fingerspelling hand, or on the signer's palm, or cup his or her hand around the signer's hand.[xci]

Further information and alternate methods can be found on the American Association of Deaf-blind's website at www.aadb.org.

Support Service Providers (SSP)

Support service providers (SSPs) relay visual and environmental information, act as sighted guides and facilitate communication for people who are Deaf-blind, using the Deaf-blind person's

 preferred language and communication mode. SSPs enable Deaf-blind persons to access their communities and connect with other people, reducing communication barriers that otherwise would result in social isolation, incapability to live independently, and inability to participate as citizens within mainstream society.[xcii]

Most SSPs are not interpreters. They can provide communication assistance for short exchanges, but not for more complex situations. An SSP can help a Deaf-blind person fill out an insurance form at a doctor's office, but a sign language interpreter would be needed during the actual medical examination. Further information about the use of SSPs can be found on the **American Association of Deaf-blind**'s website at www.aadb.org/information/ssp/ssp.html.

Helpful Tips

Communication, stimulation, and companionship are essential to human beings. Deaf-blind people need this as well. Some helpful tips to keep in mind:[xciii]

❑ Touch is especially important for Deaf-blind people. It is their link with the world. It can show you are nervous, withdrawn, friendly, tired, or bored. You may be uncomfortable "holding hands" during pauses, but it is best to wait for the Deaf-blind person to break contact. It keeps that link and makes it easier for the Deaf-blind person to get your attention.

- Communication options: POP (print on palm), tactile, CV (close vision), distant signing, tracking, limited space/tunnel vision, tactile fingerspelling, sim-com (if the person still has some residual hearing), as well as others.

- Begin slowly with a new person until they are used to you and you see how best to communicate. This is particularly true since most interpreters working with Deaf-blind individuals are also working as support service providers (SSP), their guide, as well.

- Remember the Deaf-blind person cannot see head nods, facial expressions, and other grammatical markers. Additional signs must be added.

- When you know the person better, touch will also include an occasional squeeze, stroke, pat on the back, walking close, or a hug of greeting and farewell.

- If the person's hands are heavy, it may mean he or she is tired or having difficulty understanding. Be aware of a need for a break in the conversation or interpretation.

- Help other people who are new to the Deaf-blind world learn how to communicate with them. Do not be surprised if people, even Deaf people, are reluctant to communicate by touch.

- All people like an interpreter with the right attitude - someone who is flexible and who is there to make communications go smoothly.

- Be careful that clothing contrasts skin color. Some Deaf-blind people are even more sensitive to bright colors than sighted Deaf people. Take off rings or bracelets, and keep fingernails trim, and free from visually distracting fingernail polish.

Do not wear strong perfumes or colognes, including some scented hand lotions.[xciv]

❑ Keep hand sanitizer around in case the individual or the SSP/interpreter has a cold.

Reasons for hearing and vision loss vary among individuals. Granted, some people inherit their sensory loss, but for many there are causes for it. Just like the rest of society, Deaf-blind individuals want to keep their independence, and with technology and other forms of assistance, much of their independence can be retained. Empowerment of Deaf-blind persons within a congregational setting can be achieved when most or all of the information and environment is accessible, perhaps by providing Braille materials, reading materials in large print, or by making the church's website accessible for those with disabilities.[39] If the Deaf-blind person has not learned braille, encourage him or her to do so. Since each Deaf-blind person is different in terms of sensory loss, open communication is a must.[40]

Common Eye Disorders

Though listing the full range of reasons why a person may be Deaf and blind is not in the scope of this book, readers are nevertheless encouraged to study further about this area of deafness. Cataracts often occur in seniors, whether deaf or hearing. A few other terms to be familiar with are:[xcv]

---

[39] Two resources on the internet are www.helenkeller.org and www.nidcd.nih.gov .

[40] RID's Standard Practice Paper: Interpreting for Individuals Who are Deaf-blind is helpful. It can be accessed by going to www.rid.org .

Legal Blindness - this is not a medical term but a legal one. It means that someone has 20/200 vision or worse in both eyes using the best pair of glasses. It can also refer to someone who has better than 20/200 vision but whose visual field is 20 degrees or less. The top number in the ratio refers to the distance the patient is in feet to the eye chart; the bottom number refers to the size of the letters or numbers.

Macular Degeneration - this is the leading cause of central vision loss among older individuals. One of the usual presenting symptoms is that there is a problem with reading. The individual then seeks out care thinking that new glasses are needed. Upon examination, it may be found that the central region of the retina, the macula, has been damaged. There are several types of macular degeneration, the first being called the "dry" type. This is characterized by a thinning of the macular tissue without any fluid build-up in the retinal tissue. Ninety percent of all macular degenerations are of this type. The "wet" type occurs when new blood vessels grow under the macula and leak fluid and blood into the surrounding area. This can cause significant damage to the retina resulting in a central blind spot. Currently, no treatment exists for this problem, but promising treatments are being explored. Low vision optical aids can sometimes help. While this problem is more common in people over age 55, it can happen in childhood; then, it is usually called Stargardt's Disease.

Glaucoma – this is an eye disease that occurs when the tiny channels that allow fluid to drain from the eye become clogged. The result is a build-up of pressure inside the eye. This increased pressure cause's damage to the optic nerve, and in time loss of vision may occur. Glaucoma usually develops without any warnings or symptoms and slowly does damage. Without treatment, glaucoma will lead to total blindness. Another type of glaucoma, acute angle-closure glaucoma, may produce noticeable blurred vision and pain either in the eyes or head. Regular eye exams are needed to routinely test for glaucoma. This condition is managed with eye drops, laser therapy, or surgery. There is no cure for glaucoma. Glaucoma is a major cause for blindness worldwide.

Usher Syndrome - this is the most common condition that involves both hearing and vision problems. A syndrome is a disease or disorder that has more than one feature or symptom. The major symptoms of Usher syndrome are hearing loss and retinitis pigmentosa, an eye disorder that causes a person's vision to worsen over time. Some people with Usher syndrome also have balance problems. Usher syndrome is inherited or passed from parents to their children through genes (random genetic mutation). Usher Syndrome 2 is diagnosed when a person is born hard-of-hearing and starts to lose his or her vision later in life. With Usher Syndrome 3, a person is usually born with normal vision and hearing, or with a mild hearing loss, and start to lose both senses later in life.[xcvi]

Low Vision Strategies

The organization, **Low Vision Resources,** has a plethora of information about vision loss and provides recommendations, as well as trainings.[xcvii]

Optical low vision devices can include:

- ❑ Magnifying spectacles
- ❑ Hand-held magnifiers
- ❑ Stand magnifiers
- ❑ Telescopes

❑ Closed-circuit televisions (CCTV)

Non-optical low vision devices can include:

❑ Large print books, newspapers, and magazines
❑ Check-writing, and other writing guides
❑ Large playing cards
❑ Enlarged telephone dials
❑ Auditory timers, clocks, and computers
❑ Computer scanners that read scanned documents

The Low Vision Resources also provides helpful information with regards to families through their Children, Youth and Family Services program (CYFS).[xcviii] CYFS provides support, information, referral, training and advocacy for the parents of Deaf-blind children from ages 0 to 21 in Minnesota. Staff trained in Deaf-blind intervention work with Deaf-blind children to assist them with accessing and learning about their environment and community, meeting childhood developmental goals, and developing communication strategies.

Outreach Ministry

Having Deaf-blind individuals being a part of worship is wonderful; moreover, providing assistance outside of worship is just as vital. Many Deaf-blind individuals live independently, with family, or even living with other roommates. Befriending them; being intentional in going out with them for coffee or to some where to eat; providing transportation to appointments; SSP assistance; if needed, connecting them to government services or national, state, or local Deaf-blind organizations; offering social and fellowship opportunities; even taking them shopping are all forms of an outreach ministry. The list is endless. It is always best to ask what their needs might be. Some Deaf-blind individuals may have reliable transportation, while others may need to be brought to these activities, including bringing them to church each week. Offering a sign language class that includes aspects of Deaf culture and ways to interact with Deaf-blind individuals can foster the fellowship for Deaf-blind people. Furthermore, hosting regular Deaf-blind events at one's church, which invites Deaf-blind individuals from the community, is a good idea as well. Hospitality, providing transportation, and recruiting volunteers should be considered for this. Consider recruiting ASL students as volunteers. If you need *social activity ideas*, go to www.notjustbingo.com/activity-calendars.html.

In order to get you started, here are several ideas to consider.

Relaxation Retreat – Have aroma therapy, serve hot tea, provide hand massages, and offer a short lecture on the importance of daily relaxation.

Baking Club – Have guests (or friends of guests) make tasty cupcakes to share at an afternoon social.

Baseball Game Party – Host a fun baseball game party that includes giving out baseball caps and interesting facts about the history of baseball and some of its legends. Serve popcorn and Cracker Jacks, even hotdogs as snacks.

Show & Tell Social – Have guests bring an item or two they have collected over the years to pass around. Individuals can share the history and meaning behind the collected item. Ice cream or a sundae bar can be offered.

Study Hall Social – Have guests come prepared with their thinking caps and play an American history trivia game.

Small hand-held American flags can be given to guests. Light refreshments can be served.

Picnic in the Park – Have guests meet at a local park for a picnic. It can be a potluck or a church group (like a women's group) can cook and bring food. Fried chicken, potato salad, chips and sodas will be a great addition.

Passover 101 – Invite Jewish guests to educate non-Jewish guests about the history and tradition of Passover. Light refreshments can be served. Other Jewish or Christian holidays/festivals can be substituted.

Holiday Party – Observe one of the national or religious holidays by having a holiday themed party. Share a brief history education about the holiday or even a trivia game about the holiday. Hors d'oeuvres, a dinner, or a potluck meal can be planned. Be sure to include specialty foods that are unique to the observed holiday.

Flea Market – Plan a flea market where individuals can bring in items to sell. This can be either an indoor or an outdoor event.

Sweet Tea Tasting Social – Serve a variety of sweet teas to guests. Educate guests about each tea. Guests will know more about teas than anyone else in their community. Butter cookies or other refreshments can be served.

Speaker Series – Have guest speakers come and provide lectures on interesting topics. Light refreshments or a potluck meal can be planned.

Yogurt and Granola Social – Plan to have a variety of different flavored yogurts with an assortment of toppings like nuts and berries. Share the history of yogurt and its significance in some cultures.

Health Seminars – Provide an education series on a variety of health topics. Light refreshments can be served.

Cookout – Invite guests to come to a cookout, using either a charcoal grill or an indoor/outdoor George Foreman grill. Hotdogs with all the fixings, potato salad, a mixed fruit salad, baked beans, potato chips, and baked cookies can spruce up any cookout. Briefly share with guests about the history of the cookout followed by an afternoon social. This can be an indoor or outdoor event.

Deaf-blind Interpreting

To locate a sign language interpreter for a Deaf-blind individual, consider contacting the following:

- ❑ A local or state interpreting agency (go to www.rid.org/search-tools/ to locate an agency).
- ❑ By contacting a local or state aging and disability office (go to www.adrc-tae.acl.gov/ and click on the ADRC tab).
- ❑ Contact an interpreter education program in your state for possible referrals; including possible interpreting students (go to https://myaccount.rid.org/Public/Search/Organization.aspx).

The Registry of Interpreters of the Deaf includes a Standard Practice Paper, which provides helpful information.[xcix] Some helpful information for communication can be gleaned from the paper.

INTERPRETING FOR INDIVIDUALS WHO ARE DEAF-BLIND

The Registry of Interpreters for the Deaf, Inc., (RID) Standard Practice Paper (SPP) provides a framework of basic, respectable standards for RID members' professional work and conduct with consumers. This paper also provides specific information about the practice setting. This document is intended to raise awareness, educate, guide and encourage sound basic methods of professional practice. The SPP should be considered by members in arriving at an appropriate course of action with respect to their practice and professional conduct.

It is hoped that the standards will promote commitment to the pursuit of excellence in the practice of interpreting and be used for public distribution and advocacy.

Individuals who are Deaf-blind

The spectrum of consumers who utilize Deaf-blind interpreting services consists of individuals with differing degrees of vision loss and hearing loss. The amount and type of vision and hearing a person has determines the type of interpreting that will be most effective for that individual. Environmental factors must be taken into account in order for effective communication to take place. In addition, many Deaf-blind individuals require support service providers (defined below) in order to fully access the environment. Each of these factors, as well as considerations for hiring interpreters, is explained below.

There is a continuum of vision and hearing loss among people who are Deaf-blind. Persons within this community are not necessarily fully deaf or fully blind. Some Deaf-blind people have a substantial amount of usable vision while others have little (limited vision and/or legally blind) or no usable vision (blind). The same is true regarding the degree of hearing. Individuals may be hard-of-hearing with usable hearing while others are profoundly deaf. The range and degree of both hearing loss and vision loss will determine critical communication factors between the consumer and the interpreter.

Factors that contribute to the diversity in communication within the Deaf-blind community include:
- type, degree and age of onset of hearing and vision loss
- whether current vision and/or hearing is stable, progressive or fluctuating
- level of language competencies in American Sign Language (ASL) or other signed language systems and/or English
- family, ethnic, socio-economic and educational backgrounds
- physical, cognitive or other disabilities

Interpreting for Deaf-blind Individuals

The type and extent of the combined hearing and vision loss determines an individual's mode of communication and needs regarding visual accommodations. Individuals who are Deaf-blind employ one or more of the following communication modes:
- sign language at close visual range (less than 4 feet) and/or within a limited visual
sign language at close visual range (less than 4 feet) and/or within a limited visual space (often a small area including and just below the signer's chin to signer's chest)
- sign language at a greater visual range (4-8 feet) to accommodate those individuals with limited peripheral vision
- sign language received at close visual range with the use of tracking [hand(s) is/are placed on the interpreter's wrists/forearms for the receiver to maintain signs within their visual range]

333 Commerce Street ■ Alexandria, VA 22314
PH: 703.838.0030 ■ FAX: 703.838.0454 ■ TTY: 703.838.0459

RID

- sign language received by sense of touch with one or two hands (tactile)
- fingerspelling received by sense of touch (tactile)
- Print-on-Palm (block letters drawn on the palm)
- speechreading at close visual range
- hearing with assistive listening devices
- reading via text-based devices and services (e.g., real-time captioning connected to a large visual display or refreshable Braille output)
- sign supported speech

Experienced interpreters who work with Deaf-blind people are knowledgeable about and sensitive to environmental factors that may significantly affect the interpreting process. Skilled Deaf-blind interpreters are able to incorporate the speaker's message while also transmitting visual, auditory and environmental stimuli that contribute to the context of the interpreted message.

Dependent on the Deaf-blind consumer's preference, the following components should be considered and may be incorporated during to the beginning of the meeting/workshop/conference:
- the layout of the room (position of windows, color of walls/platform background, tables, chairs, doors)
- specific visual background (signer's shirt in contrast to skin color, high-necked collar, minimal jewelry/accessories)
- seating positions (need for distance or proximity; logistics for teaming)
- auditory factors (background noise; use of assistive listening devices)
- identify who is speaking and location of the speaker the speaker's emotional affect and gestures
- unspoken actions and reactions of people in the room
- information from handouts, PowerPoint slides, other audiovisual materials
- when a person enters or exits the room

The amount of information incorporated is at the discretion of the Deaf-blind consumer and also requires considerable skill and judgment on the part of the interpreter.

Arranging for interpreting services

A person who is Deaf-blind presents unique circumstances for gathering information about the world around him or her as well as the people and interactions encompassed within it. Interpreters and support service providers (SSPs) are often the essential link to the array of information people who are Deaf-blind need in order to be informed, active participants within society. Careful matching of a qualified interpreter and a consumer who is Deaf-blind is critical so that the intricate and individualized interpreting needs are met.

Interpreters must be versatile and flexible because of the unique communication needs of Deaf-blind individuals. For the same reason, the ratio of interpreters to consumers must be appropriate so that these needs can be satisfactorily met. The number of Deaf-blind individuals in an environment will greatly influence the number of interpreters or interpreting teams that will be needed.

In situations involving one Deaf-blind individual, only one interpreter or interpreter team may be needed. When two or more Deaf-blind individuals are present, more teams may be required. For example, one team might interpret via tactile sign language (hand-over-hand communication) with a single consumer, while another team may interpret at close visual range with a group of two to four consumers and yet another team may provide audible interpretation using an FM system. Team interpreting is standard practice for any event of an hour or more in duration and/or because of the complexity of content or for platform situations.

Interpreting For Individuals Who Are Deaf-blind.

STANDARD PRACTICE PAPER

Another reason two or more interpreters may be needed is that interpreting can be physically and mentally demanding, which may require frequent rest breaks or relief (in addition to their teaming responsibilities). For assignments under one hour with a person with close or low vision, one interpreter may be sufficient though the need for additional rest times should be considered. Any assignment with a tactile consumer with duration over thirty minutes however, should utilize a team of two interpreters due to the physical demands of that type of communication. An interpreting team may include one or more interpreters who are deaf. In these instances, the deaf interpreter receives the speaker's message visually (either from the speaker directly or through another interpreter), processes the message, and then transmits it in a style that is suitable to that particular Deaf-blind individual.

Professional standards of practice when arranging for interpreting services include:
■ asking for consumer preferences regarding communication mode(s) and specific interpreter(s)
■ engaging interpreters who are skilled in working with Deaf-blind consumers
■ engaging an appropriate number of interpreters
■ agreeing on the specific role and responsibilities of the interpreter prior to the event
■ arranging for any special communication equipment needed (e.g. microphones, FM systems)
■ ensuring that the visual environment is conducive to communication for the Deaf-blind participant(s)
■ ensuring that the interpreters hired wear clothing which is in high contrast to their skin tone and with a crew neckline or higher; clothing material should not be made of shiny or patterned fabric or be heavily buttoned and should not reflect light
■ ensuring that the interpreters hired minimize the use of jewelry and accessories allowing 15 to 30 minutes prior to the assignment to establish communication, rapport and preferences before interpreting begins
■ note that not all interpreters are qualified to work with Deaf-blind consumers

Support Service Providers

Individuals who are Deaf-blind may request additional services that are not typically associated with interpreting for individuals who are deaf. For example, an individual may wish to receive an orientation to a conference hall where they will be attending activities for the day, ask that someone be available to function as a guide to the restroom or request assistance through a buffet. These types of services are often performed by a SSP, a specially-trained guide who is familiar with the Deaf-blind person's communication needs and is able to provide environmental information and assistance before, during and/or after a scheduled event takes place. Qualified interpreters accepting assignments with Deaf-blind consumers should be aware of and sensitive to these potential needs. It must be noted that while interpreters can often function as SSPs, it is not the case that a SSP is necessarily a qualified interpreter; although they may be able to facilitate brief, informal communication.

Deaf-blind Camps

Deaf-blind camps have been established for several decades. It provides an opportunity for Deaf-blind individuals to come and enjoy activities, fellowship, and experience a sense of belonging. Since Deaf-blind camps are a popular venue for outreach ministry, the following list has been compiled to consider supporting and/or for participating.

Alaska
Camp Abilities: A Developmental Sports Camp for Children who are Blind, Deaf-blind, or have Multiple Disabilities (for youth)
Dept of Physical Education
350 New Campus Drive
Brockport, NY 14420
585-395-5361 voice
www.brockport.edu/camp-abilities
llieberm@brockport.edu

Maryland
Deafblind Camp of Maryland, LLC
911 Regina Drive
Baltimore, MD 21227
 info@deafblindcampofmd.org

New York
Camp Helen Keller (for youth)
Helen Keller Services for the Blind
One Helen Keller Way
Hempstead, NY 11550
Bill Dale, Camp Director
516-485-1235, ext. 607 or
email: info@helenkeller.org
www.helenkeller.org

North Carolina
Camp Dogwood (for adults)
Helen Keller National Center
404-766-9625 Voice 2820 TTY
monika.werner@hknc.org
www.nclf.org

Cleveland Sight Center's Highbrook Lodge (youth and adults)
Contact Information: Cleveland Sight Center
C/o Cleveland Society for the Blind
1909 East 101st Street
Cleveland, OH 44106-8696
Greg McGrath, Camp Coordinator
www.clevelandsightcenter.org

Tennessee
Tennessee Organization of the Deaf-blind (TODB) Camp
(for youth and adults)
C/o John Forbes
4040 Woodlawn Drive, Unit #34
Nashville, TN 37205
jcforbes@bwsc.net

Texas
Texas Commission for the Deaf and Hard-of-hearing (for youth)
4800 North Lamar
Austin, TX 78756
www.dars.state.tx.us
www.gssjc.org/residentcamp/misty.asp

Camp Summit (for youth and adults)
2915 LBJ Freeway, Suite 185
Dallas, TX 75234
972-484-8900 voice
L.braziel@campsummittx.org
www.campsummittx.org

Utah
Adventure Learning Program & other Year-Round
Recreational Activities
(for youth and adults)
Contact Information: National Ability Center
P.O. Box 682799
Park, City, UT 84068
Jenn Carpenter, Adventure Learning Manager
435-649-3991 ext. 609 voice/TTY
nac@nac1985.org
www.nac1985.org

Washington
Seabeck Deaf-blind Retreat Camp (for teenagers and
adults)
C/o The Lighthouse f/t Blind
P.O. Box 14959
Seattle, WA 98114
206-436-2231 TTY 206-436-2133 voice
dbretreat@seattlelh.org

Deaf-blind Organizations

Deaf-blind organizations often have a clearing house of information for resources, conferences, events, and how to obtain additional support. The following is a compiled list of national organizations, which also have chapters (by state).

American Association of the Deaf-blind
8630 Fenton Street, Suite 121
Silver Spring, MD 20910
301-495-4402 TTY/VP; 301-495-4403 Voice
301-495-4404 Fax
Email: aadb-info@aadb.org
Website: www.aadb.org

Helen Keller National Center for Deaf-blind Youths and Adults
Administrative Offices/Training Program
141 Middle Neck Road
Sands Point, NY 11050
Main Switchboard: (516) 944-8900 8:00 am to 3:45pm
Fax: (516) 944-7302
TTY: 516-944-8637
Videophone: (516) 570-3626 or (866) 351-9089
Email: hkncinfo@hknc.org
Website: http://www.hknc.org/
Locate state representatives at
www.hknc.org/FieldServicesREGREPADD.htm

National Center on Deaf-blindness
345 N. Monmouth Ave.
Monmouth, OR 97361
info@nationaldb.org
Website: https://nationaldb.org/
Family specialists are located at
Website:
https://nationaldb.org/members/list?type=Family+Speci
alist

National Family Association for Deaf-blind
141 Middle Neck Road
Sands Point, NY 11050
Phone: 800.255.0411
Fax: 516.883.9060
Email: NFADBinfo@gmail.com
Website: http://nfadb.org/
NFADB State Affiliates: http://nfadb.org/who-we-
are/state-affiliates/

iCanConnect
The National Deaf-Blind Equipment Distribution
Program
Telephone: 800-825-4595
Website: www.iCanConnect.org
iCanConnect advertises and promotes the National Deaf-
Blind Equipment Distribution Program, and provides
technical support and service information to people
experiencing combined hearing and vision loss who may
be eligible for the program's services.

National Federation of the Blind
200 East Wells Street (at Jernigan Place)
Baltimore, MD 21230
Phone: 410-659-9314
Fax: 410-685-5653
Website: https://nfb.org/search/gss/deaf
Has resources for living, working, learning, recreation, products and technology, and publications.

Case Study – DeafCAN!

DeafCAN! (Deaf Community Action Network) is located in West Chester, PA. It is a human service program of Christ the King Deaf Church (a Lutheran church) in providing SSP services for Deaf-blind individuals, as well as other social services for its community. DeafCAN! has established formal SSP services by training support service providers to assist Deaf-blind individuals in their communities. SSPs will work with 35 Deaf-blind consumers, up to 15 hours each month, in

- ❑ Navigating and communicating for shopping, medical appointments, banking, etc.
- ❑ Participating with families, neighbors and their communities
- ❑ Handling and understanding email/phone calls and other home communication needs.
- ❑ Pursuing employment and other participation in their communities
- ❑ Assisting with travel by either driving or using public transportation[c]

Bill Lockard, the program director, who serves with his wife, Rev. Beth Lockard, the executive director, says, "With all the services that DeafCAN! provides, it is wonderful when those who had received services wish to return and volunteer – paying it forward for others."

Questions for Reflection

1. Do you know of any individuals who are losing their hearing and/or losing their sight? If so, how might your faith community show compassion and mercy to them?
2. Community is very important for many people. What ways can your church provide aspects of community to those who are losing their sight and/or their hearing?
3. How can some of your church's general ministry be adapted to accommodate Deaf-blind individuals?
4. What ways can your church show support to Deaf-blind individuals?
5. James **4:6** reads, *But He gives us more grace. That is why Scripture says: "God opposes the proud but shows favor to the humble."* How can your church share more grace to Deaf-blind individuals and their families?

Conclusion

In conclusion, this chapter provides an overview of a Deaf-blind ministry; it discussed the more common communication modes, the common eye disorders, low vision strategies, and interpreting considerations. Support service providers were also discussed and common outreach ministry ideas with Deaf-blind individuals were suggested. If a Deaf-blind individual has not had any Deaf-blind training, helping the individual consider training, like at the Helen Keller Center in New York, is suggested.

Chapter 6 – Overview of a Multicultural Church

In this model of Deaf ministry, the multicultural church or congregation incorporates hearing culture and Deaf culture, and can include d/Deaf, hard-of-hearing, late-deafened, Deaf-blind and hearing people. There are variations in how a person becomes deaf or hard-of-hearing, level of hearing, age of onset, educational background, communication methods, and cultural identity. How people "label" or identify themselves is personal and may reflect how identification with the Deaf community, the degree to which they can hear, or the relative age of onset. For example, some people identify themselves as "late-deafened," indicating that they became deaf later in life. Other people identify themselves as "Deaf-blind" due to having hearing and vision loss. Some people believe that the term "people with hearing loss" is inclusive and efficient. However, some people who were born Deaf or hard-of-hearing do not think of themselves as having lost their hearing.

According to Carol Padden and Tom Humphries in <u>Deaf in America: Voices from a Culture</u> (1988), they point out "this knowledge of Deaf people is not simply a camaraderie with others who have a similar physical condition, but is, like many other cultures in the traditional sense of the term, historically created and actively transmitted across generations." The authors also add that Deaf people "have found ways to define and express themselves through their rituals, tales, performances, and everyday social encounters."[ci]

In multicultural church model, Deaf culture and sign language is often interwoven into the context of the hearing church's ministry or vice versa.[cii] Often, one will see both hearing individuals and d/Deaf individuals in the fabric of leadership, frequently using interpreters or other modes of communication between both language systems (e.g. ASL and English).

When a church is made up of d/Deaf, hard-of-hearing, late-deafened, Deaf-blind, and hearing members, this too takes on the paradigm of a multicultural ministry. Merging various cultural values, while respecting one another's communication needs, these show social diversity and inclusiveness for all. Frequent cultural mediation and a leadership who values inclusiveness will make this a successful ministry. For this ministry to work effectively, the congregations will likely use interpreters, CART (captioning), assisted listening devices, and visuals (e.g. large print bulletins and multimedia).

Flexibility and creativity, as well as continued respect of varying cultures and language systems are needed. Those who are bi-cultural, multicultural, or a "culture broker" often bridge the gap between cultures by selecting, combining, and synthesizing aspects of both cultures (hearing and Deaf), which is part of culturally mediation.[ciii] If Deaf-blind interpreting is needed, it is helpful to recruit d/Deaf individuals who are willing to team interpret for them. Coordinating and scheduling captionists, as well as recruiting these volunteers ahead of time are helpful.

The Lutheran Deaf Mission Society includes one aspect of this ministry model in its teaching and understanding of Deaf ministry models. It describes it as a multi-staffed, multi-directional ministry.[civ]

Multi-staffed, Multi-directional Ministry

This version is characterized by a hearing congregation that has a commitment to missions with Deaf people, so as to provide a staff person (full-time or part-time) who is responsible for this outreach. This model differs in that a mission to Deaf people is incorporated into the entire ministry of the hearing congregation and the Deaf Christians are viewed as integral members of the hearing parish. This model will differ from the description of an interpreted ministry, since in this model; the interpreter or church worker is viewed as part of the staff to help the church be inclusive rather than integrate people with hearing loss.

Advantages – A few advantages to this model include:
1. This model provides for integration of Deaf people into the life of the hearing congregation.
2. This model provides more opportunities to reach Deaf youth who are mainstreamed in local schools.
3. Programming can be planned—either separate from the hearing part of the congregation or jointly—as best meets the needs of the situation.

Disadvantages – A few disadvantages to this model include:

1. The Deaf people, being a small minority in the congregation, may feel overwhelmed by the hearing majority, and thus limit their participation in congregational life and activities.
2. Unless a significant number of caring hearing members in the congregation learn to communicate in sign language, Deaf people will feel isolated because of the communication barrier.

Considerations - Additional considerations to this model include:

1. This model depends on the dedication of the congregation to the ministry and on the active support of the entire staff, especially the pastors.
2. As with any team ministry, care must be exercised to insure a compatible working relationship between staff members.

Dual Parish: Deaf & Hearing

Another scenario that falls into the multicultural church model is what The Lutheran Deaf Mission Society calls a Deaf and Hearing Dual Parish.[cv] This model has two congregations, one hearing congregation and one Deaf (or Deaf and hearing combined) congregation. It assumes that at least 50% of the pastoral work time is devoted to the Deaf church when:

❑ One pastor serving two congregations (in the same or in separate locations);
❑ An assistant or associate pastor in a larger hearing church also serving a Deaf congregation (with the same options concerning location);

❑   Two pastoral workers (2 clergy or 1 pastor and 1 lay worker) serving two congregations as a team (both fully qualified for mission outreach among Deaf people).

Advantages - A few advantages of this model can include:

1. This model provides greater opportunity to serve both hearing and Deaf members of the family (when both congregations are in the same location).
2. This model provides numerous opportunities to reach Deaf children/youth that are mainstreamed in local schools.
3. This model provides the hearing pastoral worker opportunity to work with people of his or her culture, as well as cross-culturally with Deaf people. This may provide some additional satisfaction from mission service than when working only in a cross-cultural setting.
4. This model provides a base with more members for the financial support of this mission, thus reducing the amount of resource sharing that is needed from the District.
5. It is possible that both groups could share the same facilities.

Disadvantages – A few disadvantages of this model can include:

1. There is a tendency for people in either congregation to feel that the pastoral worker is involved too greatly in the other congregation's mission, especially when one worker serves two churches.

2. Extensive work in two cultures may tempt a
    person to be too busy to regularly feed himself
    through studying God's word which might lead to
    "pastor burn-out."
3. The hearing congregation—which may be seen as
    the "dominant" partner—often relegates the Deaf
    congregation to the status of "second-class
    citizenship."
4. Dedication of the hearing parish to continuing
    the dual mission outreach whenever there is a
    change in pastoral workers may pose a problem
    to the longevity of the mission with Deaf
    members.

Considerations - A few additional considerations for this
model include:

1 . As with any team ministry, care must be exercised
    to insure a compatible working relationship
    between staff members.
2 . Communication between the two congregations
    is important. When difficulties arise, a neutral
    third party may be helpful.
3 . Periodic review is essential to insure that each
    congregation is receiving the mission focus it
    requires. If either or both grow significantly,
    additional staff or a division of the dual parish
    may be required.
4 . An average attendance of 100 people in the
    hearing church and 30 people in the Deaf church
    may mark the upper limits of the number of
    people that can effectively be served by one
    pastor.
5 . Essential to the success of this model is a position
    description with careful delineation of tasks and
    time allotted for the tasks.

6 . Also essential is regular communication between the parties involved (i.e. District, hearing congregations, and the Deaf congregation). This should include minimally quarterly reports and an annual re-evaluation and if necessary redefinition of position description and times allotted.

Multicultural Framework

The work by Zuniga, Nagda, and Sevig (2002) provides a framework to foster engagement between various social identity groups, which can be one paradigm used in the multicultural ministry model. The following components of this model for cultivating engagement include:[cvi]

- ❏ **Sustained Communication** – This enables groups to explore issues more fully, develop empathetic connections, and find strength and value in each other's' perspectives. Allows for listening without judgment, appreciating different perspectives, and asking questions, all of which help build trust.
- ❏ **Consciousness Raising** – This is a process that encourages individuals to recognize, question, broaden, and challenge individual, cultural, and institutional beliefs and behaviors that cause estranged and oppressive relations between various cultures.
- ❏ **Bridging of Differences** – This refers to building connections across differences and commitment to social justice. This involves developing empathy and understanding, building collaborative ties, and supporting action for change.

- ❑ **Social Justice Perspective** - Throughout these interactions, Zuniga, Nagda, and Sevig (2002) recommend maintaining a social justice perspective, which fosters salient conversations between social group interactions. This is to help with prejudice reduction and relationship building across social groups. Encouraging periodic reflection is also helpful.
- ❑ **Faith** – What comes before or with the social justice perspective is the incorporation of God into the interactions. When building moments of grace and experiencing this throughout conversations and programs, this will help the primary focus to be the congregation's relationship with God. Remember, it's all about grace, mercy, and love. Plus, it was Jesus who said to love one another (John 15:17).

Case Study - Bethany Community Church

A multicultural church in Laurel, Maryland, Bethany Community Church offers a fascinating model in which the Deaf and hearing congregation hold their own worship service in sign language, while is integrated into the life of the overall church.

The church's website states: *The purpose of our Deaf ministry here at Bethany is to help Deaf people begin and grow in a personal relationship with Jesus Christ. Our Deaf Ministry Team, led by a dedicated group of Deaf leaders, is the catalyst for a range of ministry opportunities for Deaf people - and, Deaf people also serve in a broad range of ministries across the spectrum of our church such as: Visual Worship and drama, communications and publicity, web team, missions, facilities and grounds maintenance, special events, children's ministry, and Bible teaching. During worship, both a high quality, professional interpreter in American Sign Language as well as real time captioning (CART) are provided. All of our music is presented in a visual format as well.[cvii]* According to the church's pastor, Kevin McGhee, "Our philosophy is one of 100% integration whenever possible, while still encouraging pure ASL environments to flourish as well. Our Deaf ministry potlucks (all ASL) have a number of hearing who attend." Bethany Community Church is doing what more churches are doing by integrating both cultures.

Case Study - Magothy United Methodist of the Deaf

Magothy United Methodist Church of the Deaf in Pasadena, Maryland is a part of a cooperative parish where it shares the facility with a hearing church (Magothy United Methodist Church). What is unique about Magothy Deaf Church's model is it incorporates Deaf culture, hearing culture, and bi-culture (CODAs) into its contextual values of the church. Both hearing and d/Deaf individuals make up the church's leadership, including substitute preaching when their pastor, who signs fluently, is unavailable.

One reason for their multicultural approach to Deaf ministry is the incorporation of hearing family members and friends, some of who sign and some of who do not, as well as CODAs (those who are bicultural). Magothy does provide sign language interpreters during worship and during special events and meetings.

Initially, Magothy Deaf Church began as a mostly Deaf church, but evolved into a multicultural church that embraces both hearing culture and Deaf culture. Between the hearing church and the

Magothy United Methodist Church of the Deaf

Deaf church, members of both congregations often share in ministry with one another (e.g. Doorstep Mission, a food pantry) and occasionally participate in one another's events.

Case Study – Calvary Community Church

Calvary Community Church is a part of the Assemblies of God denomination, located in Los Angeles, California. It is a church where both Deaf and hearing people fellowship together. It also emphasizes the moving of the Holy Spirit, and encourages its members to be filled with the Spirit with the evidence of speaking in other tongues. They also encourage members to seek the Spiritual gifts resident in the apostles and members of the New Testament Church. You will see conversations in sign language flowing freely in their church. The church believes it pleases God when hearing and Deaf people worship together as equals. For hearing members who do not sign, there are white boards with markers placed throughout the church.[cviii]

Questions for Reflection

1. Are there any attitudinal barriers that may be deterring your church from growing in its ministry with d/Deaf, hard-of-hearing, late-deafened, and Deaf-blind people?
2. Are there any cultural differences that cause discomfort or awkwardness for members in your church (identifying them is helpful)? If so, how might you resolve them?
3. How can your church expand its current ministry to include various cultures and languages (e.g. ASL and English)?

4. Ministry often causes us to stretch beyond our comfort zone. What might be holding your church back from expanding its ministry to be more inclusive of d/Deaf, hard-of-hearing, late-deafened, and Deaf-blind people?

5. Zechariah 7:8-10 reads, *8And the word of the LORD came again to Zechariah: 9"This is what the LORD Almighty said: 'Administer true justice; show mercy and compassion to one another.10Do not oppress the widow or the fatherless, the foreigner or the poor. Do not plot evil against each other.'* (NIV) How can your church be more open and accommodating to individuals from various backgrounds?

Conclusion

In conclusion, this chapter discusses the dynamics of the multicultural church model, which has both Deaf culture and hearing culture being merged in the whole church or in certain aspects of the ministry. A helpful visual of a multicultural congregation that is inclusive is the following image from The Equal Rights Center.

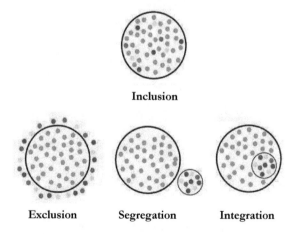

Inclusion

Exclusion   Segregation   Integration

Contributing examples of this model by the Lutheran Church, as well as case studies that emphasize this model were also included. The kinds of ministry involvement by those in the multicultural church can be similar to what is mentioned in the Deaf church model (i.e. visiting d/Deaf shut-ins, providing religious education at Deaf schools, offering a sign language class to the community, ministering to d/Deaf prisoners, involvement at a Deaf camp, and so on). Since the multicultural church or congregation includes hearing culture and a hearing membership, as well as possibly sharing a facility with another hearing congregation, the multicultural church may have ministry involvement that focus on hearing people's needs (i.e. food pantry and soup kitchen type ministries).

Chapter 7 – Overview of the Deaf Advocacy Model

Another form of Deaf ministry is the Deaf advocacy model. This often includes support to Deaf ministries and organizations in the Deaf community. Also, this type of ministry is done by (1) prayer, (2) case advocacy, (3) financially partnering with Deaf churches, (4) supporting a Deaf organization's mission and/or ministry, and (5) by offering support through resources and advocacy so the church or congregation may be autonomous and/or inclusive.

While Jesus was a prophet, a king, and a priest, he was also an advocate. In fact, Jesus often advocated in his public ministry. At the end of Luke 4, we see the work of social justice in Jesus, as he heals and restores sick individuals so they can have their rightful place in their society. There are plenty of examples in the gospels of Jesus standing up to authorities on behalf of the poor, those with a disability, and the sick.

Human Services

One aspect of Deaf advocacy is human service work. Broadly defined, the National Organization for Human Services defines human services as meeting human needs through an interdisciplinary knowledge base, focusing on prevention as well as remediation of problems, and maintaining a commitment to improving the overall quality of life of service populations.[cix] In terms of church life, we call this ministry, as the church often tries to improve the quality of life to those in their faith community and in its community-at-large through compassion/mercy programs, case management, advocacy, family ministries, spiritual life, and so on.

The Law Pertaining to Deaf People

For advocacy purposes, it is helpful to know the laws that support Deaf people. Federal law mandates the prohibition of discrimination of people with disabilities. Guidelines[cx] from the Department of Justice stipulate:

❑ *American with Disabilities Act (ADA):* The ADA prohibits discrimination on the basis of disability in employment, State and local government, public accommodations, commercial facilities, transportation, and telecommunications. It also applies to the United States Congress.
  o Title I requires employers with 15 or more employees to provide qualified individuals with disabilities an equal opportunity to benefit from the full range of employment-related opportunities available to others.
  o Title III covers businesses and nonprofit service providers that are public accommodations, privately operated entities

offering certain types of courses and examinations, privately operated transportation, and commercial facilities. Public accommodations are private entities who own, lease, lease to, or operate facilities such as restaurants, retail stores, hotels, movie theaters, private schools, convention centers, doctors' offices, homeless shelters, transportation depots, zoos, funeral homes, day care centers, and recreation facilities including sports stadiums and fitness clubs.

o Title IV addresses telephone and television access for people with hearing and speech disabilities. It requires common carriers (telephone companies) to establish interstate and intrastate telecommunications relay services (TRS) 24 hours a day, 7 days a week. Title IV also requires closed captioning of federally funded public service announcements.

❑ The *Individuals with Disabilities Education Act (IDEA)* (formerly called P.L. 94-142 or the Education for all Handicapped Children Act of 1975) requires public schools to make available to all eligible children with disabilities a free appropriate public education in the least restrictive environment appropriate to their individual needs.[cxi]

Complete descriptions of these guidelines, plus several others, are accessible through the Department of Justice. Notable, however, is that the ADA *does not apply* to religious institutions or churches. Sadly, the church has the discretion whether or not to provide and pay for an interpreter. The d/Deaf person's spiritual growth may be underdeveloped, and centuries of exclusion may continue because of lack of communications access at local churches.

Deaf Self-Advocacy

Self-advocacy does not come easily for some people. Sometimes trying to figure out what exactly are one's needs and how to ask for accommodations can be challenging. The Deaf Self-Advocacy training program is an initiative through the National Consortium of Interpreter Education Centers. Consultation and training is provided, which teaches d/Deaf individuals about self-determination, the law, ethics related to interpreters, video relay interpreting, preparation for self-advocacy, and connecting to other resources.[cxii] There is a fine line between advocating and taking over, and empowering individuals to advocate for themselves is always recommended. Additional information can be found at www.interpretereducation.org/deaf-self-advocacy/.

In addition to the training, the University of North Carolina in Greensboro, offers an advocacy curriculum in its Deaf program, which it suggests the following advocacy tips for self-advocating:

- ❑ Encouraging Deaf, hard-of-hearing, late-deafened, and Deaf-blind people to express their communication preference, their needs and other rights in order to be treated equally and fairly in an appropriate way.
- ❑ Informing and encouraging d/Deaf, hard-of-hearing, late-deafened, and Deaf-blind individuals to make their own choices regardless of the beliefs and values of the advocate.
- ❑ Educating d/Deaf, hard-of-hearing, late-deafened, and Deaf-blind individuals to be independent and doing things for themselves

when possible. In other words, the advocate allows the d/Deaf, hard-of-hearing, late-deafened, and Deaf-blind individuals to take control of their own life and making their own decisions.

❑ Empowering d/Deaf, hard-of-hearing, late-deafened, and Deaf-blind individuals to accept responsibility for themselves and the consequences of their decisions.

❑ Educating and encouraging d/Deaf, hard-of-hearing, late-deafened, and Deaf-blind individuals to ask for clarification when needed.

❑ Helping and educating d/Deaf, hard-of-hearing, late-deafened, and Deaf-blind individuals to identify their needs in order to succeed and be able to state those needs themselves.[cxiii]

Case Advocacy

Case advocacy assists those with housing, education, medical, legal, and financial needs. The difference between case advocacy and case management is case advocacy is usually limited to temporary assistance and case management often provides on-going assistance. To identify what benefits one may be entitled to, go to **www.benefits.gov**. Various benefits to look for include housing, education, disability assistance, energy assistance, food/nutrition, child care support, healthcare, Medicare/Medical Assistance, living assistance, and others.

Public Benefits

Through the Social Security Administration, the following benefits are sometimes approved for those with hearing loss.

Supplemental Security Income - Supplemental Security Income (SSI) and Social Security Disability Income (SSDI) can be applied for through the Social Security Administration (SSA) by going to a local field office or by applying online at SSA's website. Social Security administers this program. The Social Security Administration pay monthly benefits to people with limited income and resources who have a disability, are blind, or age 65 or older. Blind or children with disabilities may also qualify for SSI.[cxiv]

According to the Social Security Administration's website, it stipulates the following:

❑ In most States, SSI beneficiaries also can get medical assistance (Medicaid) - to pay for hospital stays, doctor bills, prescription drugs, and other health costs.

❑ Many States also provide a supplemental payment to certain SSI beneficiaries.

❑ SSI beneficiaries may also be eligible for food assistance in every State except California. In some States, an application for SSI also serves as an application for food assistance.

❑ SSI benefits are paid on the first of the month.

❑ To get SSI, you must be disabled, blind, or at least 65 years old and have "limited" income and resources.

❑ In addition, to get SSI, you must also:
  ▪ be a legal resident of the United States, and
  ▪ not be absent from the country for a full calendar month or more or for 30 consecutive days or more; and
  ▪ Be either a U.S. citizen or national, or in one of certain categories of qualified non–citizens.

Social Security Disability Income – Social Security pays benefits to people who can't work because they have a medical condition that's expected to last at least one year or result in death. This type of benefit is called Social Security Disability Income (SSDI).[cxv]

In general, to get disability benefits, you must meet two different earnings tests:

1. A recent work test, based on your age at the time you became disabled; and
2. A duration of work test to show that you worked long enough under Social Security.

According to the Social Security Administration, one will want to apply for disability benefits as soon as one becomes disabled. Processing an application for disability benefits can take three to five months. Applications can be found online at www.socialsecurity.gov. Be prepared to provide information such as:

- ❑ Your Social Security number;
- ❑ A copy of your birth or baptismal certificate;
- ❑ Names, addresses and phone numbers of the doctors, caseworkers, hospitals and clinics that took care of you, and dates of your visits;
- ❑ Names and dosage of all the medicine you take;
- ❑ Medical records from your doctors, therapists, hospitals, clinics, and caseworkers that you already have in your possession;
- ❑ Laboratory and test results;
- ❑ A summary of where you worked and the kind of work you did; and
- ❑ A copy of your most recent W-2 Form (Wage and Tax Statement) or last year's tax return. [cxvi]

The Social Security Administration uses a screening process to determine benefits that includes the following:

1. Are you working?
2. Is the medical condition "severe"? (SSA has criteria they follow.)
3. Does your impairment meet or medically equal a listing? (Based on the SSA list of conditions.)
4. Can you do the work you did before?
5. Can you do any other type of work?

Tax Credit for Providing ADA Accommodations

According to the IRS Disabled Access Credit, form 8826, businesses accommodating people with disabilities may qualify for some of the following tax credits and deductions[cxvii]. According to the form, businesses that provide qualified interpreters or other methods of making audio materials available to d/Deaf individuals; are eligible for a tax deduction.

The Disabled Access Credit provides a non-refundable credit for small businesses that incur expenses for the purpose of providing access to persons with disabilities. An eligible small business is one that that earned $1 million or less or had no more than 30 full time employees in the previous year; they may take the credit each and every year they incur access expenditures. The Disability Access Credit applies to the deaf, vision impaired, mobility impaired with disabilities and the elderly.

Filing Discrimination Complaints

Unfortunately, some Deaf people are discriminated against in a number of ways. The National Association of the Deaf (NAD) has the NAD Law and Advocacy Center as a part of its organization. If d/Deaf individuals are unable to resolve rights issues or legal matters relating to discrimination, the law and advocacy center can be contacted for guidance, referrals, and possibly assistance.

The law and advocacy center advocate on legislative and public policy issues of concern to the deaf and hard-of-hearing community and represent select cases. The types of discrimination assistance the law and advocacy center has previously helped with and offer suggestions for include:[cxviii]

- ❑ Air travel
- ❑ By businesses
- ❑ By state and local government programs and services
- ❑ Health care and mental health services
- ❑ In higher education
- ❑ Public transportation (buses, metro, and trains)
- ❑ Employment discrimination
- ❑ Federally funded programs
- ❑ Housing discrimination
- ❑ Police discrimination
- ❑ Other types of discrimination and legal problems.

To learn more about filing complaints, go to www.nad.org/about-law-and-advocacy-center/file-complaint.

Senior Resources

The National Association of the Deaf worked with the Deaf Seniors of America organization and collaborated on establishing a resource list that includes many states. The following resource categories are listed on the NAD website:cxix

- ❑ Government agencies
- ❑ Independent living and residential facilities
- ❑ Assisted Living Facilities
- ❑ Nursing facilities
- ❑ Hospice facilities/services
- ❑ Social gathering sites

Information about these and more can be read by going to http://nad.org/senior-resources.

Mental Health and Substance Abuse Treatment Providers

When in ministry, it is common to make referrals to community resources. The Rochester Institute of Technology (RIT) hosts a national directory of substance abuse treatment providers, which includes some mental health providers (some providers incorporate both into their practice).[cxx] Some of the providers are d/Deaf or are hearing with sign fluency. Other providers may use interpreters or other accommodations in their practice. The website for providers is located at www.rit.edu/ntid/saisd/national-directory.

At the time of this writing, there is only one all d/Deaf and hard-of-hearing inpatient drug treatment unit in the United States. It is **Minnesota Chemical Dependency Program**. More information about this program can be located at www.mncddeaf.org/.

Domestic Violence

Domestic violence is prevalent in the Deaf community like it is in any other community. Most churches experience this in some way, such as a member of the community seeking refuge or a church family shares it with a pastor or church leader. While intimate partner violence is one aspect of domestic violence, it can occur among other family members. Identifiable signs and tactics of domestic violence include: (1) coercion and threats, (2) intimidation, (3) emotional abuse, (4) isolation, (5) minimizing, denying, and blaming, (6) using children, (7) economic abuse, and (8) male privilege.[cxxi]

<u>Power and Control Wheel</u>

The following equality wheel is provided to identify what the opposite abusive behaviors are, which can be helpful when explaining what healthy versus non-healthy relationships ought to look like. These identifiable signs include: (1) non-threatening behavior, (2) respect, (3) trust and support, (4) honesty and accountability, (5) responsible parenting, (6) shares responsibility, (7) economic partnership, and (8) negotiation and fairness.

181

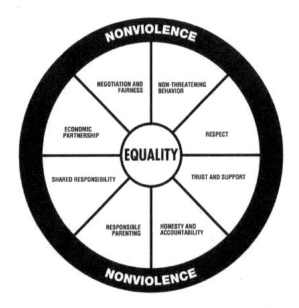

Equality Wheel

According to Deaf Hope, an agency that works with d/Deaf and hard-of-hearing survivors of domestic violence, the agency offers the following Deaf-related examples of domestic violence:[cxxii]

- ❑ Intimidation through gestures, facial expressions, or exaggerated signs, floor stomping and pounding on the table or door
- ❑ Signing very close to a victim's face when angry
- ❑ Criticizing the victim's American sign language (ASL) skills or communication style
- ❑ Not informing the victim when people try to call on the phone or try to catch their attention
- ❑ Excluding the victim from important conversations

- Leaving the victim out in social situations with hearing people
- Talking negatively about the Deaf community
- Wrongly interpreting to manipulate the situation if the police are called
- Not allowing children to use ASL to talk with the victim
- Not allowing children to be proud of deaf culture
- Criticizing the victim's speech and English skills

The **National Domestic Violence Hotline** offers d/Deaf and hard-of-hearing individuals support and assistance and referrals for follow up support. It can be reached by video phone, email, instant messaging, and by live chat on its website. It also has suggestions for a personal safety plan on its website. It can be reached by going to its website at www.thehotline.org/help/deaf-services/.

The National Domestic Violence Hotline recommends as a part of a safety plan the following:

- Open a checking or savings account in your own name.
- Leave money, an extra set of keys, copies of important documents and extra clothes and medications in a safe place or with someone you trust.
- Open your own post office box.
- Identify a safe place where you can go and someone who can lend you money.
- Always keep the shelter phone number, a calling card or some change for emergency phone calls with you.
- If you have pets, make arrangements for them to be cared for in a safe place.

Items to keep in mind in <u>personal safety planning</u> are:^{cxxiii}

Identification
- ❑ Driver's license
- ❑ Birth certificate
- ❑ Children's birth certificates
- ❑ Social security cards

Financial
- ❑ Money and/or credit cards (in your name)
- ❑ Checking and/or savings account books

Legal Papers
- ❑ Protective order
- ❑ Lease, rental agreement and house deed
- ❑ Car registration and insurance papers
- ❑ Health and life insurance papers
- ❑ Medical records for you & your children
- ❑ School records
- ❑ Work permits/green card/visa
- ❑ Passport
- ❑ Divorce and custody papers
- ❑ Marriage license

Other
- ❑ Medications
- ❑ House and car keys
- ❑ Valuable jewelry
- ❑ Address book
- ❑ Pictures and sentimental items
- ❑ Change of clothes for you & your children

Employment Assistance

The Department of Rehabilitation Services (DORS), also known as Vocational Rehabilitation (VR), assists people with physical, emotional, intellectual, developmental, sensory and learning disabilities go to work and keep their jobs by providing services such as career assessment and counseling, assistive technology, job training, higher education and job placement. DORS/VR is supported by the Department of Education's Rehabilitation Services Administration (RSA).[cxxiv]

DORS/VR will assign a counselor who will talk with you about DORS/VR services and find out if you are eligible for these services. Many DORS/VR counselors are specially trained to work with specific groups like high school students or individuals who are deaf/hard-of-hearing, blind or have persistent mental illness. Go to https://rsa.ed.gov/about-your-state.cfm (under the contacts tab) to locate a state office. Most DORS/VR counselors can also provide referrals for other needs as well.

The **Ticket to Work program** through the Social Security Administration offers employment assistance for those who receive SSI and SSDI. Ticket to Work is a free and voluntary program that can help Social Security beneficiaries go to work, get a good job that may lead to a career, and become financially independent, all while they keep their Medicare or Medicaid.[cxxv] It often will provide resume assistance, mock interviews, and help overcome criminal background barriers, and in other ways. More information about the SSA sponsored program can be found at www.chooseworkttw.net/.

Resources by State

Gallaudet University's Clerk Center offers a list of commission offices by state. These commission offices offer advocacy, have referrals to various healthcare related agencies, have a list of interpreting agencies, and some employment assistance. It can be found by going to www.gallaudet.edu/clerc-center/info-to-go/national-resources-and-directories.html.

Additional Disability Resources

Disability.gov is a federal government website that has information on disability programs and services nationwide.[cxxvi] The types of assistance that one can connect to are benefits, community life, education, housing, healthcare, and employment, technology, and transportation. This is a good place to start if one is unfamiliar to community resources.

Case Management Needs Assessment

One part of the Deaf advocacy model is the provision of case management. The Commission on Case Manager Certification defines case management as a collaborative process that assesses, plans, implements, coordinates, monitors, and evaluates the options and services required to meet the client's health and human service needs. It is characterized by advocacy, communication, and resource management and promotes quality and cost-effective interventions and outcomes.[cxxvii]

Identifying an individual's needs is often the first step in providing assistance. The following is a generic case management needs assessment form that can be used when providing case management for d/Deaf, hard-of-hearing, late-deafened, and Deaf-blind individuals.

Case Management Needs Assessment
Check All that Apply

Client Name: Date:

Social Needs	
Protective Services	
Financial Assistance (living expenses)	
Home Aid Services	
Respite Care	
Shelter Services	
Foster Care	
Adoption	
Clothing	
Food	
Housing Issues	
Independent Living	
Recreational (Big Brother, Mentor, YMCA, etc.)	
Socialization	
Other:	
Educational Needs	
Psychological Testing	
Resource Classes	
Special Schools	
Home-Bound Instruction	
Residential Schools	
Alternative Programs	
General Educational Development (GED)	
Other:	

Mental Health Needs	
Inpatient Hospitalization	
Residential Treatment Services	
Psychological Testing	
Specialized Treatment (Substance Abuse, NA)	
Health Needs	
Health Education and Prevention	
Screening and Assessment	
Primary Care	
Acute Care	
Long-term Care	
Dental Care	
Medication Assistance	
Other:	
Vocational Needs	
Career Education	
Vocational Assessment	
Vocational Skills Training	
Work Experiences	
Job Finding, Placement & Retention Services	
Other:	
Additional Needs	
Alcohol and Drug Abuse Treatment	
Self-Help and Support Groups	
Advocacy	
Transportation	
Legal Services	
Volunteer Programs	
Other:	

Nuts and Bolts of Advocacy

The work of advocacy will often be a part of the church's work. It can be in a moment of educating someone, a full writing campaign to legislatures, and works in between. Not surprising, the church is known for doing social justice and will often include advocacy in this focus of ministry. This section orients readers about advocacy. The following is from the Registry of Interpreters for the Deaf and can be adopted for your personal use.[cxxviii]

What is advocacy?

The American Heritage Dictionary defines advocacy as "the act of pleading or arguing in favor of something, such as a cause, idea, or policy; active support." That's true, but it can be even simpler. Advocacy allows people and groups to share their opinion with policymakers. These policy makers are usually your elected officials and they vote on many important issues that affect you and people like you. But policymakers can't represent you and your views effectively if you don't communicate with them. Advocacy is a powerful tool to help promote the goals and interests of the Deaf community.

When to Advocate

You should advocate anytime there is a policy proposed that will affect you. But you don't have to wait for someone to propose a change to get involved. Be proactive! If you have an idea for a new law or policy, contact your elected officials. They have the ability to propose legislation that their constituents request. So, if you have an idea, share it – that idea might become a law.

Where to Advocate?

In general, advocacy can happen at all levels of government and in many different ways. Whether you decide to focus on local, state, or federal issues will depend on you and your interests. Some issues are more appropriately addressed at the state and local level. Still others are better addressed through federal legislation and/or regulation. For example, policies related to Vide Relay Service (VRS) are promulgated through the Federal Communications Commission (FCC), a federal agency. Conversely, many states have enacted legislation regulating interpreters practicing within their borders.

Why Advocate?

Many advocates start because they witness or experience what they perceive as an injustice. Perhaps you are a certified interpreter losing opportunities to uncertified interpreters because your state doesn't have a licensure requirement. Or perhaps you are having a hard time convincing organizations and businesses that you are a professional who should be compensated for your time and work. Each advocate has a different reason for becoming more involved, however, most get involved because they encountered a situation that made them say, "Something has to be done!" This situation defines your core issue or cause and will become the basis of your advocacy efforts.

How to Advocate

Everyone approaches advocacy differently, but some principles hold true no matter your approach. First and foremost, be honest. Your credibility as an advocate depends on whether policymakers can trust what you say.

Don't exaggerate facts or statistics and don't make up information when you don't know the answer to a question. Be respectful of the policymaker and his or her time. Stay informed so that you can provide as much information to support your opinion as possible. And finally, be persistent. Changing policy takes time and it's important that you remind policymakers about your issue. Something as simple as a short email can serve as an important tool to keep your issue fresh in a policymaker's mind.

Writing Tips

Sending a letter or an email is a great way to communicate your thoughts and feelings to policymakers because it allows you to think about your message, write it down, and then edit it until you feel comfortable with what you are sending. It is also a good alternative to calling on the phone if you are concerned you may get "stage fright" or trouble understanding what is being said.

Here are some general guidelines for writing letters and emails to your representative:

- ❏ Your letter or email should address a single topic, issue, or bill.
- ❏ If you are mailing your letter, typed, one-page letters are best.
- ❏ The best letters and emails are courteous, to the point, and include specific supporting examples.
- ❏ Always say why you are writing and who you are. (If you want a response, you must include your name and address, even when using email.)
- ❏ Provide detail.
- ❏ Be factual not emotional.

❏ Provide specific rather than general information about how the topic affects you and others.

❏ If a certain bill is involved, cite the correct title or number whenever possible.

❏ Close by requesting the action you want taken: a vote for or against a bill, or change in general policy.

❏ As a general rule, emails are usually shorter and more to the point.

❏ ALWAYS THANK HIM OR HER FOR TAKING THE TIME TO READ THE LETTER/EMAIL.

Personalized letters and emails can have a big impact on policymakers. Whenever possible, write your own email or letter, even if you borrow points from a form letter. The message can be simple and to the point.

Case Study - Supporting a Habilitative Day Program

Deaf advocacy can be seen as human service type work. In one Maryland community, a hearing church partnered with a Deaf organization that had a habilitative day program for d/Deaf consumers. A habilitative day programs are in many communities where clients/consumers receive habilitation services 3, 4, or 5 days a week. Habilitiative services are health care services that help one to keep, learn, or improve skills and functioning for daily living. This Deaf habilitative day program provided lunch for the d/Deaf consumers three days a week and the consumers were expected to provide their own lunch on the other two days. A church in the community connected with the organization with the habilitative day program and provided lunch on the other two days. This showed the faith community's hospitality to its community, helped the d/Deaf consumers to save money because most of the d/Deaf consumers were low-income individuals (e.g. receiving SSI or SSDI), and helped show the church the needs in their own community. This form of Deaf advocacy is also a form of compassionate ministry and provides mercy.

Case Study – Mark Koterwski

Mr. Mark Koterwski is a Deaf lay minister associated with the Heartland Ephaptha Ministry (HEM), a Lutheran Deaf ministry that is located at the Peace Lutheran Church – both of which are a part of the South Dakota Synod. Mr. Koterwski is the president serving HEM. HEM is affiliated with the Evangelical Lutheran Deaf Association (ELDA). Also, he has been doing Deaf advocacy for a number of years in South Dakota. As a part of his ministry, he provides consultation, teaches sign language classes, teaches human service related workshops, mentors interpreters, and occasionally works with undocumented residents.

Mr. Koterwski performs Deaf advocacy in both his regular employment and in his ministry with HEM. In his work as a Deaf advocate, Mr. Koterwski does some case management and often

Mark Koterwski

makes referrals to community resources. In fact, being knowledgeable of community resources is recommended to all advocates. When it comes to Deaf advocacy, he recommends the following to be more effective:

1. Be knowledgeable with the law as it pertains to Deaf people and disability.

2. Understand public benefits, such as Supplemental Security Income (SSI), Social Security Disability Insurance (SSDI), Medicare, Medical Assistance, and so on in order to assist others who are attempting to navigate the government system.
3. Empower the d/Deaf individual to speak for him/herself, only assisting with advice if asked for. An advocate does not want to take over for the person needing assistance.
4. If needing to advocate on the behalf of others, try to do so with diplomacy (e.g. not threatening to sue). Educating the entity of what is needed or what the reasonable accommodation need is will at times be helpful. Doing this by phone, email, or in person is preferable.
5. Writing a letter to the entity or organization is sometimes warranted; moreover, it shows it was done by writing.
6. If these fail or provide unsatisfactory results, filing a complaint with the Department of Justice (DOJ) or with the Equal Employment Opportunity Commission (EEOC) may be warranted.

Case Study – Hearing Church Support

Magothy United Methodist Church in Pasadena, MD often shares a facility with Magothy United Methodist Church of the Deaf, a chartered Deaf church in the Baltimore Washington Conference. Magothy Deaf church is not a Deaf ministry of the hearing church, which is why it falls under the category of Deaf advocacy. Magothy hearing church budgets annually interpreting costs for whenever there are shared events. At one point, early on in the Deaf church's history, the hearing church used to provide some financial support. Also, Magothy hearing church provides office space in its educational building for the Deaf church's ministerial leadership. In a sense, Deaf advocacy is the model that the Magothy hearing church is doing.

Along with Magothy hearing church's advocacy/support to the Magothy Deaf church, the two churches frequently support one another's churches by attending one another's events. One example is Magothy hearing church hosts a monthly pancake breakfast that some of the d/Deaf members attend. Another example is some of the church members of Magothy hearing church attend the Deaf church's soup fest, offered on the first Saturday of the month (offered a few months during the year). One ministry that the two churches do together is the food pantry ministry.

Case Study – Deaf Immigrants and Refugees

DeafCAN! (Deaf Community Action Center) in West Chester, Pennsylvania often works with d/Deaf undocumented individuals. Part of the services DeafCAN! offers are literacy classes and case management services. DeafCAN! collaborates with Christ the King Deaf Church, a Deaf Lutheran church served by Pastor Beth Lockard.[cxxix]

The United Methodist Church has the **Justice For Our Neighbor** (JFON) program through a United Methodist immigration agency, where it offers legal clinics in some states. To locate a JFON clinic, go to its website at www.njfon.org. At the Baltimore clinic, a Hispanic family with deaf members was provided legal services, helping family members to achieve citizenship. The clinic provided both spoken language interpreters and sign language interpreters throughout the process.

Case Study – National Black Deaf Advocates

The National Black Deaf Advocates (NBDA) is an organization that has been in existence since 1982. It came about when African American Deaf leaders were concerned that Deaf and hard-of-hearing African Americans were not represented adequately in leadership and policy decision-making, thus influencing the establishment of NBDA. It has many chapters throughout the United States. According to NBDA, it describes advocacy as a problem-solving procedure to protect personal and legal rights. NBDA suggests four types of advocacy, which are (1) self-advocacy (to advocate for oneself), (2) individual advocacy (to advocate for another), (3) system advocacy (to change the system), and (4) legal advocacy (to change the law). For more information about advocacy, the types of advocacy, its conference and event schedule, and other services it offers, go to www.nbda.org.

Questions for Reflection

1. What ways is your church already advocating in its community?
2. Are there any social workers or human service providers in your church or community that might be willing to help your church to consider a new form of Deaf ministry? If so, speak to them about Deaf advocacy.
3. Are there any Deaf ministries in your community that your church can collaborate with and/or support?
4. Love, mercy, and grace are trademarks of Christ's presence in the world. How might your church do more of this within the Deaf community?

5. How can your faith community be advocates with other Deaf churches or Deaf ministries where you live?
6. Psalm 106:3 reads, *How blessed are those who keep justice, Who practice righteousness at all times!* (NIV) How can your church be more active in social justice? What needs do you see in your community?

Conclusion

In conclusion, the Deaf advocacy model provides examples of how hearing churches can partner and collaborate with Deaf ministries and Deaf churches. The human services aspect of this model and the provision of case advocacy were also touched on, as well as highlighting common biopsychosocial needs and services for d/Deaf, hard-of-hearing, late-deafened, and Deaf-blind individuals and their families. Understanding what advocacy is and the various forms of it were also discussed.

Chapter 8 – Overview of the Deaf Missions Model

The Deaf ministry model, Deaf missions, often includes doing outreach mission efforts to marginalized individuals or groups in the community (e.g. bringing dinner to group homes or visits to a nursing home). Also, this may be a one time or an irregularly scheduled type of outreach mission or support, which includes planning and/or joining mission trips, either domestically or abroad (e.g. Jamaica).

International Deaf Missions Opportunity

The **International Christian Center for the Deaf** (ICCD) leads a few Deaf mission trips a year. ICCD is located in the state of Virginia. Countries ICCD do mission work in are Cuba, Bahamas, and Mexico. Often, their mission trips are focused on renovating Deaf schools. Their website is www.iccd.net/.

After the devastating earthquake in the country of Haiti on January 12, 2010, many churches and organizations around the world have given assistance to Haiti. One organization established the **Deaf Haiti Academy** in 2013, in which allows d/Deaf students to come to school, either as a day student or to stay in its dormitory. The school partners with churches and organizations and encourages short mission trips in visiting the school. More information about this Deaf mission opportunity can be read on their website at www.haitideafacademy.com/.

Through the **Touching Lives Worldwide, Inc**., this non-profit organization is involved with a Deaf school in the Dominican Republic. They invite missionaries to come to the school for short-term mission trips. More information can be found on its website at www.touchinglivesworldwide.org.

Silent Word Ministries International also offers international mission trips. Part of their requirements is to belong to a church, be able to work as a part of a team, and be able to support your own way. Their website is at Silent Word Ministries International http://international.silentwordministries.org.

DOOR International sends missionaries to help train and translate the Bible. Deaf and hearing missionaries receive in-depth training in order to be most effective at their mission site. Their website is www.doorinternational.com.

Some Deaf churches are involved in international Deaf mission trips. Joining a Deaf group that already has established relationships in other countries can be helpful when first getting into this type of ministry. Often, international Deaf mission trips involve work with a Deaf school or a Deaf class at a hearing school.

Denominations Doing Deaf Mission Work

Some of the mainline denominations have Deaf movements or caucuses. Some of them are involved in doing Deaf mission work. The following is a short list of denominations doing Deaf mission type work.

Denominations & Organizations Involved in Deaf Missions
Adventist Deaf Ministries International
www.adventistdeaf.org/
Deaf Baptist Fellowship
http://deafbaptistfellowship.com/
Episcopal Congress of the Deaf
www.ecdeaf.org/
LCMS Deaf Missions, Lutheran Church - Missouri Synod
www.lcmsdeaf.org
Silent Word Ministries International
http://international.silentwordministries.org/
Southern Baptist Congress of the Deaf
www.sbcdeaf.org/
United Methodist Congress of the Deaf
www.umcd.org
United Pentecostal Church-International
Deaf Evangelism
www.deafevangelismministry.com/
World Deaf Assemblies of God
www.wdag.org/

Domestic Deaf Missions Opportunity

Some groups are able to do mission work in the United States. In fact, having d/Deaf individuals join a hearing group is an alternative to doing Deaf mission work. Ensuring on-going communication by having an interpreter with the group is recommended.

The **North American Mission Board** (NAMB) is affiliated with many mission sites in the United States and Canada. Mission work includes disaster relief,

Appalachian regional ministry, Vacation Bible School (VBS), home renovations, and other types of missions. The NAMB website is www.namb.net/.

Deaf Schools List

Deaf Connections, a clearing house for d/Deaf related information maintains a list of Deaf schools in other countries. Perhaps there are no other mission teams doing work in one of the countries listed. Its website is www.deafconnect.com/deaf/school.html. Going for culture sharing (religion would be part of that), bringing materials, and so on might be a way to open the door for doing mission work in another country. While those traveling to another country may have their own agenda, it's important to follow the destination's lead of what they need and/or want.

Deaf Missions Considerations

Participating in Deaf missions overseas is a wonderful opportunity. Nan McCurdy and Miguel Mairena are missionaries through The United Methodist Global Ministries. In the following, they share some helpful considerations when preparing and visiting other countries to do mission work.[cxxx]

When you consider the cost of an international trip, it just doesn't make sense to have the primary focus on work, given that we can spend a fairly small amount of money and put local people to work. (I think the groups that just want to work should find a U.S. location for their trip.) When the trip also includes a major emphasis on learning and on relationship building, I believe a lot of good can come out of international mission experiences for the groups and for the people they work with in the country—if they go with an open heart.

1. Contact your hosts and get any materials or orientation they provide. Take seriously suggested advance reading. If you don't receive reading suggestions, search them out.
2. Listen to your hosts both before and during the trip and try to abide by their orientations.
3. If your hosts do not include at least one day of learning as described above – ask them if they could set up, or find someone to set up, the kinds of meetings described above, and let them know you are prepared for the extra costs of honorariums for speakers.
4. Find someone to facilitate a group dynamics workshop to get to know one another in advance of the trip.
5. Gifts and donations should go to churches and organizations and not to individuals. Individual gift-giving erodes community cohesiveness.
6. If you plan to do an international trip every few years, attempt to find an organization or church to partner with. In this way, over time, people in both communities have a chance to get to know one another, understand the other's joys and suffering, and grow in love and respect.
7. Gather for shared prayer and study in the time prior to your departure and ask your church to hold you in prayer during your trip.
8. Expect to be changed by the experience.

Mission Trip Planning Guide

The NAMB offers a brief pre-planning guide to mission work. The following is helpful to planning mission work.[cxxxi]

1. **Age** The recommended age for all volunteers on a mission trip to another location is 15 or older. Exceptions might include children of sponsors, and unusually mature young people under the age of 15 who do not occupy leadership roles. Check with the country you are visiting for any special requirements.

2. **Discover** - What are your skills? Where do you feel God is leading you to go? What is your interest? What is the size of your volunteer missions group? Read through the project requests, which are attached, and select one or more that fit what you feel God is calling you to do.

3. **Visit** - Successful mission trips include a pre-site visit to review the site, to secure the housing arrangements, to discuss with the contact person the project, and to pray. This is an excellent time to do a prayer walk or a prayer drive.

4. **Goals** - what would you like to see accomplished through and on this mission trip. Write it down and share it with your prayer partners. Ask yourself this question, "What do we feel God wants to accomplish through us on this mission trip?" Be flexible if they need to change so the Spirit can do its work.

5. **Ratio** of sponsors to youth should be not less than 1 to 8.

6. **Daily conduct** - Orientation and pre-trip planning should help all volunteers understand conduct requirements. Daily conduct should include the avoidance of the use of tobacco products, drugs, alcoholic drinks, vulgar and lewd language, immodest dress, and reckless behavior, etc. All volunteers should conduct themselves

daily so as to present a positive Christian witness to everyone around, including other volunteers.

7. **Local Culture** - The project area may be culturally diverse and distinct from that of the volunteers. Volunteers must be as sensitive to and appreciative of that culture as if they were in a foreign country. This means that all volunteers need to listen and learn, be open to new ideas, and be capable of making adjustments to the local culture.

8. **Servanthood** - The local churches, associations and missions organization are the primary ministers to their area. Volunteers must cooperate with and follow local leadership. Additionally, volunteers will want to comply and cooperate within their team.

9. **Finances** - Unless otherwise specified all volunteer groups will be responsible for: travel cost, food and lodging, supplies and equipment, materials for construction projects, and group insurance while in transit and while on site. (Information about travel and accident insurance is available from the ARM national office.)

10. **Organization** - Each volunteer group will want to organize in an effective and detailed manner. The following type leaders may be needed: Project director – usually the pastor, other staff minister or an experienced mature lay person. Coordinators – for large projects such as; VBS, surveys, health clinics, sports clinics, construction projects, and overall financial coordinator. Drivers – only adults with current license, adequate insurance and good driving record. Sponsors – for youth, group leaders, teachers, and persons with any needed specialized skill or certification.

11. **Planning** -All participants need to work together to develop schedules and activities that are mutually acceptable and workable. A pre-project site visit is recommended, if at all possible. Then frequent contact by phone, letter or e-mail with the project sponsor is necessary to assure the project will accomplish the desired results. Pre-project planning will help volunteers know how to adjust their plans and schedules to best meet the local ministry situation. This will also assure the volunteers that good planning is being done in advance of their arrival. (Some sponsor groups require pre-project orientation for volunteer group leaders.) The use of mission site videos in pre-project planning can enhance volunteers' understanding and excitement for the project.

12. **Involving Your church** - Once your church has selected and adopted a project, several actions should be taken.

    a. Initial contact from the local project leadership should be established. The church or association that made the request should provide you with additional project information and confirm your visit dates and project details. This should include name, address and phone numbers of your contact person.

    b. Your church and mission team should begin praying for the project. Team members will want to gather frequently for Bible study and prayer in preparation for the mission experience. The whole church will want to begin praying for the mission team, the project sponsor, and for the physical and spiritual project goals. All team members should be trained in personal witnessing.

    c.   You will want to make a pre-project visit to the project location. This visit should be pre-arranged with the project sponsor and contact person. Expenses for this visit should be included as part of the overall mission trip budget. Church has responsibility for financial support including adequate insurance, dependable transportation, and needed materials. Details about the project including all materials and local housing arrangements should be discussed. You may find the check list below a helpful pre-project planning guide.

13. **Celebrate** - Work with your pastor and plan a time to share with your church about your mission trip.

Case Study – Carol Stevens

Carol Stevens has been doing Deaf mission work in The United Methodist Church for twenty years, both local missions and global missions. Ms. Stevens has traveled to Jamaica, Kenya, and Zimbabwe. She emphasizes the importance of doing an exploration/scouting trip prior to bringing a whole team. Building meaningful relationships, trust and respect for the people and their desires and needs and culture is essential for a God-filled mission experience.

In 1997, the scouting trip to Kenya identified many needs among them the needs at the Njia Primary School. There were 5 d/Deaf students who walked many miles each day to attended school, yet did not have a teacher who signed. A year later, Ms. Stevens brought a team to Kenya where the team met with Njeru Mucheri, a very wise and visionary special education administrator who was very concerned about the absence of communication for the d/Deaf students. Carol asked if there were any Deaf people who knew sign language who could come to the school and bring language to the students and teacher. Because Deaf people are so marginalized in that area the thought of a Deaf person had never crossed his mind. He knew of a Deaf woman by the name of Beatrice who was picking tea in the fields. She was invited to meet the d/Deaf students at Njia School. By the time the Deaf mission team left to return to the United States, Beatrice was hired as a teacher's assistant and began teaching the d/Deaf children and staff sign language. In addition to being a teacher she was an excellent role model for the Deaf students and for the teachers. As a part of the on-going financial support, the Deaf church Ms. Stevens belonged to provided $700 a year (a year's salary in Kenyan currency) to the teacher's-aid position. Later Beatrice was hired by the school and the government and is still employed there. Beatrice brought language to the school which now has 150 Deaf students and a staff of signing teachers.

Ms. Stevens also shared that there is always some hesitancy in sending funds overseas. With so many needs, it is easy for the funds to be "reallocated". Be a wise steward and do all you can to assure that the money is being used for the needs that the people that are at the mission site identify as most important. Ask for status updates with photos to be sent so that there is more accountability, and pray. As the wife of the local bishop of the Methodist Church of Kenya, Judy Kaburu shared with Ms. Stevens, once the money is given it is really a matter of trust because she (Ms. Stevens) is thousands of miles away

There was a Deaf Kenyan woman by the name of Mukami Lawi (her Christian name is Margret) that Carol's mission team met. Rev. Peggy Johnson who was on the scouting team met with her and discerned that Mukami had a heart for the Lord, which included a call to ministry. She was given assistance by having Mukami flown to the U.S. to attend Preacher's License School (United Methodist-related training) and could get other Deaf Ministry training. This helps her to be recognized as a valued Deaf person to become a minister in her country with the Deaf. Because Mukami is Deaf she would not traditionally be given opportunities for theological training. Later she was accepted and received the university training needed to become the first Deaf person ordained in the Methodist Church of Kenya where she serve Deaf people throughout Kenya. Mukai brought to the US her enthusiasm, tenacity and strong Christian commitment. Much was learned from her. This is a reciprocal relationship and highlights how the Kenyan Deaf person is a gift to us. Mukami is very involved in doing Deaf ministry in parts of Kenya and has serviced as the president of the organization of international Methodist Deaf Ministries

In 1999, Ms. Stevens and her team joined hearing United Methodist leadership from her annual conference on a trip to Zimbabwe. Ms. Stevens and her small team did exploratory work and followed up with leads they had for doing Deaf mission. This led to Ms. Stevens and her team to meet two people who were doing work with Deaf people who later became partners in developing Deaf ministry. This again emphasized to Ms. Stevens the importance of building relationships with the people in the country they visited and to inquire to what their needs are (not making assumptions or bring their own agenda). In 2000, a team of 20 Deaf and hearing people traveled to Zimbabwe as a Deaf mission's team. Besides bringing supplies, American d/Deaf leaders were model for those in Zimbabwe (emphasizing d/Deaf individuals are capable of leadership), and they helped bring attention to, make known the needs of, and promote Deaf awareness to hearing denominational leadership in Zimbabwe. The interpreters on the team were a novelty because at that time there were no interpreters in Zimbabwe. Several bright young people who were orphans became fascinated with signing and joined with the Deaf people in the area and became interpreters. They all worked together to establish 2 thriving Deaf Ministries

Ms. Stevens connects to resources here that often partners with her Deaf missions abroad. Ms. Stevens has gone on a number of other trips to Kenya and Zimbabwe. Each time she goes she always brings along new team members. The joy of mission trips is not only in the ways that God's uses all of the people involved to minister to each other, but also in the life-transformational changes that occur in the hearts of the people on the team.

Carol Stevens

Questions for Reflection

1. What mission needs can be found in your own community? In your own state?
2. Might there be individuals or a group of church members willing to join others in Deaf mission work? If so, pray about joining one.
3. The Apostle Paul's ministry often included mission work when he traveled. What new opportunities can your church be involved in?
4. Sharing supplies, materials, and education are ways to do mission work. In what ways can these be disseminated in communities that are in need?

5. 1 Peter 4 reads, *⁸Above all, love each other deeply, because love covers over a multitude of sins. ⁹Offer hospitality to one another without grumbling. ¹⁰Each of you should use whatever gift you have received to serve others, as faithful stewards of God's grace in its various forms.* (NIV) What gifts does your faith community have for doing mission work?

Conclusion

In conclusion, this chapter discusses the Deaf missions model, which included suggestions for planning your own mission project. Also discussed were potential international missions projects and domestic missions projects, as well as ways to connect with denominations that often do Deaf mission work. While international mission trips is one aspect of Deaf missions, the mission contributions and support, along with the relationships with d/Deaf, hard-of-hearing, late-deafened, and Deaf-blind individuals and communities is what distinguishes this ministry model from other Deaf ministry models.

Chapter 9 – Overview of a Disability Ministry

This chapter provides a general overview of a disability ministry, which can include hearing loss. Not surprisingly, there is some overlap between a Deaf ministry and a disability ministry in terms of accessibility, advocacy, empowerment, and inclusion. Considerations for possible barriers, accommodations, and general advice for inclusion are discussed. Also included are ministry considerations.

Often, what distinguishes a disability ministry from the other Deaf ministry models is the stressing of disability rights, promoting disability awareness, the emphasis of disability access, and the work of disability advocacy. Also, the value of Deaf culture and the desire to grow a ministry specifically made up of d/Deaf, hard-of-hearing, late-deafened, and Deaf-blind individuals are not typically at the forefront of a disability ministry.

Remember, individuals with disabilities are children of God and are a needed part of the church. Jesus' friendship and advocacy for those with disabilities are in all the gospels. In fact, in Luke 14, Jesus shares a parable of a king who invited such people.

> [21] *"The servant came back and reported this to his master. Then the owner of the house became angry and ordered his servant, 'Go out quickly into the streets and alleys of the town and bring in the poor, the crippled, the blind and the lame.'"*

Inviting everyone, including people with disabilities, into our faith communities is underscored in this verse.

Types of Disabilities

According to Johns Hopkins University, there are a number of disabilities, which are not limited to[cxxxii]

- ❑ Blindness or Low Vision
- ❑ Brain Injuries (e.g. Difficulty with organizing thoughts and/or processing information, with social interactions and possibly with short-term memory)
- ❑ Deaf, Hard-of-Hearing, and Late-Deafened
- ❑ Learning Disabilities (e.g. Difficulty with oral and/or written expression, with reading comprehension, with time management, with problem solving, and interpreting social cues)
- ❑ Medical Disabilities (e.g. Cancer, Epilepsy, Lupus, substance abuse, and diabetes)
- ❑ Physical Disabilities (e.g. Resulting from congenital conditions, accidents or diseases)
- ❑ Psychiatric Disabilities (e.g. Ranges from behavioral and/or psychological problems that can include anxiety, mood swings, and psychosis)

❑ Speech and Language Disabilities (e.g. May result from hearing loss, cerebral palsy, or physical conditions resulting in articulation)

❑ Invisible Disabilities (e.g. Asthma, chronic pain, mental illness, allergies, chemical sensitivity, and arthritis)

Barriers

There can be a number of reasons why individuals who are d/Deaf, hard-of-hearing, late-deafened, Deaf-blind, or who have a disability do not attend church, some due to barriers. [cxxxiii] They can include:

❑ Architectural barriers – Are your church doorways wide enough for wheelchairs? Can individuals navigate the worship space, classrooms, and restrooms in your church? What does the building communicate about the commitment and values the congregation holds towards individuals with disabilities (e.g. not having ramps)?

❑ Attitudinal barriers – This is usually inadvertent through events and activities that were planned without consideration for individuals with disabilities in mind. Sometimes individuals encounter words and actions (sometimes unintentionally) that are demeaning, paternalistic, or condescending. As well-meaning as comments may be, they can neglect to affirm their gifts and contributions.

❑ Communication barriers – This type of barrier can include issues regarding sight, sound, language, and listening (e.g. not offering large print bulletins or not having listening devices).

❑ Programmatic barriers –Some churches do a wonderful job for inviting participation in church programs, but sometimes no consideration is given for individuals who are d/Deaf, hard-of-hearing, late-deafened, Deaf-blind, or who have a disability, as some may need assistance in order to participate (e.g. transportation needs).[cxxxiv]

While these may be church-related reasons for why individuals with disabilities do not attend church, there can be personal reasons why individuals and families do not attend. A few personal reasons can be:[cxxxv]

❑ Limited transportation
❑ Past experience (of exclusion or inhospitable attitudes)
❑ Not being invited
❑ Service provider (may feel it is not his/her job to attend to the spiritual needs of the individual).

Welcoming

All people need to feel welcomed and the congregation (not just the ushers) is responsible in ensuring individuals and families experience this. Often, we expect a welcoming attitude from leadership or pastors, but hospitality is a congregational responsibility. Hospitality can be seen in ways such as saying hello, remembering a name, or asking how someone's week was, inviting someone to lunch, recognizing the contributions of individuals, and getting to know someone on a personal level.

Considerations for welcoming people with disabilities, including hearing loss, do not happen only in the sanctuary. The following areas within the church are worth examining.

- ❑ Awareness (are there barriers of exclusion)
- ❑ Accommodations (that include invitations)
- ❑ Welcoming church members
- ❑ Local outreach (partnering with local agencies), which has a plan to do so
- ❑ Leadership (recruiting lay people with disabilities)[cxxxvi]

The following survey provides further consideration for welcoming in the different areas and life of the church

---

Indicators of Welcome

Perspectives

Whose perspectives were sought as a part of the reflection process?
- ☐ Clergy
- ☐ Person(s) with disabilities
- ☐ Community members
- ☐ Children/youth program leaders
- ☐ Adult program leaders
- ☐ Support providers
- ☐ Other _____

Presence and Participation

What steps have been taken to identify individuals with disabilities?

What steps have been taken to identify individuals with disabilities beyond the church?

In what ways are individuals with disabilities and their families participating in the following ways in the church?

	Actively	Some-times	Never	Unsure
Worship	☐	☐	☐	☐
Fellowship	☐	☐	☐	☐

	Actively	Some-times	Never	Unsure
Religious education (children and adult)	☐	☐	☐	☐
Bible Study	☐	☐	☐	☐
Summer programs	☐	☐	☐	☐
Greeters, ushers & other worship assistants	☐	☐	☐	☐
Choir or worship team	☐	☐	☐	☐
Church committee	☐	☐	☐	☐
Outreach ministries	☐	☐	☐	☐
Social activities	☐	☐	☐	☐
Other _____	☐	☐	☐	☐

What barriers seem to be hindering their involvement in these areas?

Architectural and Physical Accessibility
Can the following areas of the building and grounds be navigated easily by people using wheelchairs, walkers, and scooters, as well as other adaptive equipment?

<u>At present, how accessible are we?</u>

	Completely	Some-what	Not at all	Uncer-tain	Comments
Sanctuaries & other worship space	☐	☐	☐	☐	_____
Classrooms & meeting rooms	☐	☐	☐	☐	_____
Fellowship Hall	☐	☐	☐	☐	_____
Nursery	☐	☐	☐	☐	_____
Restrooms	☐	☐	☐	☐	_____
Playgrounds & recreation areas	☐	☐	☐	☐	_____
Gymnasium	☐	☐	☐	☐	_____
Parking lots & sidewalks	☐	☐	☐	☐	_____

	Completely	Some-what	Not at all	Uncer-tain	Comments
Doorways & hallways	☐	☐	☐	☐	_____
Church offices	☐	☐	☐	☐	_____
Kitchen & eating areas	☐	☐	☐	☐	_____
School building & childcare center	☐	☐	☐	☐	_____
Other_____	☐	☐	☐	☐	_____

Which three architectural barriers are the most pressing?
1.
2.
3.

To what extent does each statement below describes our church?

	Absolutely	Some-what	Not at all	Uncer-tain
Worship services				
Greeters, ushers, & other worship assistants know how to extend welcome and offer assistance to people with disabilities.	☐	☐	☐	☐
People with disabilities are supported to sit with friends, family, or whomever they choose.	☐	☐	☐	☐
Faith partners are available to sit with, befriend, and support people with disabilities, if desired.	☐	☐	☐	☐
Worship experiences are designed to engage multiple senses and allow for participation in various ways.	☐	☐	☐	☐

	Absolutely	Some-what	Not at all	Uncer-tain
Congregational leaders are willing to explore alternate ways for participating in worship and the sacraments, as necessary.	☐	☐	☐	☐
People with disabilities are contributing to worship services in varied ways, including as greeters or choir members.	☐	☐	☐	☐
The congregation expresses comfort with people who worship in different ways (e.g. making noises, rocking, flapping their hands).	☐	☐	☐	☐
The congregation is periodically asked about chemical sensitivities, food allergies, or other issues.	☐	☐	☐	☐

Religious Education	Absolutely	Some-what	Not at all	Uncer-tain
Children with disabilities participate in the same activities and classes as their peers without disabilities.	☐	☐	☐	☐
Activities are adapted and supports are provided so that children with disabilities can participate in activities to the greatest extent possible.	☐	☐	☐	☐
Religious curricula appeals to children who learn, participate, and contribute in a variety of ways.	☐	☐	☐	☐

	Absolutely	Some-what	Not at all	Uncer-tain
Basic information, training, and support are provided to lay volunteers who work with children with disabilities.	☐	☐	☐	☐
Teachers and helpers are ready to include children with disabilities, in their classes from the moment families first arrive.	☐	☐	☐	☐
Topics related to hospitality, inclusion, disabilities, and community periodically are woven into education curricula.	☐	☐	☐	☐
Youth with disabilities participate in preparation classes for membership, confirmation, bar/bat mitzvah, and other rites of passage.	☐	☐	☐	☐
Adults with disabilities are included in religious education programs.	☐	☐	☐	☐
Schools and daycare programs sponsored by our congregation include children with disabilities.	☐	☐	☐	☐
Other _____	☐	☐	☐	☐
People with disabilities contributes on planning teams and serve in leadership positions.	☐	☐	☐	☐

	Absolutely	Some-what	Not at all	Uncer-tain
Efforts are made to discern the gifts of people with disabilities and connect them with opportunities to share their gifts.	☐	☐	☐	☐
People with disabilities are serving in varied capacities within the congregation.	☐	☐	☐	☐
People with disabilities are serving in varied capacities beyond the congregation.	☐	☐	☐	☐
Other _____	☐	☐	☐	☐

Outreach	Absolutely	Some-what	Not at all	Uncer-tain
Intentional efforts are made to invite people with disabilities and their families to participate in congregational life.	☐	☐	☐	☐
Accessibility symbols and images of people with disabilities are included in our materials and advertising.	☐	☐	☐	☐
Transportation to congregational activities is provided or arranged for individuals who cannot drive.	☐	☐	☐	☐

	Absolutely	Some-what	Not at all	Uncer-tain
Visitation programs are extended to people with disabilities and their families, as well as those who are homebound.	☐	☐	☐	☐
We actively seek out ways to address unmet needs of people with disabilities living in our community.	☐	☐	☐	☐
Members are informed of opportunities to support people with disabilities within and outside the congregation.	☐	☐	☐	☐
Other _____	☐	☐	☐	☐

General Awareness	Absolutely	Some-what	Not at all	Uncer-tain
Our policies and practices clearly communicate our desire to worship and serve alongside people with disabilities.	☐	☐	☐	☐
Our vision to be inclusive is frequently shared with members and broadcast throughout the community.	☐	☐	☐	☐
Reflection on our accessibility and hospitality is conducted at least annually.	☐	☐	☐	☐

	Absolutely	Some-what	Not at all	Uncer-tain
Basic disability awareness is communicated through sermons, bulletin inserts, newsletters, religious education curricula, and other avenues.	□	□	□	□
Accessibility and support needs are considered when congregational events are planned.	□	□	□	□
Our resource library includes books and materials about disabilities, as well as resources for family members.	□	□	□	□
Our clergy and ministry leader's are familiar with disability issues related to specific programs, roles, and responsibilities.	□	□	□	□
Other _____	□	□	□	□

Families	Absolutely	Some-what	Not at all	Uncer-tain
Families feel welcomed and included in the congregation.	□	□	□	□
Families contribute to discussions on congregational accessibility.	□	□	□	□
If respite care is available, families are aware of it.	□	□	□	□
Support groups are available to interested parents, siblings, and others within our congregation.	□	□	□	□

	Absolutely	Some-what	Not at all	Uncer-tain
Financial support is available to people with disabilities and their families, as it is to all members of the congregation.	☐	☐	☐	☐
People with disabilities and their families know who to contact to ask for support and assistance.	☐	☐	☐	☐
Clergy and care ministers feel equipped to provide spiritual care and support to people with disabilities and their families.	☐	☐	☐	☐
Other _____	☐	☐	☐	☐

Partnerships with Community Groups	Absolutely	Some-what	Not at all	Uncer-tain
We have developed relationships with agencies and organizations serving people with disabilities in our community.	☐	☐	☐	☐
We have invited people with disabilities and advocacy groups to provide us with feedback about our materials, programs, and activities.	☐	☐	☐	☐
Staff from service and support organizations are helping us to improve our capacity to welcome and support people with disabilities.	☐	☐	☐	☐

	Absolutely	Some-what	Not at all	Uncer-tain
We know where to turn when we need more information about specific disability-related issues.	□	□	□	□
We advocate for laws, policies, and resources that improve the quality of life for people with disabilities and their families.	□	□	□	□
Other _____	□	□	□	□

Other Indicators	Absolutely	Some-what	Not at all	Uncer-tain
We have developed a written plan describing how we will improve our accessibility and welcome.	□	□	□	□
Intentional efforts are made to support people with and without disabilities to develop meaningful social relationships.	□	□	□	□
A key person or group in our congregation is committed to making sure that the needs of people with disabilities are being addressed.	□	□	□	□
People with disabilities and/or their family members are involved in visioning and planning for the future of the congregation.	□	□	□	□

	Absolutely	Some-what	Not at all	Uncer-tain
We have a process for identifying the emotional, spiritual, practical, and other support needs of congregational members.	☐	☐	☐	☐
Other _____	☐	☐	☐	☐

Plan of Action

List up to five goals for improving our congregation's welcome and accessibility. What specific steps will we need to take to realize those goals? When will we aim to accomplish each goal? Who will be responsible to ensuring that each goal is followed through to completion?

Goals	Next Steps	Completion Date	Person Responsible
1.			
2.			
3.			
4.			

Comments

Permission given. Carter, E.W. (2007). Including People with Disabilities in Faith Communities: A Guide for Service Providers,Families, and Congregations. Paul H. Brooks Publishing Co, Inc.

Respectful Language

The Indiana Governor's Council for People with Disabilities challenges us to think carefully about how we use words:[cxxxvii]

"Be sensitive when choosing words. The reality is that people with disabilities succeed not 'in spite of' their disabilities but 'in spite of' an inaccessible and discriminatory society. They do not 'overcome' their disabilities so much as 'overcome' prejudice. You can help by using nonjudgmental terms and phrases that portray an image of dignity and respect."

ACCEPTABLE	NOT ACCEPTABLE
cerebral palsy/paraplegia/physical disability	crippled, spastic
cognitive or intellectual impairment	retarded, mongoloid
communication disorder/unable to speak, deaf	dumb/deaf-mute, hearing-impaired
disability	handicap
psychiatric disability	insane, crazy, deranged
uses a wheelchair	wheelchair bound/confined to a wheelchair
has or had a disability	stricken, victim, or suffering from
accessible parking/seating/restrooms	handicapped parking/seating/restrooms

Church Training

Churches that are unfamiliar with deafness and other disabilities can be at a loss of how to provide hospitality or assistance to individuals and their families. Most denominations have specific groups, boards, and/or agencies that provide education and resources to local churches. For further training and preparation for working with this population, the **Christian Institute on Disability (CID)** through the Joni & Friends International Disability Center provides online training, either as a class or by their certification program.[cxxxviii] Classes are 16-weeks long. Joni & Friends is on the forefront of disability ministry and the church and is should be remembered when discussing disability ministries. The CID website is at www.joniandfriends.org/christian-institute-on-disability/.

The **Western Theological Seminary** also offers a certification program (Graduate Certificate in Disability and Ministry). More information on this specialty certification can be found at www.westernsem.edu/academics/degrees/gcdm.

The **Special Friends Ministry**, affiliated with First Baptist Orlando, believe that the church should be a place of welcome for ALL people, including persons with disabilities. Simply, because everyone is made in God's image. It offers a Youtube channel that includes a plethora of helpful strategies for beginning and maintaining a disability ministry. The Youtube channel is www.youtube.com/user/specialfriendsfbo/featured. Training videos featured on the Youtube channel are (1) managing behaviors, (2) meltdown 911, (3) everyday mission for special needs parents, (4) serving in a special needs ministry, (5) disability theology, and many more.

Locating State and Local Resources

Whether planning to begin an accessibility ministry or you are blessed to have a new family join the church, there may be times where churches will need to provide resources or referrals to agencies in the community or surrounding areas. **The Aging and Disability Resource**

Center has several resource centers in many states. In case there is not a center, the national website has alternative resources through state and local organizations. The website can be reached by going to www.adrc-tae.acl.gov.

In addition, Gallaudet University offers a national website for d/Deaf students with disabilities network. This website is http://deafwdisabilities.grou.ps/home. It also includes information for thirteen types of disabilities.

Disability.gov is a federal government website that has information on disability programs and services nationwide. The types of assistance that one can connect to are benefits, community life, education, housing, healthcare, and employment, technology, and transportation.[cxxxix] This is a good place to start if one is unfamiliar to community resources.

Family Caregivers Advice

Caregivers of individuals with disabilities will need assistance themselves, as often caregiving can be challenging. The Center for Disease Control and Prevention provides suggestions for family caregivers that the church, sometimes an extended family to the family, should be aware of.

Be Informed – a number things to be aware of are[cxl]

❑ Gather information about the family member's condition, and discuss issues with others involved in the care of the family member. Being informed will help one to make more knowledgeable health decisions and improve understanding about any challenges the family might face.

❏ Notice how others care for the person with disability. Be aware of signs of mental or physical abuse.

Get Support – How to get support includes the following.

❏ Family members and friends can provide support in a variety of ways and oftentimes want to help. Determine if there are big or small things they can do to assist you and your family.

❏ Join a local or online support group. A support group can give one the chance to share information and connect with people who are going through similar experiences. A support group may help combat the isolation and fear one may experience as a caregiver.

❏ Don't limit your involvement to support groups and associations that focus on a particular need or disability. There are also local and national groups that provide services, recreation, and information for people with disabilities.

❏ Friends, family, health care providers, support groups, community services, and counselors are just a few of the people available to help a caregiver and his/her family.

Be An Advocate – You can be an advocate. The following is suggested by the Center for Disease Control and Prevention.[cxli]

❏ Be an advocate for family members with a disability. Caregivers who are effective advocates may be more successful at getting better service. (The disability coordinator or a disability ministry committee within the church can also be advocates.)

☐ Ask questions. For example, if the family member with a disability uses a wheelchair and the caregiver wants to plan a beach vacation, find out if the beaches are accessible via a car, ramp, portable walkway mat, or other equipment. (The disability coordinator can ask these questions to better accommodate the person with a disability.)

☐ Inform other caregivers of any special conditions or circumstances. For example, if a family member with a disability has a latex allergy, remind others of the interaction. (For example, a Sunday school teacher may need to know these regarding class activities.)

☐ Document the medical history of the family member with a disability, and keep this information current. (This may be helpful for the disability coordinator to know.)

☐ Make sure an employer understands the circumstances and limitations. Discuss any ability to travel or to work weekends or evenings. Arrange for flexible scheduling when needed. (The church can be supportive and empathetic if there is employment stress.)

☐ Become familiar with the Americans with Disabilities Act, the Family Medical Leave Act, and other state and national provisions. Know how and when to apply them to your situation. (This can be done when educating the congregation on disability awareness events at the church.)

Be Empowering – Empowering others is important. This includes:[cxlii]

❑ Focus on what the family and the family member with a disability *can* do.
❑ Find appropriate milestones and celebrate them.
❑ If someone asks questions about the family member with a disability, let him or her answer when possible. Doing so helps empower him or her, but engages him or her with others.
❑ When appropriate, encourage the person with a disability to be as independent and self-assured as possible. Always keep health and safety issues in mind.

Take Care of Yourself – Caring for one's self is crucial. The following are helpful reminders for how to do it.[cxliii]

❑ Take care of yourself. Caring for a family member with a disability can wear out even the strongest caregiver. Stay healthy for yourself and those you care for.
❑ Work hard to maintain your personal interests, hobbies, and friendships. Don't let caregiving consume your entire life. This is not healthy for you or those you care for. Balance is key.
❑ Allow yourself not to be the perfect caregiver. Set reasonable expectations to lower stress and make you a more effective caregiver.
❑ Delegate some caregiving tasks to other reliable people.
❑ Take a break. Short breaks, like an evening walk or relaxing bath, are essential. Long breaks are nurturing. Arrange a retreat with friends or get away with a significant other when appropriate.

❑ Don't ignore signs of illness. If you get sick, see a health care provider. Pay attention to your mental and emotional health as well. Remember, taking good care of yourself can help the person you care for as well. Exercising and eating healthy also are important.

Ways to Keep Balance in the Family – How to keep balance in the family are suggested here.[cxliv]

❑ Family members with a severe disability may require extra care and attention. Take time for all family members, taking into account the needs of each individual. For example, it's important for parents of a child with a disability to also spend time with each other and with any other children they might have.
❑ Consider respite care. "Respite" refers to short-term, temporary care provided to people with disabilities so that their families can take a break from the daily routine of caregiving.

Respite Care

One way churches can assist families is to offer respite care. Respite care provides temporary or short-term care to family members caring for a member with an illness or disability, helping to improve physical and emotional health for the caregiver.[cxlv] Respite care also prevents or delays more costly out-of-pockets, reduces the risk of abuse or neglect, and helps keep family members safe and stable.[cxlvi]

Church respite programs can also work with other community-based resources. The types of respite services are emergency respite, in-home respite, sitter-companion services, a specialized facility, and a therapeutic adult day care.[cxlvii] **The ARCH National Respite Network** has a respite locator on its website at http://archrespite.org/respitelocator. This same organization provides information for how to obtain respite training, either generalized or for specialized populations.

The way the church can provide respite care within the home can be in the form of housecleaning, grocery shopping, providing general maintenance, preparing a meal, offer a break to the caregiver by providing companionship to the person with a disability, do yard work, and provide assistance to doctor's appointment.[cxlviii]

There are a number of ways of providing respite. The following are creative <u>faith-based models</u> for providing respite.

1. Financial Support – a church may be unable to have their own respite care program, but may instead help fund another existing respite program in the community.

2. Respite Site - allow others to use their facility as a place to provide respite, like in a child care area during the afternoon or evening.

3. Support Group Respite - sponsor a support group. During the meetings, there may need to be child care or elder care provided as well.

4. Respite Vouchers - no direct services are provided, but vouchers may be provided to the family to help cover caregiver's cost of hiring a provider.

5. Adopt-a-Family Program - a congregation provides care for a family needing respite.

6. Family Caregiver Cooperatives - two or more families needing respite trade off care for each other's child, children, adult, or aging family member who is the care recipient.

7. Trained Respite Providers - a faith community can create a provider registry by training church members to become direct respite service providers, either for pay or as volunteers.[cxlix]

Some Common Causes of Disabilities

Having more than one disability means the individual has multiple disabilities. Often it is not known what causes a disability or multiple disabilities. With some children, however, the cause can be determined. Some causes can include:

- ❏ Chromosomal abnormalities
- ❏ Premature birth
- ❏ Difficulties after birth
- ❏ Poor development of the brain or spinal cord
- ❏ Infections
- ❏ Genetic disorders
- ❏ Injuries from accidents[cl]

Advice for Sunday School Teachers

Helpful suggestions from the Center for Parent Information and Resources for teachers can be applicable for volunteers in church settings working with a child with a disability or multiple disabilities. Modifications or accommodations are most often made in the following areas:[cli]

Scheduling. For example,

- ❏ giving the child extra time to complete assignments or tests
- ❏ breaking up testing over several days

Setting. For example,

- ❑ working in a small group
- ❑ working one-on-one with the teacher

Materials. For example,

- ❑ providing audiotaped or CD lectures or books
- ❑ giving copies of teacher's lecture notes
- ❑ using large print books, Braille, or books on CD (digital text)

Instruction. For example,

- ❑ reducing the difficulty of assignments
- ❑ reducing the reading level
- ❑ using a student/peer tutor

Student Response. For example,

- ❑ allowing answers to be given orally or dictated
- ❑ using a word processor for written work
- ❑ using sign language, a communication device Braille, or native language if it is not English

Also, **supplementary aids and services** that the Center for Parent Information and Resources suggest are[clii]

- ❑ adapted equipment—such as a special seat or a cut-out cup for drinking
- ❑ assistive technology—such as a word processor, special software, or a communication system
- ❑ training for staff, student, and/or parents
- ❑ peer tutors

- a one-on-one aide
- adapted materials—such as books on tape, large print, or highlighted notes; and
- collaboration and consultation among staff, parents, and/or other professionals

Disability Friendly Sunday School Programs

The following tips are provided for Sunday school programs that may have children with a disability or multiple disabilities. It is always a good practice to ask the parent or guardian what is most effective for his or her child so he or she can get the most out of the class.[cliii]

Physical Disabilities

- If children are physically unable to create a craft, or participate in an activity, allow them to borrow your hands. But don't forget to use their imagination. Make them active participants by encouraging them to direct your actions. Ask questions such as, "Should we make a bird or an elephant? Big ears or little ears? A tail or no tail? What color is the bird?"
- Provide larger toys, crayons, utensils or dolls for children who have difficulty grasping items.
- Some children will have an easier time painting or coloring if the paper is taped to the table surface. Others may be more successful (and have more fun) at toe painting than finger painting.
- When singing, tap the rhythm lightly on child's hand or leg. Engage the children in lots of motions or sign language. Encourage kids to use jingle bells or drums, flags, scarves or streamers to praise with (especially for those with less fine

motor control who may have difficulty with the motions).

❑ For children whose grasp is weak, bring strips of Velcro to fasten everything from a paintbrush to a rhythm instrument to a child's hand or wrist. This will help stabilize the object as the child holds it.

❑ Objects (craft supplies, etc.) can be placed on a Rubbermaid non-slip pad to hold them in place.

❑ During playtime, position children in a comfortable and safe way that will allow them to have maximum range of motion.

Blind and Visually Impaired

❑ Avoid using vague words when giving instruction, especially words associated with visual space ("The glue is over there."). Instead use a familiar point of reference ("The glue is just above your paper by your right hand.").

❑ Allow child time to feel the props, stage, craft materials, or game pieces before beginning.

❑ Use sound cues, musical toys, and interesting textures or sounds to enhance the child's play experience.

❑ Use vivid, bright colors for children with limited visual ability. They can enjoy and respond to colors, even if they can't clearly see objects.

❑ If a child has some vision, place craft or lesson materials on a larger sheet of black paper. This helps bring the other materials into focus.

❑ If a child is to color on paper, place craft paper on a larger piece of sandpaper. This will help the child know where the edges of the paper are.

❑ Describe and talk about colors, lights, shapes and sizes of objects in the child's surroundings.

❑ During music, ask if you can gently guide the child's hands or arms to teach them the motions.

Deaf and Hard-of-Hearing

❑ Compensate for loss of hearing by making the most out of the senses of sight and touch. Use visual and physical examples as you explain directions.

❑ Remember body language and facial expressions are part of communication. Be animated so that what they cannot hear from your voice they can read in your posture and face. But remember that over-exaggerating may actually make it more difficult to understand.

❑ As often as possible, get to the child's eye level so he can comfortably see your face when you speak.

❑ If he or she is able, encourage the child to communicate about his surroundings and experiences. Ask open ended questions such as, "Tell me about what you are making", or "What was your favorite part of the drama?"

Mental Disabilities

❑ Avoid long lists of instructions. Allow a child to finish one step before explaining the next.

❑ Repeat instructions frequently, using the same words or phrases.

❑ When necessary, gently turn the child's head to face you or the activity to help focus attention.

❑ Limit choices. Too many choices might be confusing or distracting.

❑ Allow child to make a simpler version of craft. Keep rules less complicated for games and activities.

- ❑ Provide well-marked boundaries for physical activity.
- ❑ If you know or suspect that a child is capable of a task, don't do it for the child.
- ❑ Avoid seating child near distractions when possible (in high traffic areas, near air conditioner, near loud children, etc.).

Learning Disabilities and ADD/ADHD

- ❑ Break instructions into short segments. If necessary, give one instruction at a time.
- ❑ Get the child's attention before talking to him.
- ❑ Expect that you will need to repeat instructions. Stay calm and patient. Be a safe person that they can request help from.
- ❑ As much as possible, maintain eye contact with the ones who have difficulties comprehending during verbal instruction.
- ❑ Whenever possible, demonstrate instructions visually. The more ways you give input, the easier it is for children to understand and remember.
- ❑ Limit choices. Too many options can be confusing and distracting.
- ❑ Allow for movement during activities if possible (lie on the floor, sit with legs out or legs crossed, kneel, stand to do craft, etc.).
- ❑ Provide reminders about time when necessary. Give 10 minute, 5-minute, and 1-minute warnings towards the end of an activity. Help the child start to wrap up a little early to aid in transitions.

Autistic and Sensory-Sensitive

- ❑ Eliminate as many non-essential distractions as possible. It may help some children to face a plain wall rather than sitting in the middle of the room or in the midst of a flurry of activity.

❑ Be aware of environmental factors to which the child is most sensitive (noises, lights, motion, personal space violations, etc.). Think through the program and be prepared to remove the child to a nearby spot that is less stimulating before anxiety escalates.

❑ Keep "escape" or comfort toys handy that can be used in a repetitive way (objects that roll, spin, rock, etc.). These allow the child to tune out distractions that may be disturbing by concentrating on the objects, especially if they are familiar with the object or use it at home.

❑ A headset to block out noises may calm some children at stressful times.

Over 50 Ways to Be an Accessible Church

From the Disability Resource Manual: A Practical Guide for Churches and Church Leaders, the following are over fifty ways to make your church more accessible with little or no cost.[cliv]

1. Use your copier to produce large-print copies of the prayer book or other materials used in worship. (Large print is 18 point and should be produced on paper which is white or off-white and produces good contrast with the type.)

2. Consider replacing fixed pews with moveable pews or chairs so that people with disabilities may be seated with the community and participate fully.

3. Cut the ends of a few pews so that wheelchair users can sit with their friends and families rather than being segregated in the back or front of the worship space.

4. If there are steps into your chancel or sanctuary, consider having a communion station on the floor of the nave. This will permit young children, those who are frail or elderly, and person with disabilities to receive the Sacrament in the same way the rest of the congregation receives.

5. Involve people with disabilities in the planning of all architectural modifications.

6. Think about converting two side by side bathrooms into one accessible unisex bathroom. Allow room enough for wheelchairs to turn around. Leave transfer space on both sides of the toilet. Make sure the toilet paper dispenser is close enough for easy reach by the person using the toilet. Make sure that sinks can be easily accessed by a wheelchair user, and do not forget to lower towel and soap dispensers so that they can be easily reached.

7. Provide a paper cup dispenser near your water fountain. This will transform an inaccessible fountain into one easily accessible to wheelchair users.

8. If any wheelchair users volunteer in your office, consider raising the height of desks and tables so that they wheelchair can fit under these surfaces.

9. Give the option to d/Deaf parishioners to sit toward the front of the nave so that they can easily see the preacher and other worship leaders. Ask the preacher and worship leaders to speak clearly and at a normal pace,

looking frequently at the congregation. Make copies of the sermon and have them available before the service as well as copies of the lessons to be read. People who are d/Deaf or hard-of-hearing may find these materials especially helpful.

10. Install long-handled hardware which is easier for everyone to use, especially those who have impaired hand function.

11 Survey your sound system to ensure that it meets the needs of those with high frequency sound loss. Consider purchasing a sound system with individual hearing devise that better meets the needs of those with hearing loss.

12. Apply brightly colored, textured strips at the top of all stairs. These strips alert people with limited vision that they are approaching stairs. People who are carrying things which block their vision will also appreciate this notice.

13. After every service, take the altar flowers and service leaflets to those who are shut-in or hospitalized.

14. Provide transportation to church for those who are elderly or without transportation.

15. Maintain regular communication with those who are unable to attend services or other parish events. This allows these people to continue to feel a part of the community, and it allows the community to monitor those persons' well-being.

16. Include the children of the parish in visits to nursing homes. Many elders enjoy short visits form youngsters.

17. Discover sources of large print or audio-recorded books, magazines and Bibles. Share this information with older parishioners whose vision are failing and may not yet be acquainted with these resources.

18. Offer a Christian Education day in which participants explore what life as a person with a disability is like. Ask your parishioners who have disabilities to share their experiences. Explore ways in which life as a person with a disability can be improved and how your parishioners with disabilities can feel more included in the life of the congregation.

19. Invite outside speakers to the parish to talk about issues and needs of persons with disabilities.

20. Show one or more of the excellent video tapes which are available about disability concerns. Prepare questions for discussion following the viewing. In interest is expressed, make plans to address the issues which still separate people with disabilities from the larger community of the church and society.

21. Plan an adult education segment to discuss the non-architectural barriers to inclusion.

22. Remove snow and ice promptly from all sidewalks and parking-lots. During the fall months, make sure that slippery leaves are also removed.

23. Survey present church lighting to ensure that the wattage is high enough and that the placement of light fixtures ensures maximum visibility.

24. Make yourselves knowledgeable about the needs of persons with invisible disabilities such as diabetes,

epilepsy, high blood pressure, mental illness, etc. In an adult education session, share this knowledge about these disabilities.

25. Develop support groups for persons with disabilities such as stroke, diabetes, epilepsy, mental illness, etc.

26. Hold all community activities in areas accessible to everyone.

27. Encourage one to one relationships between persons who are elderly and youth and young couples.

28. Enlist the expertise of your parishioners who are carpenters, plumbers, contractors, teachers, social workers, nurses, etc. to accomplish simple accessibility and disability awareness tasks. For example, if you are creating an accessible bathroom, raising the height of the toilet, moving the toilet paper roll closer to the toilet, etc. are easily accomplished by parishioners who are handy.

29. Develop a section of disability resources in your parish library.

30. Look for educational opportunities about disability concerns in your community. Gather several interested parishioners and parish leaders to attend programs. Publicize these events in your bulletins and newsletters.

31. Encourage parishioners to designate memorial gifts for accessibility projects.

32. Organize a beep baseball game, inviting one of the organized teams of blind people to play a team of your own blindfolded parishioners.

33. Visit accessible churches in your area, noting especially the non-architectural ways these churches demonstrate their accessibility and inclusion.

34. Consult local nursing homes to ascertain whether your congregation might invite their residents to become members of your congregation.

35. Share your facilities with organizations which serve people with disabilities.

36. Consider getting involved in congregate dining, meals on wheels, or your own feeding program for those who are in need. Join other parishes in the area in this effort.

37. Set aside a separate bulletin board to display material concerning your own accessibility projects.

38. Explore ways of including people with disabilities in the education and ministry as well as the worship of your congregation.

39. Explore ways of working with other congregations and denominations on projects related to disability access and ministry.

40. Suggest that your parishioners volunteer their time at a day care center, rehabilitation facility or hospital as a way of coming to know persons with disabilities better.

41. If you have persons who are blind or visually impaired in your congregation, install signage in Braille or raised letters.

42. If you have persons in your congregation who are deaf or severely deaf, install a fire alarm which is light cued. Before installing this kind of alarm, however, make sure that there are no persons with epilepsy in the congregation since this light alarm may cause seizures for them.

43. In an educational program or in a sermon, explore the differences between "healing" (wholeness) and "cure". All people can receive God's healing grace. Not all of us will be cured.

44. Because two-thirds of working-age people with disabilities are unemployed (even though they are able to work and want to do so) and because many members of your congregation are employers make sure they are knowledgeable about the issues around employment of persons who have a disability both from the point of view of the employer and the point of view of those who have disabilities.

45. Convene a team of parishioners who are willing to call your legislators on behalf of legislation about transportation and housing. Join with other churches in your community on this project.

46. Survey your neighborhood to ascertain whether there are unmet needs among those who are elderly, home-bound or have a disability.

47. Many activities such as skiing, roller skating and camping can be enjoyed by people who have a disability especially when they are partnered with someone. Encourage your parishioners to look for the fun and fulfillment in these activities.

48. Educate your congregation about environmental illnesses. Survey your cleaning supplies being mindful of those with environmental sensitivities. Encourage everyone to curtail the wearing of perfumes and aftershave as well. For some, the use of incense will be a problem. At the very least, when incense is to be used, notify the congregation beforehand.

49. Designate your church campus as a non-smoking area.

50. Let your diocese or district and your council of churches know about your concern that people with disabilities must be welcomed into the ministry of the church.

51. Set aside parking spaces in your parking lot or in front of your church for people with disabilities. Mark these spaces with an appropriate sign.

52. Provide appropriate Christian Education curricula for children with disabilities. Most children with disabilities can be mainstreamed. When this seems inappropriate, find material suitable to the child's abilities.

53. Encourage families with children with disabilities to bring their children to church. Encourage the members of the congregation to be welcoming, even if a child is not always quiet during the service. Welcome children with disabilities to participate in the celebration of the Sacraments of Baptism, Eucharist and Confirmation.

54. Accept the God-given gifts that people with disabilities bring to the community.

55. Partner with neighboring parishes to provide disability programming for the community.

56. Establish a peer mentoring program between your young people and young people who have a disability.

57. Understand, accept and celebrate your own limitations. All of us who are who we are because of, rather than in spite of, our limitations. Encourage people with disabilities to teach us the lessons of imperfection and limitation.

Disability Access Symbols

The following disability access symbols are often used to notify accessibility to patrons. Consider using them in the church bulletin or in other ways to advertise accessibility at your church. If your church does not offer some of these types of access, have your leadership or disability committee determine how they can be added.

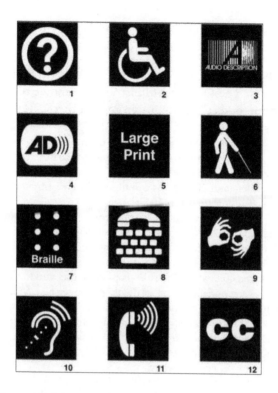

1. Universal Information Symbol
2. International symbol Accessibility
3. Symbol indicating Audio Description for Theatre & Live Performances
4. Audio Description for TV, Films & Video
5. Large Print / Accessible Print Symbol
6. Symbol indicating Access for Individuals Who Are Blind or Have Low Vision
7. Braille Symbol
8. Telephone Typewriter Symbol
9. Sign Language Interpretation Symbol
10. Assistive Listening Systems Symbol (Ear)
11. Assistive Listening System Symbol (Telephone)
12. Closed Captioning Symbol

Disability Theology

The following is provided by Tim Vermande, a member of The Disability Ministries Committee of The United Methodist Church, to promote a theological conversation about disabilities.

The word "theology" comes from Greek roots designating the study of God. Such a proposal is, to say the least, audacious. How can a human mind hope to understand God? How can human language pretend to communicate the ineffable?

What can we do when attempting such an effort? Perhaps, for a place to begin, we can join with St. Anselm, who wrote of "faith seeking understanding." Theology can help us understand our faith in God and, by extension, what God calls us to do in the world.

One understanding of theology that we take from Paul's first letter to the church at Corinth is that the body of Christ is composed of many parts. Each part has a unique function. Together, all of the parts create a functioning body, and each part, while uniquely different, is also necessary.

The primary concern of disability theology is to understand the nature of this diversity in humans. We are created in the image of God, but exhibit many variations. Some of these variations may seem to be limiting, but on careful examination, are human views of different ways of understanding or doing things. Theological study reminds us that "Yahweh does not see as mortals see; they look on the outward appearance, but Yahweh looks on the heart" (1 Samuel 16.7, NRSV), and that we need to look further than the outside, beyond the body and its differences.

Theology is also a reflection on life experience. Therefore, we place value on how people live and where they find God's presence and direction. When we meet to worship, we express this search through our rules for living together. The Bible is a record of how we have come to understand the practical aspects of living in community. [In our various communities,

252

we have rules and laws that express our understandings of how to best live together.] [In the United Methodist Church, these rules are expressed in the *Discipline* and *Book of Resolutions*.] Although neither perfect nor followed perfectly, they tell us what we aspire to be.

Theology also reminds us that God calls every person to some variety of the work that comprises living together with this diversity. It also reminds us that this work includes helping others with the needs that we all face. And therefore, it also reminds us to strive to reach everyone, and that sometimes this requires knowledge of how those needs are understood and absorbed in different ways by some.

Finally, theology reminds us that we all stand equally before God. In the context we have set out of diverse gifts within a body, people with disabilities have gifts of their own to bring. These gifts may be different but they are vital to its health. Therefore, we speak of *ministry with* and not ministry *to* people with disabilities.

Among people who are Deaf or live with multiple differences, we seek to promote the inclusion of all people. Deaf theology also asks what faith has to tell us about Deaf people, about being Deaf and deaf, and the resulting challenges to mainstream theology. As such, it joins with other theologies of liberation, whether racial or disabilities. In doing that, it brings to every person a new sense of identity and self. [clv]

Case Study – Calvary United Methodist Church

In Frederick, Maryland, Calvary United Methodist Church offers an adult Sunday school for individuals with disabilities. They offer this weekly class by incorporating additional volunteers in order to best serve and lead the class of Sunday school students. There is a wide range of disabilities present in the class and attendance varies from week to week. Their volunteers receive training and a background check. More importantly, Calvary has made a commitment to spiritual formation that includes people with disabilities, not just in worship, but in religious education as well.

Case Study – Boston Avenue United Methodist Church

A respite care program was established by Boston United Methodist Church after it did a community needs assessment to determine how it can reach out to both its own members and to its community. After a brief interview with Ms. Shelly Owens, a deaconess, Ms. Owens shared she is one of the respite caregivers for their home-bound ministry program. Trained caregivers go to the homes of those who are homebound, providing support, encouragement, and moments of mercy.[clvi]

Case Study – A Mennonite Church

A family of a church has a son with multiple disabilities. The family's son lived in a dilapidated apartment and several members of the Mennonite church helped to make home improvements for the son (a form of deaf mission). Once the work was completed, the church members saw the need to continue the relationship with the son and began to take him out weekly for lunch. In addition, the members agreed to provide respite care for the parents while they went out-of-town on travel.[clvii]

Questions for Reflection

1. What ways might your church be deterring individuals with a disability from growing in their faith?

2. What ways can individuals with a disability serve in leadership roles within your church? What is holding them back?
3. What barriers need to be removed so individuals with a disability can live out their full potential within the life of the church?
4. How might your church policies be adapted in order to include individuals with a disability?
5. Leviticus 19:14 reads, "*You shall not curse the deaf or put a stumbling block before the blind, but you shall fear your God: I am the Lord.*" (NIV) What ways is your church being a stumbling block to Deaf people or others with disabilities in your faith community?

Conclusion

This chapter explained the difference between a disability ministry and Deaf ministry, though there are some similarities between the two. It also discussed various disabilities, which can include hearing loss. While many culturally Deaf people do not consider themselves as having a disability, some do. In addition, culture plays a big part in how one self-identifies as being Deaf or having a disability. Furthermore, many churches are unaware of how to be in ministry with people with disabilities and their families. Accommodations, attention to family caregivers, consideration of starting a respite care ministry program, and hospitality were discussed as ways to do this form of ministry. Further reading is recommended and The Church and People with Disabilities: Awareness, Accessibility and Advocacy by Peggy A. Johnson is an excellent resource to explore further disabilities and the church. It is a must have book for any church library.

Chapter 10 – Starting a Deaf Ministry

Starting a Deaf ministry at your church is a wonderful idea. As Christians, we should always be looking to see who is missing from our pews (and from the Lords Table). There are a few books that offer suggestions and insight for starting and maintaining a Deaf ministry, such as

- ❑ A Guide to Deaf Ministry (by DeAnn Sampley)
- ❑ Deaf Ministry: Make a Joyful Silence (by Peggy A. Johnson and Bob Walker's)
- ❑ Signs of Love: A Guide for Deaf Ministry (by Lori Buck).

Johnson and Walker's book includes a devotional for small groups. Along with this, this chapter also provides some helpful insight for starting your Deaf ministry.

Often, the identity of the Deaf ministry (the model) will be developed as it grows.

Strategies for Beginning a Deaf Ministry

So, what can you do to build a Deaf ministry? The following are strategies that includes pray, enlist leadership support, gather a team, begin small, educate the team and congregation, assimilate into the church, and adjust and grow the ministry.[clviii]

1. **Pray** - Prayer is the best place to start. Pray for God's wisdom for yourself and for discernment for leaders in your church. Ask God to call people to serve in the ministry and to bring Deaf, hard-of-hearing, or Deaf-blind people from your community into the life of your church. Be faithful in prayer. The most important starting point for any ministry effort is prayer. It is interesting to note that Jesus Himself took the time to pray to the Father before He selected the twelve apostles. Prayer helps us remember to put God first in all that we do. It reminds us to rely solely on the Lord for wisdom, guidance, and strength. In prayer we can also ask God to help us view others through Gods eyes instead of our own. For these reasons, prayer ought to undergird all you do in your church's Deaf Ministry. Pray for:

- ❑ Your church will recognize the need to welcome people who are d/Deaf, hard-of-hearing, late-deafened, and Deaf-blind.
- ❑ For opportunities to develop friendships with individuals who are d/Deaf, hard-of-hearing, late-deafened, and/or Deaf-blind.
- ❑ For each member of the group that is setting up a Deaf ministry. Ask that you would work well together as a team. (Read Matt 9:38)

- ❑ God would move the hearts of people to serve in the Deaf ministry.
- ❑ Your church's Deaf ministry would serve as a role model to the surrounding community.
- ❑ For the people whom the ministry will be serving, both those from within the church body, and those from the community.

What is God laying on your heart? Jot that down to share with your church leadership.

2. Enlist Leadership Support - Leadership support must be obtained for a strong Deaf ministry. It is vital to stay connected with your minister(s) and any governing boards for their support and commitment. Follow the normal protocol for starting a ministry at your church. Questions to answer:[clix]

- ❑ Have you talked with your pastor or minister? This is so important! You need your pastor's support and approval, someone to turn to with questions and for help.
- ❑ Have you talked with any other governing board(s)? This also is very important! You want enthusiastic support from your church board.
- ❑ How does a Deaf ministry fit the mission of your church? Review your church's mission statement. Follow the normal protocol for starting a ministry at your church. There may be several times in the process that you need to seek leadership approval.

3. **Gather a Team** - A team is at the heart of any successful ministry. Gather a core leadership team to oversee the ongoing development of the ministry. It also takes many willing volunteers to build and support a growing inclusive program.

Begin With Prayer - Ask for wisdom as you consider and invite prospective candidates. Pray for volunteers who will become good matches for the Deaf ministry. Ask the Lord to provide a team with a diverse range of spiritual gifts, skills, and talents, to meet a wide variety of needs.[clx]

Define the Purpose and Goals - It's essential to know what you plan to do before you can find the team members who are rightly equipped to help you. Will you focus solely on d/Deaf people? Focus on hard-of-hearing, late-deafened, and Deaf-blind people? Do you want to start a Deaf fellowship by having a weekly dinner? Or have a weeknight Bible study at a group home? Clearly stating your purpose and goals will help you determine what kinds of volunteers you need. Write a brief list of "jobs" along with a brief description for each one. Then when you're ready to talk with potential volunteers, you'll have a better idea of the abilities and skills that are needed.

Recruit the Volunteers - You can search for Deaf ministry team members by:

- ❑ Asking for recommendations from other church leaders.
- ❑ Placing an announcement in the church bulletin.
- ❑ Making announcements in Sunday school classes and at the worship service.

Developing a Prayer Team - A prayer team can serve two important purposes for your Deaf ministry.[clxi] First, by sharing prayer requests with others in your church, you can increase Deaf awareness. Second, by having such a team, you create a spiritual support. The people who join your prayer team do not have to come from the Deaf ministry team/committee. You may want to invite participants who have a burden for people with disabilities. This prayer team can be comprised of two, three, or four people who get together at regular intervals—such as weekly or bi-weekly. Before each meeting, give them a list of the prayer requests and praises they can bring before the Lord. Inform the pastor of the prayer requests and praises. The pastor may share some of them with the congregation so they can see how God is working in the Deaf ministry.

4. **Begin Small** - Begin with the people and resources that God provides. You can't go too slowly, but you can try to move too fast. Develop a plan utilizing resources which will accommodate the current needs of worshipers who are d/Deaf, hard-of-hearing, late-deafened, and Deaf-blind. Look for available resources and wait for God to provide the increase.

Start Small and Build Well - As you begin to build your Deaf ministry, remember the Giant Oak tree is grown over a period of years, even decades. It starts from a very small acorn and develops a root system that sustains the tree throughout the many seasons of sunshine, rain, growth... all seasons are important and over time they lead to stability.[clxii] It has been said that a ministry can fail if it grows too fast, but there are not failures because a ministry grew too slow. So remember to, try not to tackle too much too quickly. Don't attempt to have 'cradle to grave' range of Deaf ministry offerings in the first year. Focus on the people God has placed in the path of the church first. These may be people from within the congregation or from nearby in the community. Some churches start their Deaf ministry with adults, others with a children's ministry based on who God has put into the church's path or the biggest need. There is not a right or wrong way to start, as long as you get started.

5. **Educate Team and Congregation** - Educate your team and the church. Obtain training resources from your denomination or other organizations such as Joni and Friends to train your team and congregation. Conduct a church survey to discover unknown needs within your congregation and to raise awareness. Start with prayer for guidance and wisdom. The team developing Deaf ministry, the congregation, and any of the children, youth or other classes that would have d/Deaf, hard-of-hearing, late-deafened, and Deaf-blind individuals may need some education on the subject of deafness and Deaf culture.

- ❑ Hold a group study on Deaf ministry
- ❑ Teach a sign language class
- ❑ Host a Deaf sensitivity workshop
- ❑ Invite an expert from the community to give a talk
- ❑ Have a book club and learn about Deaf culture, Deaf history, and the work your denomination does (in Deaf ministry).

6. **Assimilate into the Church** - Assimilate Deaf people into the fabric of the church.[clxiii] Look for ways to include in existing church programs. When possible, allow Deaf people to use their spiritual gifts to serve the church body. Your church may find that it's possible to include Deaf children in regular Sunday school classes with their peers. The Deaf ministry committee leader, parents of the d/Deaf or hard-of-hearing child, Sunday school teacher, and a pastor or elder meet together to devise a plan that ensures the inclusion experience will be positive and successful for all involved.[clxiv] Once you get to spend some time with people who are d/Deaf, hard-of-hearing, late-deafened, Deaf-blind you learn they are not that much different from you. They have needs, desires and want the option to know the Word of God.

7. **Adjust and Grow the Ministry** - The needs of children and adults who are d/Deaf, hard-of-hearing, late-deafened, or are Deaf-blind are ever changing. Be ready to adjust to them as new opportunities become available. If a plan is not working, try something new. Have the Deaf ministry continue to meet either bi-weekly or monthly to continue evaluating the progress of the ministry. Begin to do outreach into your community, by attending any Deaf-related events such as Dingo (Deaf version of Bingo), a Deaf club, Deaf coffee chat, other Deaf churches or Deaf ministry events, disability-related events, and by doing outreach ministry to those who are in group homes, psychiatric hospitals, in prisons (many state Deaf resource offices have deaf-related referral resources to identify what is near you). Google deaf events in (and put your state), there will be several listings.

Assessing the Needs

A Deaf ministry grows over time. Start out simple, and start with those God has placed in the church or in the local neighborhood. As individual and family spiritual needs are attended to, other opportunities will arise that allow the ministry to grow. Each and every church is unique, so there is no one path or exact set of things you need to get started, but it is a process. Start out by utilizing the individual and communal resources God has already provided. Resources can include individuals in your church who work and are aware of communication needs, who can sign, who is hospitable, and so on. Resources also include your current church facilities. God has supplied the resources for the ministry; God has called your church to do in your community. Having someone to talk with can help shed light on workable

263

answers to what seem like insurmountable challenges. Consider the following:[clxv]

- ❑ Education and training for your church
- ❑ Hosting a Deaf awareness event for the congregation
- ❑ Establishing a team to lead the effort
- ❑ Deciding to mainstream or have a standalone classroom that is only for Deaf people
- ❑ Truly assimilating those who are d/Deaf, hard-of-hearing, late-deafened, and Deaf-blind
- ❑ Have Deaf people serve the congregation.

Essentials for Implementing a Deaf Ministry

There are five essentials to making your Deaf ministry successful:[clxvi]

1. **Set Objectives and Goals** – You'll want to begin by determining your goals. There are two immediate benefits of doing this. First, you'll know exactly what you should be doing. Second, everyone on the Deaf Ministry committee/team will be able to work in harmony because you're all aiming toward the same thing.

2. **Develop a Calendar** – Once you've decided your goals; you are ready to plan a schedule for making those goals become a reality. As you plan your schedule, keep in mind the three levels of <u>Deaf ministry: Awareness, Response, and Outreach</u>. On your calendar, schedule events and activities that will enhance awareness. Next, implement your response. That is what you need to do to make your church more accessible. Finally, include steps for reaching out to people who are d/Deaf, hard-of-hearing, late-deafened, and Deaf-blind, and invite them to

your church.

3. **Identifying a Budget** - Now that you have determined your goals and the time frame for achieving those goals, you are ready to determine the costs of establishing, maintaining, and expanding the Deaf ministry. Some denominations have funding grants that are specific for start-up ministries such as this. Be sure to check. One major advantage of setting a budget is that it enables you to plan ahead and determine the best way to spend your money. When determining your budget, remember to consider any resources you might already have available. For example, if you want to begin a transportation ministry, it may not be necessary to purchase a van. Someone in your church may be willing to loan a van that can be adapted for such use on Sundays.

4. **Managing the Deaf Ministry/Outreach Team (s)** – Once your Deaf ministry is up and running, how do you keep the team members motivated and working together? You can take a number of steps to help your team reach its maximum potential.

Encourage Frequently - A pat on the back or a kind word goes a long way. People need to know when they're doing a good job. Well-placed encouragement helps team members know they are appreciated and they have a valuable role. The apostle Paul frequently used encouragement in his ministry. For example, in Romans 1:8 he told the Christians at Rome that he thanked God because their faith —is spoken of throughout the whole world.

Create Motivation – In the Christian race, Paul said that he ran so as to get the prize (Phil.3:14). Paul knew the award that awaited him upon winning the race and that motivated him. Similarly, we can motivate our Deaf ministry committee/team.

Maintain Mutual Support – Set up opportunities for the Deaf ministry committee/team to get together to share personal needs, frustrations, prayer requests, and praises. These meetings will allow people to take turns offering support to one another. When we share our problems and burdens, we get the support we need to help us keep going. In any type of ministry, the temptation to quit or give up can become overwhelming. The solution is to bring everyone together to guild up one another. Make a goal of having your team members meet frequently – perhaps once a month.

Pray Together – As you share burdens, frustrations, and problems, lift them up to the Lord. When you pray together as a group, it reinforces that you are turning your circumstances over to God's own care.

Write Thank-You Letters – If you appreciate someone, put it in writing. A simple thank-you note speaks volumes to the recipient. People enjoy getting a surprise thank-you card in their mailbox. It can serve as a morale booster when they least expect it. You'll notice that the one common thread running throughout these suggestions for managing your team is cultivation of a positive, can-do attitude. Ministry is hard work that can be made much easier and more enjoyable when it's backed by frequent support, encouragement, and love.

5. **Maintaining Resources and Supplies** – Designate one or more members of the Deaf ministry committee/team to be responsible for overseeing the resources and supplies used by the ministry. This coordinator can put together a list of resources that are available through the church or people in the congregation. This person will also want to work with the

budget committee to determine what types of supplies are needed, when, and where.

Suggestions for Building a Deaf Ministry

According to Silent Word Ministries, an organization that has been in existence since 1966, it suggests a number of ways to promote Deaf ministry.[clxvii] It recommends:

- ❏ Church literature – in tracts and flyers – should include a statement about the Deaf ministry. Examples: "All services interpreted for the Deaf." or "Deaf Bible Class."
- ❏ Website – List the Deaf ministry with equal emphasis as other ministries.
- ❏ Fliers – For Deaf ministry activities and special events, mail or hand-deliver them. Share them at Deaf gatherings or organizations which serve Deaf people.
- ❏ Create a Deaf culture atmosphere.
- ❏ Encourage the church to be friendly to Deaf people. Smile, shake hands, and learn a few "welcome" signs. Learn to be patient with communication
- ❏ Greeters – Should know where the Deaf class/fellowship meets in the church, know a few signs, carry pen & paper, and be alert for "quiet" visitors who may be d/Deaf, hard-of-hearing, late-deafened, and Deaf-blind.
- ❏ Deaf class signs (advertisements) placed appropriately and prominently.
- ❏ Access – Deaf class should be easily accessible to all ages and disabilities. Interpreted section should be near the front with an easy view of the

platform. Many Deaf people appreciate seeing the Pastor's expression as he/she speaks.

❑ Deaf Bible Class – Lessons should be clear, informative, heart-touching, and life-changing. Interaction (questions and answers, sharing) is a valued part of Deaf culture.

❑ Pulpit – Welcome d/Deaf visitors when appropriate. Treat Deaf people much the same as hearing people. Pastor should not normally talk with interpreter during the message. Also, most interpreters find it helpful for the pastor to brief them regarding difficult terminology or illustrations and main point of sermon. Allow for delay when addressing Deaf people, as the interpreter usually has a lag time in the interpreting process.

❑ Involvement – Encourage Deaf people to become involved in the overall ministry – the nursery, usher, Deaf choir, prayer, teaching, yard work, cleaning, etc.

❑ Study Deaf culture – Many things are a little different in the Deaf world. Examples: Clapping is done by raising and shaking hands. When leaving a group, say good-bye to everyone.

Overcoming Attitudinal Barriers

Let's take a look at attitudes and better understand the role they have in building relationships. Two of the greatest influences on our attitudes are background and knowledge. Background includes our family, our education, our insecurities, and our religious and cultural upbringing.[clxviii]

In certain religious or social systems people who are d/Deaf or have a disability are often shunned, viewed as cursed, an object or charity, shame, dishonor, lowest class of society.

Wrong attitudes can also prevent us from building relationships with d/Deaf, hard-of-hearing, late-deafened, and Deaf-blind people. A few stereotypes:[clxix]

- ❑ People who are d/Deaf or people with disabilities are being punished for their sins. If only they had enough faith, they would confess their sins and be healed.
- ❑ I'm afraid of the unknown, and because d/Deaf, hard-of-hearing, late-deafened, Deaf-blind, and/or people with disabilities represent the unknown, I'm afraid of them.
- ❑ I do not know how to communicate in sign language.

The apostle Paul gives us practical suggestions for building relationships with people. God has gifted every Christian with a unique function, a special role, in the church. The purpose of our spiritual gifts is to build up one another. It is vital that we use our gifts to serve others and that we allow opportunity for others to use their gifts to serve us. Romans 12:6-8 tells us, "*Having then gifts differing according to the grace that is given to us, whether prophecy, let us prophesy according to the proportion of faith; or ministry, let us wait on our ministering: or he that teacheth, on teaching; or he that exhorteth, on exhortation: he that giveth, let him do it with simplicity; he that ruleth, with diligence; he that sheweth mercy, with cheerfulness.*"(KJV) In Romans 12:9-21 Paul tells us we are to love others. He also lets us know how we can show love to others. "*Be devoted to one another in brotherly love.*"(v.10a) "*Honor one another above yourselves.*" (v10b), "*Share with God's people who are in need.*"(v.13a), "*Practice hospitality*" (v.13b), "*Rejoice with those who rejoice; mourn with those who mourn.*"(v.15), "*Live in harmony with one another.*"

(v.16a) *"Do not be proud, but be willing to associate with people of low position."* (v.16b)

Throughout our communities, we see efforts being made to ensure that Deaf people or people with disabilities have greater access to the world around them. We see closed captioning on television sets and at the movies, more places are providing interpreters, new technology is helping to restore hearing for those who want it, and so on. Even though progress is being made, there is still a long way to go. The barriers, both communicational and attitudinal, are still many in number. What is unfortunate however is that d/Deaf, hard-of-hearing, Deaf-blind, and people with disabilities have found that churches lag far behind in the efforts to eliminate barriers. The one place anyone should feel welcome, regardless of his or her physical condition, is the church. You have an opportunity to let your church shine out to the community as a place where d/Deaf, hard-of-hearing, Deaf-blind, and people with disabilities are truly welcome.[clxx]

Deaf Ministry or Deaf Awareness Sunday

One way to start a Deaf ministry or to build it is to have a Deaf ministry Sunday or a Deaf Awareness Sunday where worship is planned around including aspects of Deaf culture and the Deaf experience. The following is an order of worship, followed by a children's message, a sample sermon, and an alternative reading response.

Planning Guide: In worship planning, remember to include d/Deaf, hard-of-hearing, late-deafened, and/or Deaf0blind persons as liturgists, ushers, communion servers, and preachers - all the ways people who are able-bodied share their gifts with the church. Have a sign language interpreter be present and interpret the service.

Order of Worship

Call to Worship[clxxi]

Leader: Jesus Christ, friend to all.

People: Give us the grace and the love to stretch out our arms wide and embrace, in your name, all those whom you love, especially those who are d/Deaf, hard-of-hearing, Deaf-blind and persons with disabilities.

Leader: Jesus Christ, hope of all the nations.

People: Help us to be a church that is welcoming and accepting, and which sees in everyone an expression of you.

Leader: Pour out your Spirit upon us, we pray.

People: That we may recognize and promote the gifts of all people, so that each of us may, in our own ways and with our own abilities, participate in the mission of Jesus Christ.

All: Give us the courage to be lights of welcome in the darkness of exclusion, a voice of gentleness in the wilderness of the unheard, and an outstretched hand of love to those longing for community that we may welcome in Christ's name all who are sent our way. Amen.

Opening Song of Praise

(Invite a guest Deaf choir, a signing choir, or invite the congregation to follow someone who is signing (copy sign) the song).

Children's Time

(See the suggestion following this liturgy.)

Scripture Reading: Acts 4:32-37 (or another reading) (Have a d/Deaf, hard-of-hearing, or a Deaf-blind person read it.)

Sermon

(Have a guest d/Deaf preacher or a person who is fluent in sign language give the message.)

Offering

(Have d/Deaf, hard-of-hearing, and/or Deaf-blind persons collect the offering.)

Doxology or the Lord's Prayer

(Have a d/Deaf, hard-of-hearing, or a Deaf-blind person sign it.)

Closing Song of Praise

(Invite a guest Deaf choir, a signing choir, or invite the congregation to follow someone who is signing (copy sign) the song).

Closing Prayer

Benediction

May the God of hope
Fill you with joy and peace
So that you may abound in hope
By the power of the Holy Spirit.
(Adapted from Romans 15)

Children's Message

The following is a children's message from the National Organization on Disabilities that can be used.[clxxii]

Preparation: Put a small jigsaw puzzle together. Apply masking tape to the back to hold the pieces together so that the entire picture shows. Remove an important piece or two, leaving holes in the picture.

Story: Explain how the puzzle was put together, whether it was hard or difficult, how many people it took. Once it was done, you realized there were important pieces missing, pieces that helped to make the picture whole. Explain that as you worked to put the puzzle together, it struck you as to how the church is like a jigsaw puzzle. We have to put the church together – piece by piece. It's hard. It takes time. It takes many pieces working together. If a piece is left out, the picture is not clear. And there are times when we don't know if all the pieces are going to fit together. With each piece, the picture becomes clearer. Ask, "Have you ever put together a puzzle, only to find there were pieces missing?"

Explain that at times people who are different from ourselves for many reasons – deafness, color of their skin, the clothes they wear, how much money they have, or where they live –are the missing piece of life's puzzle. They are often not seen as a piece of the whole picture, and that makes the picture not be complete. Only when we accept everyone for the gifts and graces they bring, can the picture of the church be made clear. We need to welcome and support the ability of all people be a contributing part of God's family.

SAMPLE SERMON
(by Bishop Peggy Johnson)

Scripture: Acts 4:32-37 (NIV)
The Believers Share Their Possessions

32 All the believers were one in heart and mind. No one claimed that any of their possessions was their own, but they shared everything they had. 33 With great power the apostles continued to testify to the resurrection of the Lord Jesus. And God's grace was so powerfully at work in them all 34 that there were no needy persons among them. For from time to time those who owned land or houses sold them, brought the money from the sales 35 and put it at the apostles' feet, and it was distributed to anyone who had need.

36 Joseph, a Levite from Cyprus, whom the apostles called Barnabas (which means "son of encouragement"), 37 sold a field he owned and brought the money and put it at the apostles' feet.

Sermon: "Heart of Barnabas"

We first meet Barnabas in Acts, chapter 4 when he is converted to Christ and sells his field, his family inheritance (don't underestimate this in this time in history) and lays the proceeds from the sale of that field at the feet of the apostles.

Barnabas gave his all. Prior to his Christian name, his name was Joseph; however, his name was changed by the apostles to Barnabas, which means "Son of Encouragement." He gave the apostles an infusion of encouragement.

Still today, there is no greater encouragement than the generosity of the Body of Christ. A female pastor went through an ice storm on her way to Dallas, TX in 1979. At the time, this pastor was attending a seminary where 98% of the students were male. She was a pioneer. At seminary, she had not received much encouragement from others; "I have never heard a woman preach" was sometimes said. Often, she was questioned about her call to ministry. In her denomination, they had a women's organization. Groups of women from various churches had helped pay her way to attend a women's conference in Dallas. There, she met many other clergywomen and was greatly warmed by the fellowship of other clergywomen. She received encouragement and continued in following her call to ministry.

When she was later assigned to an all Deaf church in Baltimore, she had a mess to clean up. There were outstanding bills from the apartment building the church was supporting (it was going to foreclosure). The tenants had fled and left unpaid electric, gas, and phone bills. Sadly, there were all kinds of inconsistencies in the checking account. One Sunday morning, this pastor and the Deaf choir traveled to a hearing church to preach and perform at. The church pastor knew of the Deaf church's plight. They took up a special offering, encouraging everyone to dig deep. After collecting and counting the offering, it was enough to pay off the outstanding bills in the church. They were greatly encouraged and the ministry of the Deaf church soared in the light of that generous help.

You too can be a "son of encouragement" like Barnabas by giving extravagantly to further the Deaf ministries or disabilities ministry in the church. Every ramp that is built, every interpreter that is provided, every accessible parking place, and every respite program that is set up, every dime that is spent on captioning: it all speaks a word of love and it encourages the soul like nothing else. Where can you give generously to help further the vital ministry you are doing (or hope to build)?

Taking the Side of the Underdog

We most likely would not have most of the New Testament if it had not been for Barnabas. Saul, who converted to Christ and became Paul, wanted to become a part of the apostles' in-crowd after his conversion and the apostles were not so sure about this stranger. Paul had sent many Christians to prison and supported the stoning of Stephen, a deacon, and saw that many others were martyred. It's hard to warm up to a guy like that. Suppose he was using a fake conversion to arrest and kill more Christians? But Barnabas had a different heart. He came alongside of this new soul in Christ and heard him out. With the wisdom of God-given discerning heart, he discovered genuine soul in Paul into the trust-circle of the Early Church leadership.

Still today there is a need for the Barnabas-spirit to come alongside the unlovely one or the questionable one and give him or her a chance. In Deaf ministry and in disability ministry, we often have this opportunity. When this female pastor we spoke about earlier had tried to enter into Deaf ministry many years before, she had a lot of, "Who are you and why do you want to do this?" look on the faces of the Deaf leaders in the city she served. She wasn't fluent in sign language. The other pastors in Deaf ministry were not very encouraging either. This female pastor was serving at a hearing church, but had a call to do Deaf ministry, yet the door seemed shut from the inside. But there was a woman by the name of Barbara. She was hard-of-hearing, but knew many Deaf people in Baltimore and she knew who didn't attend church. Barbara told the pastor, "So you want to do Deaf ministry? Well, then write your best sermon and preach it in sign language and then preach it at your hearing church and I will gather you a row of Deaf people to come see you preach." The pastor practiced for a week and hoped some Deaf people would show up. Then on that Sunday,

Barbara had herded a whole row of Deaf people to the front pew. Barbara endorsed the pastor. The Deaf and hearing people saw her preach and several of them kept coming back. A new Deaf ministry was born. Two years later this pastor became the pastor of a Deaf church in Baltimore and all of those Deaf people who attended her hearing church had then joined the Deaf church. What would she have done without Barbara?

There is a wonderful ministry happening in the Central Congo area with Deaf children. One pastor from Pennsylvania had a vision for a ministry with children in the remote villages. Surprisingly, children have no Christian education whatsoever. They hang around in the windows of the church during worship for adults, but no age-level education is offered. Well, it is now thanks to the pastor from Pennsylvania. The Pennsylvania pastor came alongside a Congolese woman named Josephine. She is a person with a mobility challenge. No one there thought she was worth anything because of her disability. The Pennsylvania pastor discerned a true heart in her and she is now employed as the Christian Education Director there and is ministering to 4,000 children. People have begun to respect her and her ministry because of the Barnabas-spirit of the Pennsylvania pastor.

Still today, you can come alongside someone who is struggling and give them a chance. I have to say that sometimes Deaf ministry and disability ministry can be a closed system. We can't afford to shut people of good will out of the mix. Sometimes we have to be discerning, but sometimes the closed system has to do with power issues and we can't afford to leave anyone out who is called to do this work. Who can you reach out to?

Out in the Margins

Another great thing about Barnabas was his work with the Gentiles, which was out-of-the-box ministry for sure. He and Paul took the Gospel of Jesus Christ outside of the bounds of Judaism. This was no little thing. It was a radical step to preach to those whom the Jews thought were not a part of the family of God's chosen people. Many thought the gospel was just for Jews and if someone wanted a new life in Christ, they had to become a Jew first. Just to give it all away without the legal requirements of circumcision and the law was unthinkable at that time. But Paul and Barnabas heard a different call from God. God was going public with this gospel and these two were bold enough to preach to those the Jews had rejected.

This is still the call of Deaf ministry and disability ministry. It is not enough to get a ramp and an interpreter and some large print bulletins and say, "we are inclusive." The larger your heart is for Christ the more you want to reach out further and further and that means reaching out to the people who are more and more severely challenged and more and more on the margins.

The female pastor and her church thought they were inclusive. They had sign language. They had a voice interpreter. They had listening devices. They even had captioning for the sign language impaired. Then they figured out that there were a lot of Deaf-blind people not able to come to church. This is intensive work. They need transportation and much mobility work and tactile interpreting that is labor intensive to say the least. We found that as we opened the door to Deaf-blind people, the church was gifted by their giftedness in music, in organizing a Deaf-blind club, and in preaching and teaching at a Deaf-blind camp. Widening the circle in that area led the church to continually widen the circle to Deaf teenagers with huge social problems, undocumented Deaf immigrants who did not use ASL, Deaf people with cognitive delays, Deaf ex-offenders, mentally-ill Deaf people, Deaf people with addiction problems, and Deaf people with HIV/AIDS. The circle got wider and wider and the Spirit was at work in providing healing, community, and providing strength.

Mentoring

Barnabas was known for his mentoring work. He worked with Paul to get him up to snuff with the apostles, but he also mentored John Mark. John Mark was a young man, wet behind the ears, not all that dependable apparently. John Mark had deserted the crew back in Pamphylia and Paul was not going to give him another chance on the next mission trip. Barnabas on the other hand wanted to keep working with him. It says in Acts 15:29 that Paul and Barnabas had a "sharp disagreement" over this. It was so much so that these two giants of faith went their separate ways. Wow! Didn't the two of them just broker a Council in Jerusalem making peace with the Gentiles and the Jews in the same chapter in Acts and now Paul and Barnabas are at odds with each other over this young man, John Mark.

Barnabas took John Mark and went off to Cyprus and Paul and Silas went off to Syria and Cilicia. They doubled the work. John Mark got the help he needed to grow under the mentorship of Barnabas. Church tradition teaches that it was John Mark who wrote the Gospel of Mark and became the bishop of Apollonia. Where would we be without mentors like Barnabas?

Mentoring is still important work in the Deaf community and the disability community. An interpreter by the name of Carol does mentoring. She is an interpreter who resources Deaf ministry in the Philadelphia area and she is constantly mentoring new interpreters, some young person with shiny eyes who wants to become an interpreter, but can't sign very well. Same with a Deaf lay servant who does Deaf ministry outreach who comes alongside teenagers and young mothers and teaches them to be empowered, how to get services, how to budget their money, how to find shelter, and has even helped an abused Deaf woman escape from her abusive husband and move to another state.

If you are going to have a Deaf ministry or a disability ministry you have to be pulling someone alongside of you and mentor him or her. Who else is going to do this? There are classes for this sort of stuff. We have to be the teachers, the mentors in bringing forth the future.

Conclusion

I thank God for the ministry of Barnabas: he gave generously, spoke up for the underdog, went to the margins and mentored the young ones. You go and do likewise. Amen.

Alternative Responsive Reading

This reading is paraphrased from I Corinthians 12:12-27 and adapted from The Banner Newspaper, May 27, 1985.

Reader 1: For just as the body is one and has many kinds of members and all the members of the body, though many, are one body, so it is with Christ. For by one Spirit we were baptized into one Body –healthy, wise, and challenged – and all were made to drink of one Spirit.

Reader 2: For the church does not consist of one kind of member, but of many. The person who is physically challenged may say, "Because I am not able to move as freely as others, I cannot do all tasks by myself. Yet I am no less a part of this body." And the person with mental retardation may say, "Because I learn new things differently than you do, I need extra help and time. Yet I am no less a part of this body." The person who is d/Deaf may say, "Because I do not hear well, I cannot sing on key. Yet I am no less a part of this body."

Reader 3: If the whole church were teachers, where would the learners be? If the whole church were well off, where would the needy be? As it is, God arranged the kinds of people in a church, each one of them, as God chose. If all were a single kind with the same mind, where would the church be?

Reader 4: As it is, many kinds of people are needed, yet there is one church. People who are able to read litanies cannot say to the non-readers, "We really don't need you." Nor can folks who are emotionally stable say that they don't need those who are emotionally challenged. On the contrary, the people of the church who seem weaker are indispensable. But God has so composed the church that there may be no discord in the membership and that members may have the same care for one another – a covenant of care for one another.

All Readers: If one member suffers, all suffer together. If one member is left out, all are hurt. If one member is honored, all rejoice together. Now we are the Body of Christ, and each one of us is a part of it!

Acquiring Sign Language Interpreters

Often, individuals who do not work within the Deaf community are unfamiliar with Deaf resources. A few ideas for acquiring interpreters are:

1. Contacting sign language interpreting agencies in your area. They're expensive, but can be helpful in a pinch.
2. Contacting the state vocational rehabilitation (V.R.) office to ask for recommended resources (they will likely have a directory).
3. Contact your state's Deaf and Hard of Hearing

Commission/Office/Coalition (they often have a list of resources or referrals).

4. Research colleges and universities in your state that offer sign language interpreting programs, as students need practicum hours. Some professors or department chairpersons may be familiar with Deaf-related resources.

5. Go to the Registry of Interpreters for the Deaf (RID) website and search for interpreters on their online directory (it's best to search by state as some interpreters do not mind traveling).

6. Do a Google search and type "sign language interpreters in (insert your city or county)".

7. Contact other Deaf ministries in your area to see if they have recommendations.

8. Ask the d/Deaf or hard of hearing person at your church, as he or she may know of potential resources.

9. Contact your denomination's Deaf ministry organization or disability ministry organization.

For fundraising ideas to pay the interpreter, try:

1. Check out this fundraiser website www.abcfundraising.com/fundraising-ideas/ideas-for-church-fundraisers/

2. Take up an annual special offering that supports the Deaf ministry budget

3. Host a periodic spaghetti fundraiser dinner

4. Apply for available grants by your denomination

5. Consider reallocating the Deaf or hard of hearing church member's offering toward the Deaf ministry budget.

Offer Sign Language Classes

One way to help a hearing congregation to be more aware and inclusive of d/Deaf, hard-of-hearing, late-deafened, and Deaf-blind people is offer a sign language class.[clxxiii] Ideally, have a d/Deaf, hard-of-hearing, or a

Deaf-blind person teach it since it is his or her language. Perhaps provide a love offering or ask each student to pay $5 per class/session he or she attends.

If your church has an internet connection, the group could take an online class through StartASL, an online company who contracts with interpreters and d/Deaf individuals to teach and tutor. Classes are FREE, at least the basic classes are; however, you can upgrade to the paid version. They website offers an ASL video dictionary as well. The website is www.start-american-sign-language.com/.

Some community colleges offer basic sign language classes; this is ideal for more formalized learning and to learn about community events. Be sure to promote it.

Additional online sign language classes are

ASL University - ASL 1 is one of four free ASL courses offered online by ASL University. Courses are separated into six units that contain five lessons each and include quizzes, numbers practice and fingerspelling practice activities. Most lessons consist of objectives, vocabulary, practice sentences and stories for translation. Each lesson contains visual diagrams and instructor-led videos to show students acceptable signing.

http://www.asluniversity.com/

Start ASL - ASL 2 is the second in a series of three progressive ASL courses. Training includes fingerspelling, reading assignments, videos, conversion sentences and various tips for perfecting skills. These courses cover topics in numbers, grammar, vocabulary and comprehension.

https://www.startasl.com/

Lesson Tutor - ASL for the Deaf is an ASL training program offered in three series that consist of 12 lessons each. Along with an explanation article, each lesson also presents visual diagrams on proper ASL form. Worksheets are available to demonstrate training. Students can utilize Lesson Tutor's ASL dictionary to translate additional signs.

http://www.lessontutor.com/ASLgenhome.html

Expert Village - Sign Language Lessons: Common Phrases is separated in 15 parts, and all training is offered through videos that are 2-3 minutes long. These videos teach students to emphasize sign images, body language and facial expression while signing.

https://www.youtube.com/playlist?list=PLA73C298C56 86C43E

Host a Deaf Awareness Event

A Deaf awareness event is a great way to bring a better understanding about Deaf culture, Deaf issues and people, and history. Holding it during Deaf Awareness Week, also called International Week of the Deaf (IWD) is ideal.

Themes for a Deaf awareness are vast. Several can include:[clxxiv]

- ❏ Celebrate the culture, heritage, and language unique to deaf people of the world.
- ❏ Promote the rights of Deaf people throughout the world, including education for Deaf people, access to information and services, the use of sign languages, and human rights for Deaf people in developing countries.[2]

- ❑ Recognize achievements of Deaf people, including famous Deaf individuals.
- ❑ Educate about the misconceptions of being Deaf and the challenges the Deaf population face during everyday life.
- ❑ Learn about types, degrees, and causes of hearing loss.
- ❑ Be exposed to sign language and other ways deaf and hard-of-hearing people communicate.
- ❑ Learn about the types of educational programs, support services, and resources that are available for those in the Deaf and hard-of-hearing community, including children.
- ❑ Gain a better understanding of Deaf culture.
- ❑ Understand that d/Deaf and hard-of-hearing individuals are just as capable, able, and intelligent as hearing individuals. There is a difference in the way those that are d/Deaf and hard-of-hearing communicate, but it is not a considered a disability by many.

There is a wide range of Deaf events that your church can host. Some include:[clxxv]

- ❑ Awareness events, public information campaigns, and distribution of material
- ❑ Displays, exhibit booths, and information tables – possibly found anywhere from a shopping mall to your local health center, community center, pool, club house, or park.
- ❑ Interpreted story hours (libraries are a good place to check)
- ❑ Open houses in schools that have Deaf and hard-of-hearing programs or at facilities that offer educational and community resources.

- ❏ Events put on by Deaf ministry programs in churches
- ❏ Sign language lessons or courses for the public
- ❏ Hearing screening
- ❏ Events with guest speakers, workshops, or panel discussions
- ❏ Film screenings (with d/Deaf actors)
- ❏ Sign language concerts or performances
- ❏ Games and other entertainment events for the community
- ❏ Show the video *Through Deaf Eyes*[41]

You may see events in your local community from any of the following:[clxxvi]

- ❏ Deaf and hard-of-hearing organizations or clubs
- ❏ Schools, colleges, and universities
- ❏ Libraries
- ❏ Churches
- ❏ Businesses
- ❏ Sign language classes (for example, sometimes high school sign language students will do community outreach events)
- ❏ Community groups and public venues

Further Ideas For Growing Your Ministry

The following suggestions have been used by Deaf ministries.

---

[41] *Through Deaf Eyes* (a Deaf history documentary) is located at www.youtube.com/watch?v=tJeAG8tZyf4.

- ❏ Hold a revival on a Saturday evening & conclude Sunday morning that includes a guest d/Deaf preacher (do these two or three times a year).
- ❏ Invite a Deaf choir (or a signing choir) from other churches to perform at your church once a month.
- ❏ Work closely with a nearby college ASL program, by offering silent dinners (or potlucks) at your church so students and others can practice signing.
- ❏ Invite sign language students from area high schools or colleges to your church, as they may have d/Deaf family members. Send invitations monthly or quarterly.
- ❏ Integrate sign language into the worship service, such as having the congregation sign a hymn or song and by signing the Lord's Prayer together. Include Deaf-related events in any church announcements.
- ❏ Do an outreach ministry (e.g. bring meals, play games, do story-telling, and so on) to human service organizations in the area who serve those with intellectual disabilities (also known as developmental disabilities), as some may have d/Deaf or hard-of-hearing clients/residents.
- ❏ Make new connections to Deaf-related organizations in the area, possibly advertising your ministry in their newsletter or have an exhibit table at one of their events.
- ❏ Start a new sign language class to the community, advertising at the public library, Starbucks, and schools.
- ❏ Do more networking via a Facebook page, Twitter, and other social media. Be sure to connect with your denomination's Deaf-related caucus or agency that has this area of focus.

❑ Connect with your state government Deaf agency (or possibly a local government agency); sometimes it is integrated with a disability agency. Often, these agencies have weekly or monthly e-news or email announcements. You may learn of area Deaf-related events. Advertise any church Deaf-related events through their electronic broadcasts.

❑ Subscribe to other Deaf ministries, Deaf churches, and/or Deaf organization's newsletter so you can be included in any news and stay informed of any locally-held events.

❑ Revamp the church's newsletter and website to make it Deaf friendly (use more pictures and visuals) that also include Deaf-related articles or Deaf-related community announcements, such as movies that are captioned.

❑ Do outreach to hard-of-hearing and late-deafened individuals in your area by advertising with the Alexander Graham Bell Association for the Deaf and Hard-of-Hearing chapter and Hearing Loss of America chapter in your state. This can include sponsoring their meeting or event by providing desserts, drinks, and finger foods (as a form of hospitality). Have a captionist for hard-of-hearing and late-deafened individuals at your church. Don't forget to advertise this to the community as well.

❑ Connect with or subscribe to sign language interpreting workshops, conferences, or events in your area or state. Some interpreting agencies may know of Deaf organizations in your area.

❑ Begin or expand a multiple disabilities ministry at your church, which often includes Deaf people with multiple disabilities. You will likely need to coordinate additional volunteers for this.

Program events for your church and/or your community can vary and it can certainly include worship, hands-on workshops, panel discussions, networking, special music, drama performances, or resource and program exhibits. Breakout sessions can include a basic sign language class, an intermediate sign language class, introduction to Deaf culture, an introduction to interpreting workshop, and learning the art of signing music. The list is endless. The following is a half-day program schedule for consideration.

Half-Day Schedule

Times	Activities
8:00-8:30	Registration, refreshments, & networking
8:30-8:45	Welcome message
8:45-9:15	Keynote speaker
9:30-10:15	Choice of breakout sessions
10:30-11:15	Choice of breakout sessions
11:30-12:45	Lunch and panel discussion
12:45-1:00	Closing message and dismissal

Stay Connected

Remaining a part of a collective is part of Deaf culture and this is helpful for social diverse groups. Stay connected with outside entities, such as local, regional, and national organizations, as well as church and denomination caucuses and movements. By doing so, your church and/or ministry will remain informed about current events and relevant issues, be updated about new policies that may affect your group or committee. Appendix A and B of this book has a list of denominations and organizations. Most of them offer newsletters and/or social media as a way of staying connected. The same is also true by having others connect with your ministry. If your church has a newsletter, include announcements and articles to keep the community informed of your Deaf ministry. Hosting an exhibit table at church or community events that highlights your Deaf ministry is another great way to stay connected as well.

Adapting English Materials for Deaf Use

Leading a Bible study or a topical study is common within the church. While there Biblical and theological resources are plentiful, they might be challenging to those who English is a second language. For many d/Deaf individuals, English is a second language. Also, when not knowing educational backgrounds for group members, the following suggestions can be used when adapting English materials.

- ❑ Teach using ASL.
- ❑ Teach at a slower pace so the content can be better absorbed.
- ❑ Teach creatively (e.g. include dramas).
- ❑ Explain terms and concepts when needed.
- ❑ Use pictures, maps, media, and Power Point slides.
- ❑ Do introductions, reviews, and debriefing during sessions.
- ❑ Periodically, ask the group questions to see if the content is being understood.
- ❑ If using videos, pause it at intervals to explain concepts or to engage the group.

Pastoral Resources

Often what is asked is, "What Bible translation should I read?" The answer is what you feel comfortable with. Having a Bible in your primary language is what is generally recommended. **Deaf Missions**, at www.deafmissions.org, has general resources that are helpful, including Scriptures signed into ASL, daily devotionals, children's storytellers, ASL sermon series, and so on. If you do not know of anyone who is in Deaf ministry, Deaf Missions is a great place to start to gather information. Along with these resources, Deaf Missions provides a variety of trainings for Deaf ministry.

Closing Thoughts

This book provides an overview of several models that can help enhance one's church, even one's community. While these are some practical approaches to starting or improving a Deaf ministry, at the heart of it are the relationships and the relationship building that will keep the ministries going. While we are faithful to the ministry, God is faithful in pouring out grace to help it grow and draw others into the body of Christ. When one discerns about beginning a Deaf ministry, pray to see what might be the motivating reasons for it and if it is indeed a call from God, then begin to talk with church leadership to begin exploring this exciting new ministry. Which model of ministry does the Spirit seem to be swaying you and your ministry team? It is certainly in God's realm to drop a ministry right into the lap of the church and how to best manage it, as well as expand it requires prayer.

While these Deaf ministry models are approaches, they are just that. Working outside the box (and outside these models) is still recommended, as the Holy Spirit brings newness in various ways and being attuned to this helps to better envision what God has in store for your church. Jesus' apostles had their own approach for doing their ministries, yet there was some overlap, but nonetheless, they were different, which can be seen in the four gospels, in the pastoral letters, the Epistles, and the other letters that make up the New Testament. Just be open to working outside the box and see what direction and plan God has in store for you.

Working with other organizations and Deaf ministries (even outside of your denomination), either collaboratively or by partnering in a new venture is a way to begin a Deaf ministry. As Jesus and his disciples traveled throughout Galilee to share the Good News, we too must do this in our communities. We cannot necessarily expect that d/Deaf, hard-of-hearing, late-deafened, and Deaf-blind people to come to our churches. Sometimes, if not most of the time, we need to go to them, build the relationships, and then invite them. Hospitality, of course, is key for when the visitors come. Follow up and inviting them to return is important too.

Deaf ministry is also about what Jesus did for the Deaf man and his community in Mark's gospel. In Mark 7, Jesus prayed with the Deaf man and said, "*Ephphatha*" (be opened). It was at this point that the Deaf man could hear and speak. This is one interpretation to the miracle story; however, the other interpretation is Jesus did not say, "Father, let him hear and speak." Instead, Jesus' intent was to heal the man and the community so everyone would "be open" to the Word of God. *Ephphatha* is spoken to all of us. Are we open to the gifts and culture that Deaf people bring? Is there room for them at the table of grace within our faith communities? While Jesus' public ministry was about sharing the Good News, it also went hand-in-hand with social justice. Stand with d/Deaf, hard-of-hearing, late-deafened, and Deaf-blind people and remove barriers, provide accommodations, and help your church to be inclusive, so they too will "be open" to their presence and the gifts they bring us. We are the ones that are blessed. Indeed.

Questions for Reflection

1. If your church already has one of these models of ministry, in what ways can it be improved?
2. What forms of grace can your faith community offer the Deaf community?
3. Sharing the gospel is part of the church's mission in the world. What ways can your church share this with the Deaf community?
4. In Matthew 5:16, Jesus said, *"In the same way, let your light shine before others, that they may see your good deeds and glorify your Father in heaven."* Shining the light of Christ is part of the church's charge. How might your church shine its light to those mentioned in this book so they can better connect to your church?
5. What ways is your church not being open to including d/Deaf, hard-of-hearing, late-deafened, and Deaf-blind people?

Conclusion

This chapter discussed strategies for starting a Deaf ministry program in a hearing church. Strategies, suggestions, and recommendations were provided that included having Deaf ministry-related events. Starting small and building it is the best way to have long-lasting relationships, which will help maintain your ministry long-term.

Afterword- Deaf Theology

By Rev. Dr. Kirk VanGilder

Any undertaking to initiate a ministry relationship with a new community should be accompanied by a great deal of prayer, preparation, and theological thinking. Similarly, any community looking to form a ministry among themselves should likewise consider these three essential practices. Prayer is something a community should do together, giving close attention to the hopes, dreams, and frustrations people express as they wait for God's guidance and calling in a new venture. This book provides a number of models and a great wealth of information that will help a community prepare for ministry. What remains important is a vital process of theological reflection that ensures that a community is continually examining who it is, what it does, and why it takes action in joining God's mission and ministry in the world. As a Deaf person who holds a Ph.D. in practical theology, I offer this afterword as a brief sketch of what this process of theological reflection might look like in the life of your congregation or community.

One of the differences between practical theology and systematic theology is its starting point. Systematic theology tends to begin with discussions about the nature of God and proceeds from that understanding of the divine presence of God to addressing how the nature of God therefore shapes how things relate to God. Practical theology, however, tends to begin with the human experience of a life lived in context. Often, practical theological reflection will begin with addressing a dilemma or problem noted where "the way we do things" doesn't seem to be working. The goal of a practical theological process then is often to answer the question, "How do we respond to this dilemma as a people of faith?" This will require a community to examine the situation, their social context, the historical development of the situation, and other factors. They will also need to explore what their faith tradition has historically said about this situation, how it has been involved in the situation, and what, if any, action or statements exist about the situation. From there, a community will begin to discuss and develop strategic plans that bring these two streams of thought together and challenge both the social circumstances and structures that have created the dilemma they are wrestling with and the assumptions of their faith tradition may have about this situation. The end goal - being a transformed set of practices and beliefs that reflect the faithful examination of this situation and have forged a response to this dilemma that reflects a renewed expression of their faith.

As the chapter on advocacy ministry indicates, Deaf people experience a great deal of marginalization, discrimination, and disenfranchisement in American society. This results in fewer opportunities for quality education, under employment, and a tendency for society to therefore view Deaf people as helpless or in need of guidance. This is not God's plan for Deaf people—or any people. Instead, the dignity and value of God's creation of Deaf people—and all people—as they are should be honored and protected by communities of faith. Therefore, a ministry with Deaf, hard-of-hearing, late-deafened, or Deaf-blind people should be one of liberation, empowerment, and building of capacity to determine and influence the course of one's own life. This applies to life in the social world as well as one's life with God in a community of believers. Thus, in all cases, a congregation interested in forming a Deaf ministry should be asking itself tough questions about their knowledge of Deaf lives, preparing themselves to listen to Deaf people and respond not only with compassion, but with a spirit that seeks justice. Similarly a community of Deaf people who may be seeking to establish a ministry to and with Deaf people from within their own social circles will need to give careful consideration as to how they will give close attention to the stories, experiences, and aspirations of those with whom they seek to do ministry.

Giving attention to Deaf lives and experiences with the world and with God will enable the development of practical theological agency among Deaf people. This is the heartbeat of Deaf theology. Deaf communities have long valued narrative means of shaping, transmitting, and preserving cultural knowledge. As ASL is not a written language, it necessitates the living and breathing practice of telling and retelling stories in conversation and performance. Therefore, Deaf theology will often follow this tendency and be far more about fostering communities of constructive conversation than producing definitive written texts. Any model of Deaf ministry, and those with hard-of-hearing, late-deafened, and Deaf-blind people should take the task of forming communities where people can explore how to think about their lives and tell their stories seriously. Furthermore, these stories need to be seen and heard by one another and by those on the outside. Being seen and heard in meaningful ways that lead to transformed relationships is the key to a successful practical theological process.

It is my hope that the helpful information and tips for ministry contained in this book can be a resource for beginning a larger and deeper process of practical theological exploration for congregations and communities. Rather than approaching this book as a 'checklist' of things to do, seek to use it as a launching pad for exploration and relationship building with Deaf people. As Yates has mentioned, the relationship between communities of faith and Deaf people is strained at best and abusive at worst. Historically, far too much theological ink has been spilt arguing about "healing" Deaf people by making them more like hearing people and "giving Deaf people what they need" than actually listening to Deaf people and learning about us. The result of this historical trend is that Christianity has far too often been on the side of social forces that marginalize, discriminate, and disenfranchise Deaf people than those that liberate, empower, and build their capacity to flourish. Therefore, many Deaf people distrust churches reaching out in ministry either out of suspicion of their motivations or weariness that, "This church will do ministry only until they reach that point where they realize they have to change how they do things, and financially support those changes, rather than change me to fit their expectations." Therefore, Deaf ministry shares a common thread with racial and ethnic ministry development in that there must be a consistent commitment to honest repentance and reconciliation.

But don't let the difficulty of this task deter you from getting started! The book you are holding provides you with crucial information for getting started. Take the risk, open yourselves to what God is calling you to do. Be ready to be transformed in ways you never expected. Trust that God will lead you and pay close attention to God's urgings—even when you find them in unexpected places!

Appendix A – Deaf Churches & Organizations

The following are Deaf and/or interpreting related organizations.

Adventist Deaf Ministries International
www.adventistdeaf.org/

American Consortium of Certified Interpreters (ACCI)
PO Box 7451
Stockton, CA 95267-0451
(209) 475-4837 Voice / TTY
www.acci-iap.org

American Association of the Deaf-blind (AADB)
8630 Fenton Street, Suite 121
Silver Spring, Maryland 20910-3803
(301) 495-4402 TTY
(301) 495-4403 Voice
(301) 495-4404 Fax
www.aadb.org

American Sign Language Teachers Association (ASLTA)
P.O. Box 92445
Rochester, New York 14692-9998
www.aslta.org

Anabaptist Disabilities Network
ADNet
3145 Benham Avenue, Suite 5
Elkhart, IN 46517
Phone: 574-343-1362
Ph. /Fax: 877-214-9838
Email: adnet@adnetonline.org
www.adnetonline.org/

The Association of Visual Language Interpreters of Canada
PO Box 29005 Lendrum
Edmonton, Alberta, Canada T6H 5Z6
780-430-9442 Voice / TTY
780-988-2660 Fax
www.avlic.ca

CODA International, Inc.
P.O. Box 30715
Santa Barbara, CA 93130-0715
www.coda-international.org
(Children of Deaf Adults)

Conference of Interpreter Trainers (CIT)
P.O. Box 254623
Sacramento, California 95865-4623
Phone: 619-594-7417
www.cit-asl.org

Concordia Theological Seminary
Church Interpreter Training Institute (CITI)
6600 N Clinton Street
Fort Wayne, IN 46825-4996
260-452-2100 voice
www.ctsfw.edu/Page.aspx?pid=727

Deaf Baptist Fellowship
http://deafbaptistfellowship.com/

Deaf Missions
21199 Greenview Rd.
Council Bluffs, IA 51503
Phone: (712) 322-5493 (Voice/TTY)
www.deafmissions.com

Deaf Video Communications
25 W 560 Geneva Road, Suite 10
Carol Stream, IL 60188-2231
(630) 221-0909
www.deafvideo.com

Episcopal Congress of the Deaf
www.ecdeaf.org/

Gallaudet University
800 Florida Avenue, N.E.
Washington, D.C. 20002
202-651-5050 (visitor's center) Voice / TTY
www.gallaudet.edu

Global Deaf Muslim
5695 Columbia Pike, Suite 201
Falls Church, VA 22041
571-421-2998 video phone
contact @globaldeafmuslim.org
http://globaldeafmuslim.org/

International Institute on Deaf Ministry
PO Box 39009
Birmingham, Alabama 35208
www.iids-inc.org/

Jewish Deaf Community Center
507 Bethany Road
Burbank, CA 91504
www.jdcc.org

LCMS Deaf Missions, Lutheran Church - Missouri Synod
1333 S. Kirkwood Road
St. Louis, Missouri 63122-7295
888-899-5031 TTY
800-433-3954 ext. 1321 Voice
www.lcmsdeaf.org and www.lcmsdeaf.org

National Alliance of Black Interpreters (NAOBI)
PO Box 5630
Evanston, IL 602045630
www.naobi.org

National Association of the Deaf (NAD)
814 Thayer Ave
Silver Spring, MD 20910
(301) 587-1788
www.nad.org

National Black Deaf Advocates
P.O. Box 564
Secane, PA 19018
president@nbda.org
www.nbda.org

National Catholic Office for the Deaf
7202 Buchanan Street
Landover Hills, MD 20784-2236
Voice - 301- 577- 1684
TTY - 301 - 577 – 4184
www.ncod.org
(Has links to many dioceses)

National Technical Institute for the Deaf
52 Lomb Memorial Drive
Rochester, NY 14623
585-475-6400 (V/TTY)
http://www.ntid.rit.edu/

**Northeastern University Regional Interpreter
Education Center**
American Sign Language Program
405 Meserve Hall
Boston, MA 02115
617-373-2463 Voice
617-373-3067 TTY
www.asl.neu.edu/riec

Registry of Interpreters for the Deaf, Inc. (RID)
333 Commerce Street
Alexandria, VA 22314
(703) 838-0030 Voice
(703) 838-0459 TTY
(703) 838-0454 Fax
www.rid.org

Silent Word Ministries International
http://international.silentwordministries.org/

Southern Baptist Congress of the Deaf
www.sbcdeaf.org/

The United Methodist Committee on Deaf and Hard-of-Hearing Ministries
www.umcdhm.org/

United Methodist Congress of the Deaf
www.umcd.org

United Pentecostal Church-International Deaf Evangelism
www.deafevangelismministry.com/

World Deaf Assemblies of God
www.wdag.org/

Appendix B - Denomination Websites

Resources listed can be used to research doctrines, history, and other useful information.

African Methodist Episcopal Church (AME)
1134 11th Street, N.W.
Washington, DC 20001
www.ame-church.com

African Methodist Episcopal Zion Church
P.O. Box 32843
Charlotte, NC 28323
www.amez.org

American Association of Lutheran Churches
801 West 106th St., #203
Minneapolis, MN 55420
www.taalc.org

American Baptist Association
4605 N. State Line Avenue
Texarkana, TX 75503
www.abaptist.org

Assemblies of God International

1445 Boonville Avenue
Springfield, MO 65802
www.ag.org

Baptist General Conference
2002 South Arlington Heights Road
Arlington Heights, IL 60005
www.bgcworld.org

Church of God (Seventh Day)
330 West 152nd Ave.
P.O. Box 33677
Denver, CO 80233
www.cog7.org

Church of the Nazarene
6401 The Paseo
Kansas City, MO 64131
www.nazarene.org

Church of the Untied Brethren in Christ
3002 Lake Street
Huntington, IN 46750
www.ub.org

Episcopal Church
815 Second Avenue
New York, NY 10017
www.ecusa.anglican.org

Jehovah's Witnesses
25 Columbia Heights
Brooklyn, NY 11201-2483
www.watchtower.org

Lutheran Church - Missouri Synod
1333 South Kirkwood Road
St. Louis, MO 63122-7295
www.lcms.org

Mennonite Church USA
421 South Second Street, Suite 600
Elkhart, IN 46516
www.mennonites.org

Orthodox Church in America
P.O. Box 675
Sysosset, NY 11791-0675
www.oca.org

Pentecostal Assemblies of the Word, Inc.
3939 Meadows Drive
Indianapolis, IN 46205
www.pawinc.org

Pentecostal Church of God
4901 Pennsylvania
P.O. Box 850
Joplin, MO 64802
www.pcg.org

Presbyterian Church (USA)
100 Witherspoon Street
Louisville, KY 40202
www.pcusa.org

Presbyterian Church in America
1852 Century Place
Atlanta, GA 30345-4305
www.pcanet.org

Roman Catholic Church Council
3211 Fourth Street
Washington, DC 20017
www.vatican.va

Seventh-day Adventist Church
12501 Old Columbia Pike
Silver Spring, MD 20904-6600
www.adventist.org

Southern Baptist Convention
901 Commerce Street, Suite 750
Nashville, TN 37203
www.sbc.net

United Church of Christ
700 Prospect Ave
Cleveland, OH 02108
www.ucc.org

United Methodist Church
PO Box 340007
1009 19th Avenue S.
Nashville, TN 37203-0007
www.umc.org

Appendix C - Glossary of Interpreting Terms

American Sign Language (ASL): a visual gestural language with its own linguistic structure and grammar; the language used by most Deaf people in the US and Canada.

audism: is the attitude or favor of those who are hearing.

bilateral deafness: A bilateral deafness or hearing loss means that both ears have a loss of hearing. A bilateral hearing loss may occur prior to or any time after birth. It may occur gradually or suddenly.

code-switching: using more than one language during a dialogue or conversation.

Code of Professional Conduct: a core set of beliefs, values, and responsibilities fundamental to the interpreting profession that serve to define the exemplary practices of the profession.

Conceptually Accurate Signed English (CASE): Uses ASL features and conceptually accurate signs while following English grammar and structure.

communicative competence: a speaker's underlying knowledge of the linguistic system and the norms for the appropriate sociocultural use of language in particular situations; when someone knows a language, he/she knows how to use the forms of the language; knows the phonology, morphology, and syntax of the language; and knows how to use the language appropriately.

consecutive interpreting: a speaker's signed or spoken discourse into another language when the speaker pauses for the interpretation to occur.

culture: a group's beliefs, values, patterns of behavior, language, expectations, and achievements which are passed on from generation to generation.

Deaf: a particular group of Deaf people who share a language, ASL, and a culture; members of this group use ASL as a primary language among themselves and hold a set of beliefs about themselves and their connection to the larger society; self-identification with the group and native or acquired fluency in ASL, not hearing loss, often determines who is Deaf.

deaf: refers to the audio logical condition of not hearing; deaf persons often do not identify with the knowledge, beliefs, and practices that make up the culture of Deaf people.

Deaf community: a cultural group comprised of persons who share similar attitudes towards deafness. The "core" Deaf community is comprised of those individuals who have a hearing loss and who share common language, values, and experiences, and a common way of interacting with each other, with non-core members of the Deaf community, and with the hearing community. The wider Deaf community is comprised of individuals (both deaf and hearing) who have positive, accepting attitudes toward deafness, attitudes which can be seen in their linguistic, social, and political behaviors.

deaf interpreter: a Deaf professional, skilled in ASL, visual gestural communication, pantomime, and other non-conventional communication systems, who, in combination with an ASL-English interpreter, facilitates communication between a hearing consumer and a deaf consumer with minimal language skills or whose native language may be neither English nor ASL (e.g., Italian sign language). Sometimes called a CDI (certified deaf interpreter).

Demand-Control Schema (DC-S): an ethical framework (schema), developed by Dr. Robert Pollard and Robyn Dean, where interpreters can assess the demands (problems or stresses) of a situation and utilize controls (solutions) for dealing with them.

discourse: in sociolinguistics, discourse refers to any use of language that goes beyond the sentence; how language is organized in conversations, how sentences in a written text are organized; the study of discourse involves the functions of language, the norms and structure of language use, and language as a signal of social identity.

dynamic equivalent: not a word-for-word translation, but a conceptual and culturally accurate interpretation.

feed: during team interpreting, team members provide support and assistance to each other, often referred to as 'feed' within the interpreting community; ideally, in team interpreting situations, while one interpreter is interpreting, the other interpreter "stands by" and provides assistance whenever needed; i.e., if the working interpreter misses or misunderstands any part of the source message or has difficulty expressing difficult concepts.

grammar: the mental system of rules and categories that allows humans to form and interpret the words and sentences of their language; the relevant components of grammar are phonology, syntax, and semantics.

hearing-impaired – This term is no longer accepted by most in the community but was at one time preferred, largely because it was viewed as politically correct. To declare oneself or another person as deaf or blind, for example, was considered somewhat bold, rude, or impolite. At that time, it was thought better to use the word "impaired" along with "visually," "hearing," "mobility," and so on. "Hearing-impaired" was a well-meaning term that is not accepted or used by many deaf and hard-of-hearing people.

Interpreter: provides signed or spoken translation of a speaker's discourse from one language into another.

lag time: the time between delivery of the original message and the delivery of the interpreted version of that message.

language style: language use appropriate to a given register.

language variation: the differences in the pronunciation/production, vocabulary and grammar of the people who use a particular language. Language variation develops because people have different ways of saying the same thing. Variation is often caused by such factors as age, sex, racial or ethnic background, geographic area, education, context, etc.

linguistic competence: the ability to produce and understand an unlimited number of utterances, including many that are novel and unfamiliar.

linguistics: The study of language. Some of the specialties within the field of linguistics are philology, semantics, grammar, phonology, morphology, comparative linguistics, and applied linguistics.

Manually Coded English (MCE): a form of signed English.

phonology: the study of the smallest contrastive units of a language. In sign language linguists use the term phonology to refer to the study of how signs are structured and organized. ASL signs have five basic parts: handshape, movement, location, palm orientation, and non-manual behaviors (facial expression, eye gaze, head tilt and body posture).

pragmatics: how the meaning conveyed by a word or sentence depends on aspects of the context in which it is used (such as time, place, social relationship between speaker and listener, and speaker's assumption about the listener's beliefs).

prosody: the study or discussion of linguistic structure, including its parts (e.g. a sign choice).

register: the situation within which the communication takes place; the relative level of formality or informality called for and used by a speaker in a particular situation; a range of language use that will be appropriate or acceptable in any given situation; register can be frozen (such as that used in courtroom or religious services), formal, consultative (used in everyday conversation between speakers who are strangers or do not know each other very well), casual and intimate (used by people who know each other very well and who interact on a regular basis). Contextual factors help determine register such as the physical setting and social activity, channel used, (e.g., written, spoken, or signed), purpose (e.g., lecture or interview), the participants, and the interpersonal dynamics involved.

register variation: the structure of a discourse may differ depending on the setting (i.e., where and when a conversation takes place; language appropriate for a certain occasion. In ASL, different signs are used in formal settings than those used in informal settings; the location of signs may also vary depending on the social setting.

semantics: the study of the system of meaning; how words and sentences are related to the objects (real or imaginary) they refer to and the situations they describe; the relationship between words/signs and concepts.

simultaneous interpreting: signed/spoken interpretation of a discourse into another language while the speaker is signing/speaking.

source language: the originating language of a discourse that will be interpreted (e.g. English [source language] into ASL [target language]).

syntax: the study of the way in which sentences are constructed; how sentences are related to each other; knowledge of the rules for making sentences; study of word order.

target language: the language into which a discourse is to be signed or spoken (e.g. English [source language] into ASL [target l

unilateral hearing loss: Unilateral hearing loss (UHL) means that hearing is normal in one ear but there is hearing loss in the other ear. The hearing loss can range from mild to very severe.

Appendix D - Glossary of Church Terms

acolyte: An acolyte is a lay person, often a child or a teenager, who performs minor duties during the worship service to assist the ministers, such as lighting candles, carrying books, directing traffic during communion, and so forth. Acolyte comes from a Greek word for follower.

Archbishop: The word *archbishop* is Greek for *chief overseer.* Therefore, *archbishop* is not a separate order of clergy, it is just a bishop who has administrative duties over fellow bishops in a geographical region. In some areas, bishops elect one of their number to be the archbishop; in other areas, the bishops rotate the office. The head of the Episcopal Church of the USA is called a *presiding bishop* rather than an *archbishop*, but the meaning is the same.

Bishop: *Bishop* is the English version of the Greek word επισκοπος (episkopos), which means overseer or supervisor. In the historic church, a bishop is a regional minister, a priest with administrative duties over a group of churches in a territory called a diocese. Only bishops can preside at the rite of ordination. An individual bishop can ordain a deacon or a priest, but it takes three bishops to consecrate a new bishop.

cardinal: Cardinals are bishops who serve as advisers to the pope. The pope can make any priest or bishop a cardinal; however, when a priest becomes a cardinal, he is consecrated a bishop.

catechumen: *Catechumen* is an ancient term, not often used as often, for a person who is taking instruction in Christianity, but is not yet baptized. In the ancient Church, catechumens were dismissed from the service between the Service of the Word and the Eucharist.

cathedral: The term *cathedral* refers to the function of a church, not its architectural style. A cathedral is a church that serves as a bishop's headquarters (or where he/she serves from).

celebrant: A term for the minister who is the moderator of a worship service that includes communion. In most cases, only a member of the ordained clergy can be a celebrant.

chancel: the chancel is the front part of the church from which the service is conducted, as distinct from the nave, where the congregation sits. The chancel is usually an elevated platform, usually three steps up from the nave. The words *chancel* and *sanctuary* are often synonyms.

chapel: A chapel can either be an alcove with an altar in a large church, or a separate building that is smaller than a full-sized church. Chapels have the same function as church buildings and are equipped the same way.

clergy: The word clergy comes from a Latin word that means "office holder." It refers to ordained ministers who are authorized to conduct the rites and sacraments of the church. Some clergy may have administrative duties at various regional and national levels of a church.

congregation: The people who have gathered for worship. The term has two meanings: (1) Those presently assembled for worship. (2) All of the people who make up the local church's constituency. In some churches the word *congregation* is only used in the first meaning, and the word *parish* is used for the second meaning.

crucifer: *Crucifer* is a Latin word meaning cross-bearer, used for the acolyte who carries the cross in a church procession. It is an ancient custom for the clergy and the other ministers to enter the church after the worshipers have already assembled. When this is done in a procession, the procession is led by the crucifer, usually a young person, bearing the cross. The crucifer is followed by the choir, the acolytes, the lay ministers, and finally the clergy; the highest ranking clergy last.

curate: *Curate* is an Anglican term for assistant pastor.

Deacon: The word *deacon* comes from the Greek word διακονος (diakonos), which means servant. The New Testament records the appointment of the first deacons in Acts 6 and lists their qualifications for office in 1 Timothy 3. Depending on the church, a deacon can be any of the following: a member of the clergy; a lay minister; or a lay administrator.

diocese Modern churches generally follow political boundaries when they set up ecclesiastical regions, even if they don't call them dioceses. In Orthodoxy, a *diocese* is called an *eparchy*. In the United Methodist Church, the word *conference* is used instead of diocese.

Elder: *Elder* is the English word which translates the Greek word *presbuteros* (or presbyter), which translates into English as priest.

Father: In Roman Catholicism, in Orthodoxy, and to some degree in Anglicanism, people often address priests as *father*.

Grace: Is defined as the love and mercy given to us by God because God wants us to have it, not because of anything we have done to earn it. We read in the Letter to the Ephesians: "For by grace you have been saved through faith, and this is not your own doing; it is the gift of God — not the result of works, so that no one may boast" (Ephesians 2:8-9).

kneeler: In churches where it is customary to kneel for prayer, there is often a long, narrow padded bar at the base of pew in front of you, which can be tilted down for kneeling and tilted up to make it easier to get in and1out1of1the1pew.

lay reader: A *lay reader* is a lay person who is authorized to read the scripture lessons and lead the congregation in certain parts of the worship service. It is not uncommon to refer to the lay reader as a *liturgist*.

lectern: There are generally two speaker's stands in the front of the church. The one on the right (as viewed by the congregation) is called the *lectern*.

Minister: *Minister* is the Latin word for doer of little deeds, as opposed to a magistrate, who is a doer of great deeds. In some churches, the word *minister* denotes a person who is charged with the spiritual care of a church. In most churches, *minister* is a generic term that includes all who assist in worship, whether clergy or lay. The following are ministers: bishops, priests, deacons, acolyte, lay readers, and crucifers.

narthex: The term for what might otherwise be called the foyer or entry way of the church.

nave: The architectural term for the place where the congregation gathers for worship, as opposed to the front part of the church from which the service is led. Many churches use the term 'sanctuary,' which is often to mean both chancel and nave.

officiant: A term for the minister who is the moderator of a worship service. This term is most often used when the service does not include communion. Depending on circumstances, the officiant may be an ordained minister, a lay minister, or a lay person.

parish: In some churches, the geographical territory of a local church. In general, the constituency of a local church; that is, all the people who are members or who informally consider it to be their church.

Pastor: Pastor is the Latin word for shepherd. This word refers to the ordained minister who is charged with the primary spiritual care of a local church.

pew: Originally, Christians stood for worship, and that is still the case in many eastern churches. The pew, a long, backed bench upon which congregants sit.

Pope: The term *pope* or *papa* originated as a term of endearment for bishops and sometimes even priests. It is a form of the word *father*. The pope is the only member of the Roman Catholic clergy who always wears white1vestments1and1clericals.

presbyter: The Greek word πρεσβυτερος (presbyteros) is used in the New Testament for people who perform the functions of clergy in the Church. It1means1elder.

Priest: *Priest* is the English word that originated from the Greek word *πρεσβυτερος* (presbyteros), which means elder. Roman Catholic priests must be unmarried at the time of their ordination and they must remain that way. In the Eastern Church, a priest must remain in the state in which he was ordained. If he was single when he was ordained a priest, he must remain unmarried. If he was married when he was ordained a priest, he may remained married, but he is not permitted to remarry if he is widowed. Anglican and Lutheran priests can marry after ordination.

priesthood: *Priesthood* is a synonym for *clergy* in Anglican, Catholic, and Orthodox churches. The phrase *priesthood of all believers* comes from 1 Peter 1:4-10 and refers to all baptized believers work in God's kingdom.

pulpit: It is used by clergy to read the gospel and preach the sermon.

rector: *Rector* is the Anglican word for the elected pastor of a financially self-supporting congregation. The term derives from the fact that if there are multiple clergy on staff in a church, the pastor has primary responsibility1for1directing1the1worship.

Reverend: The term *reverend* is an adjective that simply indicates that a person1is1a1member1of1the1clergy.

sacristy: In historic church architecture, the sacristy is the room or closet in which communion equipment, linen, and supplies are kept. It is usually equipped1with1a1sink.

sanctuary: In historic church architecture, the front part of the church from which the service is conducted, as distinct from the nave, where the congregation sits. The term 'sanctuary' is often used to mean both chancel and nave because the two are not architecturally distinct.

shrine: A shrine is a building or a place that is dedicated to one particular type of devotion that is limited to commemorating an event or a person.

thurifer: A thurifer is a person who carries and swings the thurible in a worship service. The thurible (or censer) is the device in which incense is burnt.

vestry: In the Anglican Communion, the *vestry* corresponds to the board of directors of a secular organization. The vestry elects the rector of the church and conducts its secular business.

Appendix E – Disability Awareness Sunday Suggestions

The following are suggestions for how to observe Disability Awareness Sunday.

Tip 1
Bulletin Insert of Disability-related Awareness Dates

Tip 2
Read Scripture Passages Highlighting Disabilities

Tip 3
Invite a Guest Speaker or a Guest Preacher

Tip 4
Include Worship Liturgy

Tip 5
Handout an Americans With Disabilities Fact Sheet As People Leave the Sanctuary

Tip 6
Have a Sunday School Class Make Up a Bulletin Board

Tip 7
Read a Few Disability-related Facts During the Announcements

Tip 8
Set up an Exhibit Table and Have Disability-related Handouts Available

Have a Bulletin Insert with
Disability-related Awareness Dates

Disability-related Awareness Dates

January
Co-dependency Awareness Month - (U.S.)
Glaucoma Awareness Month - (U.S.)
Weight Loss Awareness Month

February
Heart and Stroke Awareness Month
February 4 – World Cancer Day
February 20 – World Day of Social Justice

March
Cerebral Palsy Awareness Month
Intellectual Disabilities Awareness Month
National Problem Gambling Awareness Month
March 12 – World Glaucoma Day
March 21 – World Down Syndrome Day

April
Alcohol Awareness Month
Autism Awareness Month
Child Abuse Prevention Month
Parkinson's Disease Awareness Month

May
ALS Awareness Month
Asthma Awareness Month
Better Sleep Month
Lupus Awareness Month
Stroke Awareness Month

June
June 6 – World Hunger Day
Men's Health Month
PTSD Awareness Month
June 15 – World Elder Abuse Awareness Day

July
July 16 - Disability (ADA) Awareness Day
Cataract Awareness Month

August

Cataract Awareness Month

Immunization Awareness Month

August 21 – National Senior Citizens Day

August 31 – International Overdose Awareness Day

September

Prostate Awareness Month

National Alcohol and Drug Addiction Recovery Month

Childhood Obesity Awareness Month

Ovarian Cancer Awareness Month

Deaf Awareness Month

October

AIDS Awareness Month

Breast Cancer Awareness Month

Depression Education and Awareness Month

Lupus Awareness Month

November

Adoption Awareness Month

COPD Awareness Month

Alzheimer's Awareness Month

Epilepsy Awareness Month

December

World AIDS Day

December 3 – International Day of Persons with Disabilities

Read Scripture Passages That Highlight Disabilities

Old Testament
Leviticus 19:14 God Tells His People in His Law
to Care for Those with Disabilities.
Deuteronomy 27:18 Moses establishes the Law
not to take advantage of persons with disabilities.
Isaiah 42:16 God shows compassion to persons
with disabilities who suffer due to being
marginalized.
Zechariah 7:8-10 The Lord emphasizes social justice and
encourages equality for all.

Gospels
Matthew 9:27-33 Jesus heals two blind men and a person unable to
speak.
Luke 14:15-24 In Jesus' parable, he emphasizes that God's house
should be filled and that we are to invite people with disabilities.
Mark 7:31-37 Jesus heals a deaf man with the emphasis of Jesus
restoring the community.
Luke 7:21-23 Jesus highlights his work as the Messiah, healing and
restoring individuals and communities.
John 5:1-15 Jesus heals a man unable to walk, highlighting that a
disability can sometimes be caused by sin (e.g. a heroin user
shooting heroin in your leg, causing an infection, and needing it to
be amputated).
John 9:1-3 Jesus heals a blind man emphasizing that a disability
isn't always caused by sin; moreover, that God's glory is revealed
through him.

New Testament
Acts 9:8, 17-19 Saul/Paul had lost his sight. He was cared for and
then had his sight returned to him.
James 5:14 James calls the community to pray for anyone who is
ill.
1 Corinthians 12:12-30 Paul teaches that everyone is equal in the
body of Christ, treating people with disabilities with more respect.

Proverbs
Proverbs 31:8 Emphasizing social justice and advocacy.

* These are just a few passages. There are a plethora of Scripture
references.

Invite a Person to Speak
or Preach About Disabilities

1. Check with a denominational leader in your district, dioceses, or annual conference, as he or she has a list of speakers.
2. Ask someone with a disability from your faith community to share his/her testimony and their experience (connect it to his/her faith).
3. Check with The Arc, which has agencies nationwide.
   www.thearc.org/find-a-chapter
   It is an advocacy organization on behalf of persons with intellectual and developmental disabilities that also offers programs and services.
   Can request someone to come and speak about their organization.
4. Check with Melwood, which has agencies nationwide.
   www.melwood.org/map
   Community support services for persons with disabilities.
   Can request someone to come and speak about their organization.
5. Check with Autism Society, which has chapters nationwide. Their website is www.autism-society.org/.
   Locate a chapter near you at http://209.200.89.252/search_site/affiliate_map.cfm.
   Provides information about autism spectrum disorders and resources.
   You can request someone to come and speak about their organization and/or chapter.

Worship Liturgy

Call to Worship

BEATITUDES FOR FRIENDS OF PEOPLE WITH DISABILITIES:

Leader: Blessed are you who take the time to listen to difficult speech, for you help me to know that if I persevere I can be understood.

People: Blessed are you who never bid me to "hurry up" and take my tasks from me and do them for me, for I often need time rather than help.

Leader: Blessed are you who asked for my help, for my greatest need is to be needed.

People: Blessed are you who understand that it is difficult for me to put my thoughts into words.

Leader: Blessed are you who, with a smile, encourage me to try once more.

People: Blessed are you who never remind me that today I asked the same question two times.

All: Blessed are you who respect me and love me as I am, and not like you wish I were.

(Adapted from Joni and Friends, Inc. Retrieved from www.joniandfriends.org/media/uploads/downloads/Beatitudes.pdf.)

Prayer of Confession

Almighty and creating God; we come before you today as people who are separated from one another by fear, prejudice, and ignorance. By our language, actions and facilities we declare insiders and outsiders in our lives and in our church. Forgive us and create in us the vision of opening our hearts, minds, and doors as wide as the love of God, so that no one is left outside. Help us to reach beyond ourselves to discover the joy of community. Give us the patience to discover that all people have gifts and abilities to share with our community of faith. We pray in Jesus name. Amen.

Adapted from Southeastern United Methodist Agency for Rehabilitation (SEMAR) 2004.

Songs and Hymns

- Ask someone with a disability to sing and/or play an instrument. If possible have them join the choir and/or worship team for the service.

- Include a song signed by an ASL interpreter or if you have Deaf, hard-of-hearing, or late-deafened, or Deaf-blind individuals present so the whole service can be interpreted.

- Ask a children's choir to perform a hymn or song in sign language. Ask a nearby high school ASL class to perform 2 or 3 songs in sign language.

- Work with the worship leader to be sure that the Scriptures, hymns and songs chosen for this day complement the theme.

- Include one or more of the over 8000 hymns written by Fanny Crosby who was blind, such as 'Blessed Assurance' or 'My Saviour First of All'.

- Show a music video of a song that is signed/interpreted.

Hand out an Americans with Disabilities Act (ADA) Fact Sheet as Parishioners Exit the Sanctuary

Americans with Disabilities Act (ADA) Fact Sheet

Overview
The Americans with Disabilities Act (ADA) is one of the most comprehensive civil rights laws prohibiting discrimination on the basis of physical or mental disability. The Act was established to promote equal opportunities for persons living with disabilities into all aspects of daily life, such as employment, public accommodations, transportation, state and local governments, and telecommunications.

Understanding What "Disability" Means Under the ADA
To be covered under the Americans with Disabilities Act as a person living with a disability, one must identify themselves with one of the following definitions:

* A person with a physical or mental impairment that substantially limits one or more major life activities;
* A person with a record of such a physical or mental impairment; or
* A person who is regarded as having such impairment.

ADA's Four Components
ADA was constructed into four major "Titles" each centered on a systemic category of accessibility. Below each Title are highlights of the protections afforded to persons with disabilities.

* **Title I – Employment:** Employers may not discriminate against an individual with a disability in hiring or promotion if the person is otherwise qualified for the position. Employers can ask about one's ability to perform a job, but cannot inquire if someone has a disability.

Employers must provide "reasonable accommodation," such as job restructuring and modification of equipment when necessary.
* **Title II – Public Services:** State and local governments must remove communication and physical barriers that restrict people with disabilities from using their services and activities. Public entities must make every effort to integrate the disabled into their existing and future services, programs, and activities, and be able to communicate "with all of the public (telephone contacts, office walk-ins, or interviews), provide for the public's use of the facilities, and allow access to programs that provide State or local government services or benefits."
* **Title III – Public Accommodations:** Restaurants, hotels, theaters, doctors' officers, pharmacies, retail stores, museums, libraries, parks, private schools, and day care centers may not discriminate on the basis of disability. Private clubs and religious organizations are exempt. Auxiliary aids and services must be provided to individuals with hearing or vision impairments.
* **Title IV – Telecommunications:** Telephone companies must provide telecommunications relay services for hearing-impaired and speech-impaired individuals 24 hours per day.

For more information visit www.ada.gov

Have a Sunday School Class
Make Up a Bulletin Board

Example 1

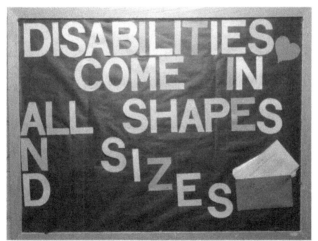

Example 2

Share Disability Facts During Announcements

5 Facts about Disabilities
From the World Health Organization

Over a billion people live with some form of disability

This corresponds to about 15% of the world's population. Between 110-190 million adults have very significant difficulties in functioning. Rates of disability are increasing, due to population ageing and the global increase in chronic health conditions.

Disability disproportionately affects vulnerable populations.

Lower-income countries have a higher prevalence of disability than higher-income countries. Disability is more common among women, older people and children and adults who are poor.

People with disabilities often do not receive needed health care.

Half of disabled people cannot afford health care, compared to a third of non-disabled people. People with disabilities are more than twice as likely to find health-care providers' skills inadequate. Disabled people are four times more likely to report being treated badly and nearly three times more likely to be denied health care.

Children with disabilities are less likely to attend school than non-disabled children.

Education completion gaps are found across all age groups in all settings, with the pattern more pronounced in poorer countries. For example, the difference between the percentage of disabled children and the percentage of non-disabled children attending primary school ranges from 10% in India to 60% in Indonesia.

People with disabilities are more likely to be unemployed than non-disabled people.
Global data show that employment rates are lower for disabled men (53%) and disabled women (20%) than for non-disabled men (65%) and non-disabled women (30%). In OECD countries, the employment rate of people with disabilities (44%) was slightly over half that for people without disabilities (75%).

(10 Facts on Disability, 2013, from World Health Organization. www.who.int/features/factfiles/disability/en/)

During the Fellowship Hour, Like After Worship, Have an Exhibit Table with Disability Materials

Consider the following disability-related materials:

* General Rules of Etiquette for Communicating with Persons with Disabilities

* Wheelchair Etiquette

* ADA Fact sheet

* Fast Facts Media Bulletin

General Rules of Etiquette for Communicating with Persons with Disabilities

1. When talking with a person with a disability, speak directly to that person rather than through a companion or sign language interpreter.

2. When introduced to a person with a disability, it is appropriate to offer to shake hands. People with limited hand use or who wear an artificial limb can usually shake hands (shaking hands with the left hand is an acceptable greeting).

3. When meeting a person with a visual impairment, always identify yourself and others who may be with you. When conversing in a group, remember to identify the person to whom you are speaking.

4. If you offer assistance, wait until the offer is accepted. Then listen to, or ask for, instructions.

5. Treat adults as adults. Address people who have disabilities by their first names only when extending the same familiarity to all others. (Never patronize people who use wheelchairs by patting them on the head or shoulder.)

6. Leaning or hanging on a person's wheelchair is similar to leaning or hanging on a person, and is generally considered annoying. The chair is part of the personal body space of the person who uses it.

7. Listen attentively when you're talking with a person who has difficulty speaking. Be patient and wait for the person to finish, rather than correcting or speaking for the person. If necessary, ask short questions that require

340

short answers, a nod or a shake of the head. Never pretend to understand if you are having difficulty doing so. Instead, repeat what you have understood and allow the person to respond. The response will clue in and guide your understanding.

8. When speaking with a person in a wheelchair or a person who uses crutches, place yourself at eye level in front of the person to facilitate the conversation.

9. To get the attention of a person who is d/Deaf, hard-of-hearing or late-deafened, tap the person on the shoulder or wave your hand. Not all people with a hearing impairment can lip read. For those who do not read lips, be sensitive to their needs by placing yourself so that you face the light source and keep hands, cigarettes, and food away from your mouth when speaking.

10. Relax. Don't be embarrassed if you happen to use accepted, common expressions such as "See you later," or "Did you hear about this?" that seem to relate to a person's disability.

This was retrieved from St. Mary's County government. The website also has handouts for specific disabilities.
http://www.stmarysmd.com/americandisabilities/resources.asp

Wheelchair Etiquette

(As written by Disability Awareness, The Rehabilitation Center, Ottawa Ontario)

- Always ask the person using the wheelchair if he or she would like assistance BEFORE you help. It may not be needed or wanted.

- Don't hang or lean on a person's wheelchair because it is part of that person's personal body space.

- Speak directly to the person in the wheelchair, not to someone nearby as if the person in the wheelchair did not exist.

- If conversation lasts more than a few minutes, consider sitting down or kneeling to get yourself on the same level.

- Don't patronize the person by patting them on the head.

- Give clear directions, including distance, weather conditions and physical obstacles that may hinder the person's travel.

- Don't classify persons who use wheelchairs as sick. Wheelchairs are used for a variety of non-contagious disabilities.

- When a person using a wheelchair "transfers" out of the wheelchair to a chair, toilet, car, or bed, do not move the wheelchair out of reaching distance.

- It is ok to use terms like "running along" when speaking to a person who uses a wheelchair. The person is likely to express things the same way.

- Don't discourage children from asking questions about the wheelchair.

- Don't assume that using a wheelchair is in itself a tragedy. It is a means of freedom that allows the person to move about independently.

Americans with Disabilities Act (ADA)
Fact Sheet

Overview

The Americans with Disabilities Act (ADA) is one of the most comprehensive civil rights laws prohibiting discrimination on the basis of physical or mental disability. The Act was established to promote equal opportunities for persons living with disabilities into all aspects of daily life, such as employment, public accommodations, transportation, state and local governments, and telecommunications.

Understanding What "Disability" Means Under the ADA

To be covered under the Americans with Disabilities Act as a person living with a disability, one must identify themselves with one of the following definitions:

* A person with a physical or mental impairment that substantially limits one or more major life activities;
* A person with a record of such a physical or mental impairment; or
* A person who is regarded as having such impairment.

ADA's Four Components

ADA was constructed into four major "Titles" each centered on a systemic category of accessibility. Below each Title are highlights of the protections afforded to persons with disabilities.

* **Title I – Employment:** Employers may not discriminate against an individual with a disability in hiring or promotion if the person is otherwise qualified for the position. Employers can ask about one's ability to perform a job, but cannot inquire if someone has a disability.

Employers must provide "reasonable accommodation," such as job restructuring and modification of equipment when necessary.

* **Title II – Public Services:** State and local governments must remove communication and physical barriers that restrict people with disabilities from using their services and activities. Public entities must make every effort to integrate the disabled into their existing and future services, programs, and activities, and be able to communicate "with all of the public (telephone contacts, office walk-ins, or interviews), provide for the public's use of the facilities, and allow access to programs that provide State or local government services or benefits."

* **Title III – Public Accommodations:** Restaurants, hotels, theaters, doctors' officers, pharmacies, retail stores, museums, libraries, parks, private schools, and day care centers may not discriminate on the basis of disability. Private clubs and religious organizations are exempt. Auxiliary aids and services must be provided to individuals with hearing or vision impairments.

* **Title IV – Telecommunications:** Telephone companies must provide telecommunications relay services for hearing-impaired and speech-impaired individuals 24 hours per day.

For more information
visit www.ada.gov

Disability Awareness Day

PEOPLE WITH DISABILITIES

consist of the nation's largest minority group, as well as the only group that any of us can become a member of at any time

1 IN 4 PEOPLE

65-69 years of age have a severe disability

56.7 MILLION PEOPLE

in the U.S. have some sort of disability

38.3 MILLION PEOPLE

have a severe disability

30.6 MILLION

people in the U.S. have a physical disability that affects the ability to walk

THE ELDERLY

are the largest population living with a disability

3.6 MILLION PEOPLE

in the U.S. use a wheelchair

AROUND 15%

of the world's population lives with disabilities

brought to you by UNlimiters.com

1/3 OF DISABLED INDIVIDUALS

require assistive technology to be able to take care of themselves at home

ABOUT 764,000

children and adults in the U.S. currently have cerebral palsy

Image Credit: Infographaholic.com

Bibliography

Aging & Disability Resource Center. (2015). Training – TAE
 Learning Network. Retrieved from www.adrc-tae.acl.gov/
 tiki-index.php?page=Training.

Alexander Graham Bell. (2015). Causes of Hearing Loss. Retrieved
 from www.listeningandspokenlanguage.org/
 Document.aspx?id=143.

Alexander Graham Bell. (2015). FAQs About Special Education
 Advocacy. Retrieved from www.listeningandspokenlanguage.
 org/FAQs_About_Special_Education_Advocacy/.

Alexander Graham Bell. (2015). Glossary Terms. Retrieved from
 www.listeningandspokenlanguage.org/Document.
 aspx?id=1012.

Alexander Graham Bell. (2015). Quick Guide for Teachers.
 Retrieved from www.listeningandspokenlanguage.org/
 Quick_Cards_to_Give_to_Teachers/.

Alexander Graham Bell. (2015). Types of Hearing Loss. Retrieved
 from www.listeningandspokenlanguage.org/
 Document.aspx?id=141.

American Association of the Blind. (2009). How Do Deaf-blind
 People Communicate. Retrieved from www.aadb.org/
 factsheets/db_communications.html.

American Association of the Blind. (2009). Support Service
 Providers – An Introduction. Retrieved from
 www.aadb.org/information/ssp/ssp.html.

ARCH National Respite Network. (2014). A Consumer's Guide
 for Family Members. Retrieved from http://
 archrespite.org/consumer-information.

Bethany Community Church. (2011). Deaf Ministry. Retrieved
 from www.bethanylaurel.org/deaf.

Boston Avenue United Methodist Church. (2015). Care
 Ministries. Retrieved from www.bostonavenue.org/
 adult/careministries.html.

Carter, E.W. (2007). Including People with Disabilities in Faith
 Communities: A Guide for Service Providers, Families, and
 Congregations. Paul H. Brooks Publishing Co, Inc.

Center for Disease Control and Prevention. (2014). Family Caregivers. Retrieved from ww.cdc.gov/ncbddd/disability andhealth/family.html.

Center for Parent Information and Resources. (2015). Supports, Modifications, and Accommodations for Students. Retrieved from www.parentcenterhub.org/ repository/accommodations/.

Christ Lutheran Church of the Deaf. (n.d.). Prison Ministry. Retrieved from www.christdeaf.org/prison.html.

Christian Reformed Church. (n.d.). Respite Care. Retrieved from www.crcna.org/site_uploads/uploads/disabilityconcerns/ disability_R13RespiteCare.doc.

Calvary Community Church. (2015). About. Retrieved from www.cccnorwalk.com/about/.

Deaf Community Action Center. (2015). Deaf-blind Services. Retrieved from www.deafcanpa.org/.

Deaf Community Action Center. (2015). Deaf-blind Services. Retrieved from www.deafcanpa.org/programs/ immigrants-refugees/.

Disabilities and Faith. (2015). Welcome to Disabilities and Faith. Retrieved from www.disabilitiesandfaith.org/.

Disability Ministries Committee of The United Methodist Church. (2014). Disability Theology. Retrieved from www.umdisabilityministries.org/ministry/theology.html.

Eckert, R.C. & Rowley, A.J. (2013). Audism : A Theory and Practice of Audiocentric Privilege. *Humanity & Society*, 37, 101-130.

Furnham, Adrian and Stephen Bochner. (1986). Culture Shock: Psychological Reactions to Unfamiliar Environments. London: Methuen.

Glickman, N.S. (1996). The development of culturally deaf identities. In N.S. Glickman & M.A. Harvey (Eds.), *Culturally affirmative psychotherapy with Deaf persons* (pp. 115-153). Mahwah, NJ : Lawrence Erblaum.

Hearing Loss of America. (2015). Cochlear Implants. Retrieved from www.hearingloss.org/content/cochlear-implants.

Hearing Loss Association of America. (2015). Hearing Aids. Retrieved from www.hearingloss.org/content/hearing-aids.

Hearing Loss Association of America. (2015). Living with Hearing Loss. Retrieved from www.hearingloss.org/ content/living-hearing-loss.

Hitching, R. (2004). The Church and Deaf People: A Study of Identity, Communication and Relationships with Special Reference to the Ecclesiology of Jurgen Moltmann . Paternmoster Publishing.

Hyde, M. & Power, D. (2006). Some ethical dimensions of cochlear implantation for deaf children and their families. *Journal of Deaf Studies and Deaf Education*, 12;11(1):102-11.

Internal Revenue Service. (2015). Form 8826, Disabled Access Credit. Retrieved from www.irs.gov/uac/Form-8826,-Disabled-Access-Credit-1.

Johns Hopkins University. (2015). Types of Disabilities. Retrieved from http://web.jhu.edu/disabilities/faculty/types_of_disabilities/.

Johnson, P. (2014). The Church and People with Disabilities. United Methodist Women.

Johnson, P. & Walker, R. (2007). Deaf Ministry: Make a Joyful Silence. Charleston, SC: Booksurge Publishing.

Joni & Friends, Inc. (2015). The Christian Institute on Disability. Retrieved from www.joniandfriends.org/christian-institute-on-disability/.

Joni & Friends, Inc. (2006). Developing a Disability Ministry. Retrieved from www.joniandfriends.org/media/uploads/PDFs/church_relations_process_map_rev2.pdf.

Joni & Friends, Inc. Avoiding Inclusion Confusion. (n.d.). Retrieved from www.joniandfriends.org/media/uploads/downloads/Avoiding_Inclusion_Confusion_rev.1__.pdf.

Leigh, I.W. (2010). Psychotherapy with Deaf Clients from Diverse Groups, 2nd Ed. Gallaudet University Press.

Low Vision Resources. (2015). Deafblind Services. Retrieved from http://visionlossresources.org/programs/dbsm.

Low Vision Resources. (2015). Low Vision Strategies. Retrieved from http://visionlossresources.org/resources-for-vision-loss/low-vision-strategies.

Lutheran Deaf Mission Society. (2013). Deaf Ministry Models. Retrieved from www.deafjesus.org/pdf/models.pdf.

The Lutheran Church – Missouri Synod. (2015). History of the LCMS. Retrieved from www.lcms.org/aboutus/history.

Marshall, L. (2013). Why Is Deaf Ministry So Hard?. Silent Blessings Deaf Ministries. Retrieved from www.silentblessings.org/deaf-ministry-so-hard-2/.

McBeth, L. (1979). <u>Baptist Beginnings</u>. Retrieved from
www.baptisthistory.org/baptistbeginnings.htm.

McCurdy, N. & Mairena, M. (2013). <u>Before You Plan that
International Mission Trip</u>. Ministry Matters. Retrieved
from www.ministrymatters.com/all/entry/3360/
before-you-plan-that-international-mission-trip-.

Minnesota Department of Human Services. (2013). <u>Deaf Culture</u>.
Retrieved from www.dhs.state.mn.us/main/idcplg?Idc
Service=GET_DYNAMIC_CONVERSION&dID=
152683.

National Association of the Deaf. (n.d.). <u>Community and
Culture – FAQ</u>. Retrieved from http://nad.org/issues/
american-sign-language/community-and-culture-faq.

National Association of the Deaf. (2015). <u>How to File a
Complaint</u>. Retrieved from http://nad.org/issues/about-
law-and-advocacy-center/file-complaint.

National Association of the Deaf. (2015). <u>Senior Resources</u>.
Retrieved from http://nad.org/senior-resources.

National Consortium of Interpreter Education Centers. (2015).
<u>Deaf Self-Advocacy</u>. Retrieved from
www.interpretereducation.org/deaf-self-advocacy/.

National Domestic Violence Hotline. (2015). <u>Warning Signs
and Red Flags</u>. Retrieved from www.thehotline.org/is-this-
abuse/abuse-defined/.

National Domestic Violence Hotline. (2015). <u>What is Abuse?</u>
Retrieved from www.thehotline.org/is-this-abuse/abuse-
defined/.

National Domestic Violence Hotline. (2015).
<u>Personal Safety Plan</u>. Retrieved from
www.thehotline.org/wp-content/uploads/
2015/05/Hotline-personalsafetyplan.pdf.

National Organization on Disability. (1997). <u>That All May
Worship: An Interfaith Welcome to Persons with
Disabilities</u>. Washington, DC.

National Organization for Human Services. (2015). <u>What is
Human Services</u>. Retrieved from www.national
humanservices.org/what-is-human-services.

North American Mission Board. (2015). <u>Projects.</u> Retrieved from
www.namb.net/arm/projects/.

Padden and Humphries. (1988). <u>Deaf in America: Voices from a
Culture</u>. Harvard University Press.

Patheos Library. (2015). <u>Roman Catholicism</u>. Retrieved from
    www.patheos.com/Library/Roman-Catholicism.html.
PBS. (2015). <u>The Black Church</u>. Retrieved from
    www.pbs.org/godinamerica/black-church/.
Peterson, A. & Swanson, C. (2007). <u>Disability Resource</u>
    <u>Manual: A Practical Guide for Churches and Church</u>
    <u>Leaders</u>. Retrieved from www.disabilitiesandfaith.org/
    resources/factsheets/50_%20PARISH_
    ACCESSIBLE_WITH_LITTLE_OR_NO_COST.doc.
Preheim-Bartel, D., Burkholder, T.J., Christophel, L.A., & Guth,
    C.J. (2015). <u>Circles of Love: Stories of Congregations</u>
    <u>Caring for People with Disabilities and Their Families</u>.
    Herald Press.
RCA Today. (2015). <u>Retiree Helps Restart Deaf Ministry</u>.
    Retrieved from www2.rca.org/page.aspx?pid=4621.
Reformed Church in America. (2015). <u>Litany for Disability</u>
    <u>Awareness</u>. Retrieved from www.rca.org/resources/
    worship-litany-disability/litany-disability-awareness.
Registry of Interpreters for the Deaf. (2015). <u>Code of Professional</u>
    <u>Conduct</u>. Retrieved from www.rid.org/ethics/code-of-
    professional-conduct/.
Registry of Interpreters for the Deaf. (2015). <u>Continuing</u>
    <u>Education</u><u>overview</u>. Retrieved from www.rid.org/
    continuing-education/.
Registry of Interpreters for the Deaf. (2015<u>). Previously Offered</u>
    <u>Certifications</u>. Retrieved from www.rid.org/rid-certification-
    overview/previously-offered-rid-certifications/.
Registry of Interpreters for the Deaf. (2007). <u>Interpreting for</u>
    <u>Individuals Who Are Deaf-blind</u>. Retrieved from
    www.rid.org.
Registry of Interpreters for the Deaf. (015). <u>Who We Are</u>.
    Retrieved from www.rid.org/about-rid/.
Rehabilitation Services Administration. (2014). <u>Vocational</u>
    <u>Rehabilitation Services</u>. Retrieved from
    https://rsa.ed.gov/programs.cfm?pc=basic-vr.
Retirement Research Foundation. (2012). <u>Toolkit for</u>
    <u>Working with the Deaf and Hard-of-Hearing</u>.Retrieved
    from www.rrf.org/wp-content/uploads/MMW-
    Deaf-Universal-Toolkit-05-24-12.pdf.Rochester Institute of
Signing Savvy. (2015). <u>Deaf Awareness Week</u>. Retrieved from
    www.signingsavvy.com/deafawarenessweek.

Silent Word Ministries. (2015). <u>Deaf Ministry Checklist.</u> Retrieved from http://silentwordministries.org/2008/12/12/deaf-ministry-checklist/.

Singleton, J.L. & Tittle, M.D. (2001). <u>A Guide for Professionals Serving Hearing Children with Deaf Parents</u>. Retrieved from http://clas.uiuc.edu/techreport/tech6.html.

Social Security Administration. (2015<u>). Benefits for People with Disabilities</u>. Retrieved from www.ssa.gov/disability/.

Social Security Administration. (2015). <u>Welcome to the Path to Work</u>. Retrieved from www.chooseworkttw.net/about/your-path-to-work/index.html.

Special Kids Network. (2006). <u>Family Guide to Respite Guide</u>. Retrieved from www.depweb.state.pa.us/portal/server.pt/document/443565/familyguidetorespitecare_pdf.

Synan, V. (2006). <u>The Origins of the Pentecostal Church</u>. Retrieved from www.oru.edu/library/special_collections/holy_spirit_research_center/Pentecostal_history.php.

Technology. (2015). <u>National Directory</u>. Retrieved from www.rit.edu/ntid/saisd/national-directory.

Theis, SL, Moss, JH, Pearson, MA. (1994). <u>Respite for caregivers: an evaluation study.</u> Journal of Community Health Nursing, 31-44.

The United Methodist Church. (2015). <u>Basics of Our Faith</u>. Retrieved from www.umc.org/what-we-believe/basics-of-our-faith.

United Methodist Congress of the Deaf. (2011). <u>Breaking the Sound Barrier: Ministry & Mission with People Who are Hard-of-Hearing or Late-Deafened</u>. Retrieved from www.umcdhm.org/download/breaking.pdf.

The University of North Carolina Greensboro.(2015). <u>Advocacy and Services for the Deaf Concentration</u>. Retrieved from http://ses.uncg.edu/pid/professions-in-deafness-programs/advocacy-services-for-the-deaf-concentration/.

Yates, L. (2012). <u>Interpreting at Church: A Paradigm for Sign Language Interpreters (3ʳᵈ Ed).</u> Charlotte, NC: Book Surge Publishing.

Zuniga, X., Nagada, B.R., & Sevig, T.D. (2002). <u>Intergroup Dialogues: An Educational Model for Cultivating Engagement Across Differences</u>. Equity and Excellence in Education, p.7-17.

Endnotes

[i] Padden and Humphries. (1988). Deaf in America: Voices from a Culture. Harvard University Press.

[ii] Minnesota Department of Human Services. (2013). Deaf Culture. Retrieved from www.dhs.state.mn.us/main/idcplg?IdcService=GET_DYNAMIC_CONVERSION&dID=152683.

[iii] Minnesota Department of Human Services. (2013). Deaf Culture. Retrieved from www.dhs.state.mn.us/main/idcplg?IdcService=GET_DYNAMIC_CONVERSION&dID=152683.

[iv] Minnesota Department of Human Services. (2013). Deaf Culture. Retrieved from www.dhs.state.mn.us/main/idcplg?IdcService=GET_DYNAMIC_CONVERSION&dID=152683.

[v] Minnesota Department of Human Services. (2013). Deaf Culture. Retrieved from www.dhs.state.mn.us/main/idcplg?IdcService=GET_DYNAMIC_CONVERSION&dID=152683.

[vi] Minnesota Department of Human Services. (2013). Deaf Culture. Retrieved from www.dhs.state.mn.us/main/idcplg?IdcService=GET_DYNAMIC_CONVERSION&dID=152683.

[vii] Minnesota Department of Human Services. (2013). Deaf Culture. Retrieved from www.dhs.state.mn.us/main/idcplg?IdcService=GET_DYNAMIC_CONVERSION&dID=152683.

[viii] Hyde, M. & Power, D. (2006). Some ethical dimensions of cochlear implantation for deaf children and their families. Journal of Deaf Studies and Deaf Education, 12;11(1):102-11.

[ix] Leigh, I.W. (2010). Psychotherapy with Deaf Clients from Diverse Groups, 2nd Ed. Gallaudet University Press.

[x] Glickman, N.S. (1996). The development of culturally deaf identities. In N.S. Glickman & M.A. Harvey (Eds.), Culturally affirmative psychotherapy with Deaf persons (pp. 115-153). Mahwah, NJ : Lawrence Erblaum.

[xi] Eckert, R.C. & Rowley, A.J. (2013). <u>Audism : A Theory and Practice of Audiocentric Privilege</u>. *Humanity & Society,* 37, 101-130.

[xii] Johnson, P. & Walker, R. (2007). <u>Deaf Ministry: Make a Joyful Silence.</u> Charleston, SC: Booksurge Publishing.

[xiii] Marshall, L. (2013). <u>Why Is Deaf Ministry So Hard?.</u> Silent Blessings Deaf Ministries. Retrieved from www.silentblessings.org/deaf-ministry-so-hard-2/.

[xiv] National Council of the Churches. (1997). "Policy: No Barriers for Deaf People in Churches." Retrieved from http://nationalcouncilofchurches.us/common-witness/1997/deaf-barriers.php.

[xv] Costello, E. (1986). <u>Religious Signing: A Comprehensive Guide for All Faiths</u>. New York: Bantam Books.

[xvi] Johnson, P. & Walker, R. (2007). <u>Deaf Ministry: Make a Joyful Silence</u>. Charleston, SC: Booksurge Publishing.

[xvii] Lutheran Deaf Mission Society. (2013). <u>Deaf Ministry Models</u>. Retrieved from www.deafjesus.org/pdf/models.pdf.

[xviii] Johnson, P. & Walker, R. (2007). <u>Deaf Ministry: Make a Joyful Silence.</u> Charleston, SC: Booksurge Publishing.

[xix] Christ Lutheran Church of the Deaf. (n.d.). <u>Prison Ministry</u>. Retrieved from www.christdeaf.org/prison.html.

[xx] Singleton, J.L. & Tittle, M.D. (2001). <u>A Guide for Professionals Serving Hearing Children with Deaf Parents</u>. Retrieved from http://clas.uiuc.edu/techreport/tech6.html.

[xxi] Johnson, P. & Walker, R. (2007). <u>Deaf Ministry: Make a Joyful Silence.</u> Charleston, SC: Booksurge Publishing.

[xxii] Hitching, R. (2004). <u>The Church and Deaf People: A Study of Identity, Communication and Relationships with Special Reference to the Ecclesiology of Jurgen Moltmann</u> . Paternmoster Publishing.

[xxiii] Hitching, R. (2003). <u>The Church and Deaf People: A Study of Identity, Communication and Relationships with Special Reference to the Ecclesiology of Jürgen Moltmann</u>. Cumbria, CA: Paternoster Press, 27.

[xxiv] RCA Today. (2015). <u>Retiree Helps Restart Deaf Ministry</u>. Retrieved from www2.rca.org/page.aspx?pid=4621.

[xxv] Lutheran Deaf Mission Society. (2013). <u>Deaf Ministry Models</u> Retrieved from www.deafjesus.org/pdf/models.pdf.

[xxvi] Registry of Interpreters for the Deaf. (015). <u>Who We Are</u>. Retrieved from www.rid.org/about-rid.

[xxvii] Registry of Interpreters for the Deaf. (015). <u>Who We Are</u>. Retrieved from www.rid.org/about-rid.

[xxviii] Yates, L. (2012). <u>Interpreting at Church: A Paradigm for Sign Language Interpreters.</u> Charlotte, NC: Book Surge.

[xxix] Registry of Interpreters for the Deaf. (2015). <u>Continuing Education Overview.</u> Retrieved from www.rid.org/continuing-education/.

[xxx] "CERTIFICATION MAINTENANCE PROGRAM." <u>Registry of Interpreters for the Deaf</u>. Retrieved from www.rid.org/cmp.html.

[xxxi] Registry of Interpreters for the Deaf. (2015). <u>Certification Overview.</u> Retrieved from www.rid.org/rid-certification-overview/.

[xxxii] Registry of Interpreters for the Deaf. (2015). <u>Previously Offered Certifications.</u> Retrieved from www.rid.org/rid-certification-overview/previously-offered-rid-certifications/.

[xxxiii] Registry of Interpreters for the Deaf. (2015). <u>Previously Offered Certifications.</u> Retrieved from www.rid.org/rid-certification-overview/previously-offered-rid-certifications/.

[xxxiv] "NIC…Moving Forward Together" <u>Registry of Interpreters for the Deaf</u>. Retrieved from www.rid.org/NICNews/index.cfm.

[xxxv] "National Council on Interpreting (NCI)." <u>Registry of Interpreters for the Deaf</u>. Retrieved from www.rid.org/nci.html.

xxxvi Registry of Interpreters for the Deaf. (2015). <u>Code of Professional Conduct.</u> Retrieved from www.rid.org/ethics/code-of-professional-conduct/.

xxxvii Registry of Interpreters for the Deaf. (2015). <u>Previously Offered Certifications.</u> Retrieved from www.rid.org/rid-certification-overview/previously-offered-rid-certifications/.

xxxviii "Explanation of Certificates." <u>Registry of Interpreters for the Deaf</u>. Retrieved from www.rid.org/expl.html.

xxxix Yates, L. (2012). <u>Interpreting at Church: A Paradigm for Sign Language Interpreters.</u> Charlotte, NC: Book Surge.

xl Yates, L. (2012). <u>Interpreting at Church: A Paradigm for Sign Language Interpreters.</u> Charlotte, NC: Book Surge.

xli Yates, L. (2012). <u>Interpreting at Church: A Paradigm for Sign Language Interpreters.</u> Charlotte, NC: Book Surge.

xlii Yates, L. (2012). <u>Interpreting at Church: A Paradigm for Sign Language Interpreters.</u> Charlotte, NC: Book Surge.

xliii Yates, L. (2012). <u>Interpreting at Church: A Paradigm for Sign Language Interpreters.</u> Charlotte, NC: Book Surge.

xliv Yates, L. (2012). <u>Interpreting at Church: A Paradigm for Sign Language Interpreters.</u> Charlotte, NC: Book Surge.

xlv Yates, L. (2012). <u>Interpreting at Church: A Paradigm for Sign Language Interpreters.</u> Charlotte, NC: Book Surge.

xlvi Yates, L. (2012). <u>Interpreting at Church: A Paradigm for Sign Language Interpreters.</u> Charlotte, NC: Book Surge.

xlvii Yates, L. (2012). <u>Interpreting at Church: A Paradigm for Sign Language Interpreters.</u> Charlotte, NC: Book Surge.

xlviii Yates, L. (2012). <u>Interpreting at Church: A Paradigm for Sign Language Interpreters.</u> Charlotte, NC: Book Surge.

xlix Yates, L. (2012). <u>Interpreting at Church: A Paradigm for Sign Language Interpreters.</u> Charlotte, NC: Book Surge.

l Clayton V & Ceil L. (2002). <u>LINGUISTICS of American Sign Language: An Introduction</u>. Washington, DC: Clerc Books, 69.

li Fant, B., Miller, B., & Fant, L. (2008). <u>The American Sign Language Phrase Book, 3rd ed.</u> New York: McGraw-Hill.

[lii] Yates, L. (2012). <u>Interpreting at Church: A Paradigm for Sign Language Interpreters.</u> Charlotte, NC: Book Surge.

[liii] Yates, L. (2012). <u>Interpreting at Church: A Paradigm for Sign Language Interpreters.</u> Charlotte, NC: Book Surge.

[liv] Clayton V & Ceil L. (2002). <u>LINGUISTICS of American Sign Language: An Introduction</u>. Washington, DC: Clerc Books, 188.

[lv] "Classroom Interpreting: EIPA Written Test and Knowledge Standards." <u>Boys Town National Research Hospital</u>. Retrieved from www.classroominterpreting.org/EIPA/ standards/ interpreting.asp.

[lvi] "Using a British Sign Language Interpreter or Communicator". <u>City of Bradford Metropolitan District Council</u>. Retrieved from www.bradford.gov.uk/health_wellbeing_and_ care/disability/using_a_british_sign_language_interpreter _or_communicator.

[lvii] Yates, L. (2012). <u>Interpreting at Church: A Paradigm for Sign Language Interpreters.</u> Charlotte, NC: Book Surge.

[lviii] Yates, L. (2012). <u>Interpreting at Church: A Paradigm for Sign Language Interpreters.</u> Charlotte, NC: Book Surge.

[lix] "The Role of Consecutive in Interpreting Training: A Cognitive View". <u>AIIC</u>. Retrieved from www.aiic.net/ViewPage.cfm/article262.

[lx] Yates, L. (2012). <u>Interpreting at Church: A Paradigm for Sign Language Interpreters.</u> Charlotte, NC: Book Surge.

[lxi] M. Joos. (1961). <u>The Five Clocks.</u> New York: Harcourt, Brace and World.

[lxii] M. Joos. (1961). <u>The Five Clocks.</u> New York: Harcourt, Brace and World.

[lxiii] Seleskovitch, D. & Lederer, M. (1989). <u>A SYSTEMATIC APPROACH TO TEACHING INTERPRETATION</u>. Translated by Jacolyn Harmer. Paris: Office of the European Communities, 124.

[lxiv] .Liddell, S.K. (2003). <u>Grammar, Gesture and Meaning in American Sign Language</u>. New York: Cambridge

University Press, 15.

lxv Lawrence, S. (1994). <u>Interpreter Discourse: English to ASL Expansion - Interpreter Discourse: English to ASL Expansion.</u> Revised ed. Jan. 2003.

lxvi Yates, L. (2012). <u>Interpreting at Church: A Paradigm for Sign Language Interpreters.</u> Charlotte, NC: Book Surge.

lxvii Yates, L. (2012). <u>Interpreting at Church: A Paradigm for Sign Language Interpreters.</u> Charlotte, NC: Book Surge.

lxviii Yates, L. (2012). <u>Interpreting at Church: A Paradigm for Sign Language Interpreters.</u> Charlotte, NC: Book Surge.

lxix Lutheran Deaf Mission Society. (2013). <u>Deaf Ministry Models.</u> Retrieved from www.deafjesus.org/pdf/models.pdf.

lxx Alexander Graham Bell. (2015). <u>Causes of Hearing Loss.</u> Retrieved from www.listeningandspokenlanguage.org/Document.aspx?id=143.

lxxi Alexander Graham Bell. (2015). <u>Types of Hearing Loss.</u> Retrieved from www.listeningandspokenlanguage.org/Document.aspx?id=141.

lxxii Alexander Graham Bell. (2015). <u>Glossary Terms.</u> Retrieved from www.listeningandspokenlanguage.org/Document.aspx?id=1012.

lxxiii Retirement Research Foundation. (2012). <u>Toolkit for Working with the Deaf and Hard-of-Hearing.</u> Retrieved from www.rrf.org/wp-content/uploads/MMW-Deaf-Universal-Toolkit-05-24-12.pdf.

lxxiv Hearing Loss of America. (2015). <u>Cochlear Implants.</u> Retrieved from www.hearingloss.org/content/cochlear-implants.

lxxv Hearing Loss Association of America. (2015). <u>Hearing Aids.</u> Retrieved from www.hearingloss.org/content/hearing-aids.

lxxvi Hearing Loss Association of America. (2015). <u>Hearing Aids.</u> Retrieved from www.hearingloss.org/content/hearing-aids.

lxxvii Hearing Loss Association of America. (2015). <u>Living with Hearing Loss.</u> Retrieved from www.hearingloss.org/content/living-hearing-loss.

[lxxviii] Retirement Research Foundation. (2012). Toolkit for Working with the Deaf and Hard-of-Hearing.Retrieved from www.rrf.org/wp-content/uploads/MMW-Deaf-Universal-Toolkit-05-24-12.pdf.

[lxxix] Association of Late-Deafened Adults. (2015). About Us. Retrieved from www.alda.org/.

[lxxx] "Assistive Listening Devices". Hearing Loss America of Association. Retrieved from ww.hearingloss.org/learn/assistivetech.asp#link1.

[lxxxi] Retirement Research Foundation. (2012). Toolkit for Working with the Deaf and Hard-of-Hearing. Retrieved from www.rrf.org/wp-content/uploads/MMW-Deaf-Universal-Toolkit-05-24-12.pdf.

[lxxxii] United Methodist Congress of the Deaf. (2011). Breaking the Sound Barrier: Ministry & Mission with People Who are Hard-of-Hearing or Late-Deafened. Retrieved from www.umcdhm.org/download/breaking.pdf.

[lxxxiii] Alexander Graham Bell. (2015). FAQs About Special Education Advocacy. Retrieved from www.listeningand spokenlanguage. org/FAQs_About_Special_ Education_Advocacy/.

[lxxxiv] Alexander Graham Bell. (2015). FAQs About Special Education Advocacy. Retrieved from www.listeningand spokenlanguage. org/FAQs_About_Special_ Education_Advocacy/.

[lxxxv] Alexander Graham Bell. (2015). FAQs About Special Education Advocacy. Retrieved from www.listeningand spokenlanguage. org/FAQs_About_Special_ Education_Advocacy/.

[lxxxvi] Alexander Graham Bell. (2015). Quick Guide for Teachers. Retrieved from www.listeningandspokenlanguage.org/ Quick_Cards_to_Give_to_Teachers/.

[lxxxvii] Johnson, P. & Walker, R. (2007). Deaf Ministry: Make a Joyful Silence. Charleston, SC: Booksurge Publishing.

[lxxxviii] American Association of the Blind. (2009). How Do Deaf-Blind People Communicate. Retrieved from www.aadb.org/factsheets/db_communications.html.

lxxxix American Association of the Blind. (2009). How Do Deaf-Blind People Communicate. Retrieved from www.aadb.org/factsheets/db_communications.html.

xc American Association of the Blind. (2009). How Do Deaf-Blind People Communicate. Retrieved from www.aadb.org/factsheets/db_communications.html.

xci American Association of the Blind. (2009). How Do Deaf-Blind People Communicate. Retrieved from www.aadb.org/factsheets/db_communications.html.

xcii American Association of the Blind. (2009). Support Service Providers – An Introduction. Retrieved from www.aadb.org/information/ssp/ssp.html.

xciii Yates, L. (2012). Interpreting at Church: A Paradigm for Sign Language Interpreters. Charlotte, NC: Book Surge.

xciv "Interpreting and working with Deaf-blind People." The Interpreter's Friend. Retrieved from www.theinterpreters friend.com/db/Ig4db.html#(2).

xcv Yates, L. (2012). Interpreting at Church: A Paradigm for Sign Language Interpreters. Charlotte, NC: Book Surge.

xcvi AADB, Inc. (2015). Frequently Asked Questions about Deaf-Blindness. Retrieved from www.aadb.org/FAQ /faq_DeafBlindness.html#cause.

xcvii Low Vision Resources. (2015). Low Vision Strategies. Retrieved from http://visionlossresources.org/ resources-for-vision-loss/low-vision-strategies.

xcviii Low Vision Resources. (2015). Deafblind Services. Retrieved from http://visionlossresources.org/programs/dbsm.

xcix Permission granted. Registry of Interpreters for the Deaf. (2007). Interpreting for Individuals Who Are Deaf-blind. Retrieved from www.rid.org.

c Deaf Community Action Center. (2015). Deaf-blind Services. Retrieved from www.deafcanpa.org/.

ci Padden, C. & Humphrie, T. (1988). Deaf in America: Voices from a Culture. Harvard University Press.

cii Johnson, P. & Walker, R. (2007). Deaf Ministry: Make a Joyful Silence. Charleston, SC: Booksurge Publishing.

ciii Furnham, Adrian and Stephen Bochner. (1986). Culture Shock: Psychological Reactions to Unfamiliar Environments. London: Methuen.

[civ] Lutheran Deaf Mission Society. (2013). <u>Deaf Ministry Models</u>. Retrieved from www.deafjesus.org/pdf/models.pdf.

[cv] Lutheran Deaf Mission Society. (2013). <u>Deaf Ministry Models</u>. Retrieved from www.deafjesus.org/pdf/models.pdf.

[cvi] Zuniga, X., Nagada, B.R., & Sevig, T.D. (2002). <u>Intergroup Dialogues: An Educational Model for Cultivating Engagement Across Differences</u>. Equity and Excellence in Education, p.7-17.

[cvii] Bethany Community Church. (2011). <u>Deaf Ministry.</u> Retrieved from www.bethanylaurel.org/deaf.

[cviii] Calvary Community Church. (2015). <u>About</u>. Retrieved from www.cccnorwalk.com/about/.

[cix] National Organization for Human Services. (2015). <u>What is Human Services</u>. Retrieved from www.nationalhumanservices.org/what-is-human-services.

[cx] "A Guide to Disability Rights." <u>U.S. Department of Justice: Civil Rights Division</u>. Feb. 2006. Retrieved 6 Aug. 2006 www.usdoj.gov/crt/ada/cguide.htm#anchor65610>

[cxi] Yates, L. (2012). <u>Interpreting at Church: A Paradigm for Sign Language Interpreters.</u> Charlotte, NC: Book Surge.

[cxii] National Consortium of Interpreter Education Centers. (2015). <u>Deaf Self-Advocacy</u>. Retrieved from www.interpretereducation.org/deaf-self-advocacy/.

[cxiii] The University of North Carolina Greensboro.(2015). <u>Advocacy and Services for the Deaf Concentration</u>. Retrieved from http://ses.uncg.edu/pid/professions-in-deafness-programs/advocacy-services-for-the-deaf-concentration/.

[cxiv] Social Security Administration. (2015). <u>Benefits for People with Disabilities</u>. Retrieved from www.ssa.gov/disability/.

[cxv] Social Security Administration. (2015). <u>Benefits for People with Disabilities</u>. Retrieved from www.ssa.gov/disability/.

cxvi Social Security Administration. (2015). <u>Disability Benefits.</u> Retrieved from www.socialsecurity.gov/pubs/EN-05-10029.pdf.

cxvii Internal Revenue Service. (2015). <u>Form 8826, Disabled Access Credit</u>. Retrieved from www.irs.gov/uac/Form-8826,- Disabled-Access-Credit-1.

cxviii National Association of the Deaf. (2015). <u>How to File a Complaint</u>. Retrieved from http://nad.org/issues/about-law-and-advocacy-center/file-complaint.

cxix National Association of the Deaf. (2015). <u>Senior Resources.</u> Retrieved from http://nad.org/senior-resources.

cxx Rochester Institute of Technology. (2015). <u>National Directory</u>. Retrieved from www.rit.edu/ntid/saisd/national-directory.

cxxi The National Domestic Violence Hotline. (2015). <u>What is Abuse?</u> Retrieved from www.thehotline.org/is-this-abuse/abuse-defined/.

cxxii The National Domestic Violence Hotline. (2015). <u>Warning Signs and Red Flags</u>. Retrieved from www.thehotline.org/is-this-abuse/abuse-defined/.

cxxiii National Domestic Violence Hotline. (2015). <u>Personal Safety Plan</u>. Retrieved from www.thehotline.org/wp-content/uploads/2015/05/Hotline-personalsafetyplan.pdf.

cxxiv Rehabilitation Services Administration. (2014). <u>Vocational Rehabilitation Services</u>. Retrieved from https://rsa.ed.gov/programs.cfm?pc=basic-vr.

cxxv Social Security Administration. (2015). <u>Welcome to the Path to Work</u>. Retrieved from www.chooseworkttw.net/about/your-path-to-work/index.html.

cxxvi Disability.gov. (2015). <u>Guide Me to Information</u>. Retrieved from www.disability.gov.

cxxvii Commission for Case Manager Certification. (n.d.). <u>Definition and Philosophy of Case Management.</u> Retrieved from http://ccmcertification.org/about-us/about-case-management/definition-and-philosophy-case-management.

cxxviii Registry of Interpreters of the Deaf. (2015). "Advocacy 101."
Retrieved from http://www.rid.org/advocacy-overview/
advocacy-toolkit/advocacy-101/.

cxxix Deaf Community Action Center. (2015). Deaf-blind
Services. Retrieved from www.deafcanpa.org/programs/
immigrants-refugees/.

cxxx McCurdy, N. & Mairena, M. (2013). Before You Plan that
International Mission Trip. Ministry Matters. Retrieved
from www.ministrymatters.com/all/entry/
3360/before-you-plan-that-international-mission-trip-.

cxxxi North American Mission Board. (2015). Projects. Retrieved
from www.namb.net/arm/projects/.

cxxxii Johns Hopkins University. (2015). Types of Disabilities.
Retrieved from http://web.jhu.edu/disabilities/faculty
/types_of_disabilities/.

cxxxiii Disabilities and Faith. (2015). Welcome to Disabilities and
Faith. Retrieved from www.disabilitiesandfaith.org/.

cxxxiv Carter, E.W. (2007). Including People with Disabilities in
Faith Communities: A Guide for Service Providers,
Families, and Congregations. Paul H. Brooks
Publishing Co, Inc.

cxxxv Carter, E.W. (2007). Including People with Disabilities in
Faith Communities: A Guide for Service Providers,
Families, and Congregations. Paul H. Brooks
Publishing Co, Inc.

cxxxvi National Organization on Disability. (2001). The Journey of a
Congregation. Washington, DC.

cxxxvii"The Power of Words: A Guide to Interacting with People
with Disabilities." (n.d.). Indiana Governor's Council for
People with Disabilities.

cxxxviii Joni & Friends, Inc. (2015). The Christian Institute on
Disability. Retrieved from www.joniandfriends.org/
christian-institute-on-disability/.

cxxxix Disability.gov. (2015). Guide Me to Information. Retrieved
from www.disability.gov.

cxl Center for Disease Control and Prevention. (2014). Family Caregivers. Retrieved from www.cdc.gov/ ncbddd/disabilityandhealth/family.html.

cxli Center for Disease Control and Prevention. (2014). Family Caregivers. Retrieved from www.cdc.gov/ ncbddd/disabilityandhealth/family.html.

cxlii Center for Disease Control and Prevention. (2014). Family Caregivers. Retrieved from www.cdc.gov/ ncbddd/disabilityandhealth/family.html.

cxliii Center for Disease Control and Prevention. (2014). Family Caregivers. Retrieved from www.cdc.gov/ ncbddd/disabilityandhealth/family.html.

cxliv Center for Disease Control and Prevention. (2014). Family Caregivers. Retrieved from www.cdc.gov/ ncbddd/disabilityandhealth/family.html.

cxlv Theis, SL, Moss, JH, Pearson, MA. (1994). Respite for caregivers: an evaluation study. Journal of Community Health Nursing, 31-44.

cxlvi ARCH National Respite Network. (2014). A Consumer's Guide for Family Members. Retrieved from http:// archrespite.org/consumer-information.

cxlvii Special Kids Network. (2006). Family Guide to Respite Guide. Retrieved from www.depweb.state.pa.us/portal/ server.pt/document/443565/familyguide torespitecare_pdf.

cxlviii Christian Reformed Church. (n.d.). Respite Care. Retrieved from www.crcna.org/site_uploads/uploads/ disabilityconcerns/disability_R13RespiteCare.doc.

cxlix ARCH National Respite Network and Resource Center. (2010). "The Technical Assistance Center for Lifespan Respite. Fact Sheet 53." Retrieved from http:// archrespite.org/.

cl Watson, S. (n.d.). Tips for working with students with severe handicaps: Severe handicaps in the inclusional setting. Retrieved from http://specialed.about.com/od/physical disabilities/a/severe.htm.

cli Center for Parent Information and Resources. (2015). Supports, Modifications, and Accommodations for

<u>Students</u>. Retrieved from www.parentcenterhub.org/
repository/accommodations.

[clii] Center for Parent Information and Resources. (2015).
<u>Supports, Modifications, and Accommodations for
Students</u>. Retrieved from www.parentcenterhub.org/
repository/accommodations/.

[cliii] Joni & Friends, Inc. Avoiding Inclusion Confusion. (n.d.).
Retrieved from www.joniandfriends.org/media/uploads/
downloads/Avoiding_Inclusion_Confusion rev.1__.pdf.

[cliv] Peterson, A. & Swanson, C. (2007). <u>Disability Resource
Manual: A Practical Guide for Churches and Church
Leaders</u>. Retrieved from www.disabilitiesandfaith.org/
resources/factsheets/50_%20PARISH_
ACCESSIBLE_WITH_LITTLE_OR_NO_COST.doc.

[clv] Disability Ministries Committee of The United Methodist
Church. (2014). <u>Disability Theology</u>. Retrieved from
www.umdisabilityministries.org/ministry/theology.html.

[clvi] Boston Avenue United Methodist Church. (2015). <u>Care
Ministries</u>. Retrieved from www.bostonavenue.org/
adult/careministries.html.

[clvii] Preheim-Bartel, D., Burkholder, T.J., Christophel, L.A., &
Guth, C.J. (2015). <u>Circles of Love: Stories of
Congregations Caring for People with Disabilities and
Their Families</u>. Herald Press.

[clviii] Joni & Friends, Inc. (2006). <u>Developing a Disability Ministry</u>.
Retrieved from www.joniandfriends.org/media
/uploads/PDFs/church_relations_process_map_
rev2.pdf.

[clix] Joni & Friends, Inc. (2006). <u>Developing a Disability Ministry</u>.
Retrieved from www.joniandfriends.org/media
/uploads/PDFs/church_relations_process_map_
rev2.pdf.

[clx] Joni & Friends, Inc. (2006). <u>Developing a Disability Ministry</u>.
Retrieved from www.joniandfriends.org/media
/uploads/PDFs/church_relations_process_map_
rev2.pdf.

[clxi] Joni & Friends, Inc. (2006). <u>Developing a Disability Ministry</u>.
Retrieved from www.joniandfriends.org/media

/uploads/PDFs/church_relations_process_map_
rev2.pdf.

clxii Joni & Friends, Inc. (2006). <u>Developing a Disability Ministry</u>.
Retrieved from www.joniandfriends.org/media
/uploads/PDFs/church_relations_process_map_
rev2.pdf.

clxiii Joni & Friends, Inc. (2006). <u>Developing a Disability Ministry</u>.
Retrieved from www.joniandfriends.org/media
/uploads/PDFs/church_relations_process_map_
rev2.pdf.

clxiv Joni & Friends, Inc. (2006). <u>Developing a Disability Ministry</u>.
Retrieved from www.joniandfriends.org/media
/uploads/PDFs/church_relations_process_map_
rev2.pdf.

clxv Joni & Friends, Inc. (2006). <u>Developing a Disability Ministry</u>.
Retrieved from www.joniandfriends.org/media
/uploads/PDFs/church_relations_process_map_
rev2.pdf.

clxvi Joni & Friends, Inc. (2006). <u>Developing a Disability Ministry</u>.
Retrieved from www.joniandfriends.org/media
/uploads/PDFs/church_relations_process_map_
rev2.pdf.

clxvii Silent Word Ministries. (2015). <u>Deaf Ministry Checklist.</u>
Retrieved from http://silentwordministries.org/2008/
12/12/deaf-ministry-checklist/.

clxviii Joni & Friends, Inc. (2006). <u>Developing a Disability Ministry</u>.
Retrieved from www.joniandfriends.org/media
/uploads/PDFs/church_relations_process_map_
rev2.pdf.

clxix Joni & Friends, Inc. (2006). <u>Developing a Disability Ministry</u>.
Retrieved from www.joniandfriends.org/media
/uploads/PDFs/church_relations_process_map_
rev2.pdf.

clxx Joni & Friends, Inc. (2006). <u>Developing a Disability Ministry</u>.
Retrieved from www.joniandfriends.org/media
/uploads/PDFs/church_relations_process_map_
rev2.pdf.

clxxi Reformed Church in America. (2015). Litany for Disability Awareness. Retrieved from www.rca.org/resources/ worship-litany-disability/litany-disability-awareness.

clxxii National Organization on Disability. (1997). That All May Worship: An Interfaith Welcome to Persons with Disabilities. Washington, DC.

clxxiii Johnson, P. & Walker, R. (2007). Deaf Ministry: Make a Joyful Silence. Charleston, SC: Booksurge Publishing.

clxxiv Signing Savy. (2015). Deaf Awareness Week. Retrieved from www.signingsavvy.com/deafawarenessweek.

clxxv Signing Savy. (2015). Deaf Awareness Week. Retrieved from www.signingsavvy.com/deafawarenessweek.

clxxvi Signing Savy. (2015). Deaf Awareness Week. Retrieved from www.signingsavvy.com/deafawarenessweek.

Index

macular degeneration, 143

Macular Degeneration, 143

mentor, 88, 89, 90

Minnesota Chemical Dependency Program, 180

models of deafness, 7

Multicultural Framework, 165

multiple roles, 100

music, 20, 61, 62, 66, 77, 78

music stand, 62

National Interpreting Certification (NIC), 47, 49

North American Mission Board, 201

outreach ministry, 25

parameters, 70

payment, 100, 102, 103

Pidgin Signed English (PSE), 72

preparation materials, 62

Prison ministry, 27

Professional Accountability, 44

professional liability insurance, 51

Relay Services, 119

resources, 51, 52, 67, 69, 123, 142

Respite care, 234

rhetorical questions, 70

RID, 43, 44, 45, 47, 48, 49, 51, 52, 54, 60, 73, 76, 78, 88, 91, 97, 101, 304

sanctuary, 51, 53, 63, 65, 101

self-monitoring, 86, 87

semantics, 315